Creating the Interactive Digital Narrative

Creating the Interactive Digital Narrative

An All-at-Once Guide to Collaborative Planning, Production, and Beyond

Bradford Gyori

BLOOMSBURY ACADEMIC
LONDON • NEW YORK • OXFORD • NEW DELHI • SYDNEY

BLOOMSBURY ACADEMIC
Bloomsbury Publishing Plc, 50 Bedford Square, London, WC1B 3DP, UK
Bloomsbury Publishing Inc, 1359 Broadway, New York, NY 10018, USA
Bloomsbury Publishing Ireland, 29 Earlsfort Terrace, Dublin 2, D02 AY28, Ireland

BLOOMSBURY, BLOOMSBURY ACADEMIC and the Diana logo are
trademarks of Bloomsbury Publishing Plc

First published in Great Britain 2026

Cover design: Megan Wilson
Cover image © Piai via Adobe Stock

A catalogue record for this book is available from the British Library.

A catalog record for this book is available from the Library of Congress.

ISBN: HB: 978-1-3504-7748-3
PB: 978-1-3504-7749-0
ePDF: 978-1-3504-7750-6
eBook: 978-1-3504-7751-3

Typeset by Deanta Global Publishing Services, Chennai, India
Printed and bound in Great Britain

For product safety related questions contact productsafety@bloomsbury.com.

To find out more about our authors and books visit www.bloomsbury.com and
sign up for our newsletters.

For the blue-sky miners.

Contents

Figures

About the Author

Bradford Gyori is an American writer and academic who relocated to the UK in 2014. He is a principal academic in digital storytelling at Bournemouth University and leads the MA in Creative Writing and Publishing.

Brad has worked as a writer-producer for networks including MTV, VH1, E!, FX, and HBO Online, and he served as the head writer for the Emmy-winning series *Talk Soup*. He holds a PhD in rhetoric and composition from Arizona State University.

His theatrical works have been presented by Steppenwolf Theatre, Phoenix Theatre, the Shelley Theatre, Poole Lighthouse, and Bournemouth Emerging Arts Fringe. He is also a company director with Doppelganger Productions.

Brad's short fiction has appeared in *No Parties Magazine*, *The Ghost Story*, *Shorts Magazine*, *Coffin Bell*, *Café Irreal*, *The Museum Journal*, and other publications. His scholarly articles have been featured in *The Journal of Broadcasting and Electronic Media*, *Media Practice in Education*, *Journalism*, *Interactive Storytelling*, *Flow*, and more.

He has designed and directed numerous interactive and immersive storytelling projects, including *Shelley's Heart*, *Target BACRIM*, and *Mr. Illusion*. For more information, visit BradfordGyori.com.

How to Use This Book

Creating an Interactive Digital Narrative (IDN) may sound intimidating, but Bradford Gyori's "All-at-Once Guide" makes it manageable. This is not a step-by-step instruction manual; the creation of an IDN involves too many moving parts to follow any rigid formula. Instead, you're encouraged to dip in and out of these chapters as needed.

Like the projects it describes, this book facilitates nonlinear exploration and rewards intellectual curiosity. It also celebrates multitasking. If you're working with others, consider assigning different team members to focus on different chapters. If you're working solo, feel free to leap around and get multiple plates spinning at the same time.

However you approach this book, rest assured, it contains everything you need to plan, create, and complete a working IDN. The information is laid out in a clear, accessible style. This is a jargon-free zone; any technical terms are quickly defined. Gyori references his own projects throughout, speaking frankly about both successes and failures. His warts-and-all approach emphasizes critical thinking and creative problem-solving.

When you encounter more design strategies than you can possibly include in a single narrative, don't panic. That's your opportunity to think strategically and decide which approaches suit the project you want to create. Choose wisely, and you'll produce an Interactive Digital Narrative that people will enjoy exploring for years to come.

Acknowledgments

The IDN projects that inspired this book were collaborative efforts, so I have many people to thank. First and foremost, I'd like to acknowledge my loving and supportive family, my partner Chris, and our two kids, Jack and Maya. You are always my alpha-through-omega readers and the best safety net and wings of inspiration a creative tightrope walker could ask for.

I also owe a big debt of gratitude to my friend and colleague Jim Pope, who has been a creative collaborator, co-conspirator, and coauthor on many IDN projects and academic articles. Another big thank-you goes to Bloomsbury Commissioning Editor Lucy Brown for reaching out and encouraging me to write this book. I am eternally grateful to Karen Fowler Watt for taking a gamble on a yank academic with a background in TV to teach Digital Storytelling at BU.

Cheers to Mat Charles, whose innovative vision and journalistic courage inspired me to leap into the narrative challenges of *Target BACRIM* with both feet. Much gratitude to the talented cast of *Shelley's Heart*: Hannaj Bang-Bendz, Robert Wallis, Mark Sillence, Matt Brackstone, Steve Rollins, Fay Elizabeth Butler, Timothy Lowe, Keely Saunders, and Samuel George. You did a great job bringing those fictional creations and their real-life counterparts to life.

Many thanks to the gifted collaborators who worked behind the scenes on the projects discussed in this book, including Steve Rafter, Shaun Osborne, Lokesh Sivakumar, Saeed Rashid, Jason Hallet, Chris Hull, Mark Phillips, Rose Perry, Emily Barrett, Alex Shore, Alexander Jones, Charlie Hargood, Rob Logan, Zhidong Xiao, Sven Wolters, and J. Urbina Peñuela. I'm grateful for the technical support and troubleshooting generously offered by Dave May, Edward Sedgley, Keith Hayward, Wez Nolan, the BU IT department, and BU Estates.

Thanks to Rev. Dr. Ian Terry for allowing us to film in St. Peter's Churchyard and Bournemouth University's Head of External Engagement, Ian Jones, and the Bournemouth Borough Council for funding support. Additional thanks go to Laura Hampshaw and Mark Brocklehurst for internal funding guidance and support.

Thanks to The Shelley Frankenstein Festival and Arts University Bournemouth, who, along with BU, sponsored the Frankenstein Unbound Conference where *Shelley's Heart Locative Version* debuted. Special thanks to Sarah Farmer of BBC South and Jason Lewis of *The Bournemouth Echo* for their news coverage of the locative launch.

I'd also like to salute the Broadcast and Multimedia Journalism Students at Bournemouth University for creating such inventive and informative iDocs. A tip of the hat to Doppelganger Productions and DP Talent for helping me recruit actors. Merci beaucoup to all our DISC (*Digital Interactive Storytelling in the Community*) facilitators and participants, including the AIM Project for At-Risk Teens, The Bishop of Winchester Academy, and The Young Offenders Initiative.

Other friends and colleagues who've provided support include John Foster, Helen Jacey, Hywel Dix, Andy Bissell, Bronwen Thomas, Julian McDougal, Andrea Francis, Leigh Hayler, Julia Round, Peter Truckel, Chris Williams, Simon Perkins, Rutherford, Mike Sunderland, Sarah Preece, Sarah Dimmer, Kirsty Reed, Joseph Amoah, Bronnie McCarthy, Roselyn Pike, Adrian Butterworth, Tom Stone, Jo Tyler, Liping Yan, Taisiia Vaskivska, Eleanor Whitelaw, Ella Betts, Ellie Beazley, Wesley Schulte, Sarah-Jane Olivant, Kay Stonham, Alex Dimitriu, Adam Topham, Dimitra Margaritidou, Jordyn Robinson, Karishma Naik, Matthew Campbell, Marcus Smith, Callum Spawforth, Dan Green, Padmapriya Nataraj, Suresh Palanisamy, Rob Munday, Rachel Bowen, Nathaniel Hobby, Rebecca Oliver, Nicola Goode, Sacha Gardner, Matthew Vass-White, Domenico Presti, Kaan Gülerdogan, Jess Spicer, Josh Rhodes, Celeste Engel, Francesca Burney, Zoe Dunne, Isabella Rega, Chamaine K. Parkin, Suchismita Ghosh, Tracy Jane Murray, Mark Berry, Vania Patel, Taisiia Vaskivska, Arianne Byers, Jon Black, Dominic Wong, Greg Sneed, Dan Barton, Mike Groom, Maisy Morris-Davies, Samuel Colwood, Lewis Stride, Annamaria Simon, Fay Sawyn, and Richard Newland.

Introduction

This book is for anyone who wants to create an **Interactive Digital Narrative (IDN)**—be they project facilitators, participants, teachers, community organizers, or solo artists. There is something here for everyone. While the chapters are full of handy tips, this is not a one-size-fits-all guide.

If an algebra textbook is well-written, every reader who solves for X will get the same result. But the creative process doesn't work that way. If every reader following the guidance in these pages produced identical projects, this book would be a failure. Creativity can't be learned through formulas—it can only be learned by analogy. There are no fixed rules, and, hopefully, no predictable outcomes—only loose guidelines and rough approximations. Teaching a creative process, therefore, requires leading by example, analyzing the pros and cons of specific works, and inspiring others to invent their own unique variations on the projects discussed.

While this isn't a paint-by-numbers guide, these chapters are brimming with practical advice accumulated from decades of creative problem-solving in the television industry (E!, MTV, VH1, FX, HBO Online) and higher education (ASU, Tribeca Flashpoint Academy, Bournemouth University). My research for this book has involved supervising, creating, and collaborating on a wide range of IDN projects.

As a principal academic in digital storytelling at Bournemouth University, I've taught the creation of **Interactive Documentaries (iDocs)** as part of the Broadcast and Multimedia Journalism degree (Gyori & Charles 2017). These projects have been showcased on the website *BUZZ* (2024). I am also the program leader for the MA in Creative Writing and Publishing, which includes the unit "Interactive Storytelling." Judging the interactive journalism category for the *New Media Writing Prize* (2024) helps me stay up to date with iDoc innovations worldwide.

In addition, I have led local community outreach projects, such as the Digital Interactive Storytelling in the Community (DISC) initiative, with my colleague James Pope (Gyori & Pope 2021, 2023). Together, we've worked with at-risk teens, secondary school students, and young offenders, helping them create branching narratives to envision alternative life paths for themselves.

Finally, my practice-research projects include the transmedia historical fiction IDN *Shelley's Heart* (Figure 0.1; Gyori 2018a, 2018b, 2019a, 2019b; Jones, et al. 2018) and the downloadable news game prototype *Target BACRIM* (Figure 0.2), co-created with journalist and educator Mat Charles (Charles et al. 2015; Gyori 2022a).

The subject matter expertise gained from these projects has involved in-depth problem-solving, and this book emphasizes both missteps and breakthroughs.

Figure 0.1 *Shelley's Heart* logo, c. 2018. Courtesy the author.

Figure 0.2 *Target BACRIM* logo, *c.* 2017. Courtesy the author.

It is impossible to accurately describe a trial-and-error creative process without acknowledging the errors. The examples featured are all drawn from projects I have worked on or supervised. Hopefully, the insights shared justify this approach. I've tried to avoid excessive self-promotion or self-flagellation, aiming instead to present a balanced, warts-and-all look at the creation of these complex projects. The IDN projects discussed here have typically been team efforts. I owe a great deal to scores of dedicated and talented collaborators. While I've avoided individual shoutouts in the main text to keep the prose streamlined, the acknowledgments section pays tribute to the amazing people I've had the pleasure of working with on these complex labors of love.

As you will see, one of these IDN narratives never made it past the prototyping stage. Another has appeared in various iterations, sometimes running smoothly and sometimes plagued by technological bugs. Similarly, the iDocs and community outreach projects discussed here showcase both flaws and flashes of inspiration. Rather than dwell on mistakes, the text identifies potential **landmines**, offers suggestions for avoiding them, and moves forward. Along the way, you'll find **pro tips** for capitalizing on creative opportunities. There are also plenty of **bonus sources** in case you want to delve deeper into a particular topic.

Each chapter concludes with both a **Success Story** and a **Cautionary Tale**. These sections provide hard-earned wisdom from the IDN trenches. Additionally, the book includes prompts for creative activities and worksheets to help you organize your IDN. The end of each chapter will reference these worksheets and explain how they can help you achieve specific production goals. Look for copies of the worksheets—which you can download and edit—on the website affiliated with this book.

Website

If you are reading a print version of this book, be sure to check out the website, available at: https://www.bloomsburyonlineresources.com/creating-the-interactive-digital-narrative

This online resource contains downloadable worksheets and clickable links related to every topic covered in this volume. It also includes an extensive amount of bonus links organized by specific topics. As you are creating a digital project, you will want to avail yourself of the many digital tools and platforms available to support you.

An All-in-One, *All at Once* Guide

The chapters in this book are numbered, but don't let that fool you. It's subtitled *An All at Once Guide* because free-range reading is both encouraged and rewarded. Feel free to pinball through the text at will. The sections of this book aren't stages to be tackled in a linear fashion. Instead, they're zones of creative potential that you and/or your team can explore in a nonlinear manner—from the beginning of the production process to the end, often working in several zones simultaneously.

Effective IDN design involves spinning a lot of plates: mapping story paths, designing story nodes, producing media assets, and user-testing prototypes, often at the same time. Clear communication is essential when you're working with a team, as there are a lot of moving parts involving different aspects of the creative process.

Making an IDN is all about managing complexity. Each chapter is a treasure trove of possibilities, but there's no reason to feel overwhelmed. No single project can incorporate all the creative suggestions on offer, so you get to pick and choose what works best for your project. Depending on the type of IDN you're creating, you might not even need certain chapters. Which ones should you skip? That's for you to decide.

Terminology

In 2015, Dr. Hartmut Koenitz coined the term "Interactive Digital Narrative" or "IDN." He defines an IDN as: "a form of expression enabled and defined by digital media that tightly integrates interactivity and narrative as a flexible cognitive frame" (92). In other words, *an IDN is a digital story that lets you do stuff.*

This book refers to a person navigating an IDN as either a "user" or a "player" depending on the context. When discussing interface design, it tends to lean on "user," and when talking about game mechanics, it employs the more appropriate "player."

As for the other terms that appear in these pages, I attempt to define them as quickly and clearly as possible. There is also a handy **glossary** at the back that you are welcome to refer to as often as you like without incurring a single penalty point.

Now, an overview of the riches that await.

Chapter 1: Plans

This chapter focuses on organization at two levels: (1) coordinating your overall production process and (2) developing a particular IDN. It raises questions related to skills, resources, and potential platforms and suggests techniques for coordinating your efforts effectively, based on different production scenarios. Topics include **budgets**, **scheduling**, **equipment**, **facilities**, and even **catering**. You'll also find tips for creative brainstorming, solidifying your **story concept**, and organizing a sensible **workflow**. Additionally, you'll learn how to create and test interactive **prototypes**— both paper and digital. The chapter also provides **aesthetic guidelines** for designing an IDN that reflects your topic and sensibilities.

Chapter 2: Paths

This chapter teaches you to think like an IDN designer. It explains how different types of **story paths** (**unilinear** and **bilinear**) are triggered by various decision points (e.g., **intro**, **skip**, **entry**, **choke**, **foldback**, **home return**). It also explores how paths and points combine to form complex narrative patterns such as **linear**, **fishbone**, **branching**, **concentric**, **parallel**, and **threaded**.

Chapter 3: Assets

This chapter covers creating media assets to enhance your IDN. Asset types include **photographs**, **videos**, **animated GIFs**, **cinemagraphs**, and **audio files**. You'll find tips for:

- **Preproduction**: scouting locations, planning shots, and testing makeup.
- **Production**: camera and microphone placement, lighting, and acting.
- **Postproduction**: video and sound editing.

Chapter 4: Nodes

This section provides instructions for creating different types of interactive project pages, also known as nodes. Examples include **launch pages**, **home pages**, **landing**

pages, **overlays**, **grids**, and **link lists**. The chapter also offers tips for assembling such pieces into a cohesive and effective IDN while focusing on interaction design principles such as **affordances**, **constraints**, **visibility**, **mapping**, **feedback**, and **consistency**.

Chapter 5: Socials

This chapter discusses how your IDN can connect with the world and foster user interaction. Embedding content from other platforms creates opportunities for users to engage with each other. Examples of interactive interfaces include **wiki pages**, **forums**, **surveys**, **polls**, **voting systems**, **aggregation tools**, **file-sharing platforms**, and **showcases** for **User-Generated Content (UGC)**. Additionally, the chapter explains how to use social media to share your IDN with potential users by effectively **linking** and **backlinking**.

Chapter 6: Curation

This chapter focuses on strategies to keep your IDN alive and functional in the long term. It includes tips for safeguarding your project against **bit rot, link rot, hacking**, and **obsolescence**. You'll also find advice for connecting with the broader IDN community and collaborating with other creators.

Conclusion

This section offers speculative thoughts on the future evolution of IDNs, touching on topics such as **Spatial Computing**, **Artificial Intelligence (AI)**, **The Internet of Things (IoT)**, **Holography**, and **Biometric Interfaces**. It concludes with a quick recap of the storytelling process before bidding you a fond farewell.

Website for this Book

Supplementary materials such as worksheets can be found on a website the publisher created for this book. Readers of the print version can also find links related to all the referenced material in this online resource. It can be accessed at https://www.bloomsburyonlineresources.com/creating-the-interactive-digital-narrative

Now What?

Before moving on, here are some additional thoughts about how this book is structured.

Scales of Collaboration

This book offers tips for creators working at the following scales:

- **Multiple teams:** Applies to a class or outreach project with eight to twenty participants divided into small teams of three to five. The number of facilitators may vary.
- **Single team:** A group of just three to five participants. The number of facilitators may vary.
- **Solo creator:** Involves a single artist driving the project, occasionally working with key collaborators such as cast, crew, or editors.

Time Frames

The chapters listed above also provide tips for creators working on projects with different time frames:

- **Three months:** The length of a typical school semester.
- **Five to seven days:** For quick turnarounds.
- **Open-ended:** May include alternating busy periods and long lulls.

Why Create an IDN?

Designing your IDN is a kind of divergent thinking accelerator. Each time you arrive at a narrative crossroads, instead of dreaming up just one possible outcome, you'll need to imagine two, three, or more. This is a fantastic workout for the imagination, keeping it elastic and resilient. IDN creators often find that this type of writing strengthens their ability to craft conventional linear narratives. When they return to traditional storytelling, they don't immediately accept the first idea that pops into their heads. Instead, they consider a range of possibilities, indulging their enhanced appetite for the surprising and bizarre. Here are just a few things you can do with interactive narratives:

- Tell a personal story.
- Explore an undersea world.
- Inhabit a different body.
- Time travel.
- Solve a puzzle.
- Collect treasures.
- Fight a dragon.
- Build a spaceship and fly to Venus.

What Does It Take to Create an IDN?

If you're dreaming of producing a **Triple-A video game** in your backyard shed, you'll need to dial down your ambitions. There's a reason such projects cost millions of dollars and take up to five years to develop—they're incredibly complex. This is why the people making them tend to be highly trained professionals specializing in areas like 3D modeling, sound design, programming, and quality assurance.

The good news is that even someone with little to no experience can create a basic IDN in just a few days, provided you set realistic goals. Many free, open-source platforms are available, and most don't require advanced technical skills. While some programs involve rudimentary coding, you can easily learn the basics with the help of free online tutorials.

This book offers all the information you need to create a fully realized IDN. If you're still feeling unsure, here are some additional resources to help you get started:

Game Studios

If you'd like more hands-on guidance than this book can provide, you might consider teaming up with a game studio. Some developers offer free assistance, while others charge a fee, so be sure to read the fine print before signing anything or sharing your contact details. Leading names in the fiction space include:

- Adventure Game Studio (Loominous & Mandarb 2003)
- Supermassive Games (Henrysson 2022)
- Quantic Studio (Cage 1997)
- Simogo (Flesser & Gardebäck 2010)
- Persuasive Games (Bogost 2003)

You can also find open-source code on developer platforms like GitHub (2024).

A nonfiction interactive production studio supporting journalists and documentarians is Crossover Labs (Atkin & Milen 2008).

Immersive, interactive, and XR storytelling studios include:

- Dreaming Methods (Alston & Campbell 2010)
- Audience of the Future (James 2019)
- Bellyfeel (Stott 1995)
- Fail Better Games (Kennedy & Arendt 2009)
- Tin Man Games (Rennison 2008)

If you're interested in creating a **story app**, consider partnering with a mobile developer such as Pocket Gems (Liu 2009) or Fan Studio (Buta 2010). You could also create something by yourself using one of the countless mobile game development engines (Kriebernegg 2015).

Funders

If your design concept is ambitious, you might need to expand your budget. Some key funders include:

- The Space (Morris 1995)
- IFTF Grants (Bortnick 2016)
- Fundbetter (Joseph 2024)

Marketing

An IDN can also be used to sell products. For example, Perrier Secret Place (Blanc 2013) is an interactive marketing campaign that consumers found immersive and engaging. Campaigns like this are often shared widely.

Education

As I've said, this book is for creators of all types, including educators. In terms of pedagogy, it has been designed with a new type of learner in mind. The digital age is forcing teachers to rethink the traditional lecture-based approach to instruction. Some lament this shift, blaming it on the advent of social media, smartphones, and the associated decline in attention spans. But there's another perspective. Education reform advocates, such as my ASU colleague James Gee (Connected Learning Alliance 2011), argue that people are learning more than ever—just in new ways, through video game mechanics, YouTube tutorials, phone apps, and similar tools. These modes of learning have one thing in common—they are all highly interactive.

Creating IDNs dovetails perfectly with the learning styles of digital natives. These projects are hands-on and collaborative. They also help participants develop meta-thinking skills, as they involve designing interactions for others to explore. Moreover, creating or navigating an IDN allows participants to experiment with low-stakes decision-making. They can explore story options that carry no real-world consequences, while considering the potential repercussions of actions taken by a **Player Character (PC)** whose identity they have temporarily assumed. Participants can also try out new identities, fostering deeper empathy for people who look, think, or behave differently from themselves. This broadens their sense of self. Such qualities make the IDN a safe space for participants to experiment with new ways of thinking, acting, and being.

If you're an educator looking to spearhead an IDN project that gives your students a hands-on, engaging experience, you don't have to go it alone. Consider reaching out to organizations like:

- Raspberry Pi Foundation (Colligan 2009)
- Scratch (Resnick 2003)
- Baamboozle (2025)

These groups offer deep subject matter expertise, as well as resources like the Raspberry Pi Tutorial Page (Hauser 2013).

Examples of IDN learning experiences include:

- The Zoo Vet (Seaton 2010)
- Minecraft Education Edition (Koivisto 2016)

Feedback

Whether you're flying solo, working as part of a team, or supervising a project being created by others, it is crucial to receive and respond to feedback throughout the production process. Feedback can come in many forms including beta testers commenting on specific interfaces, designers analyzing the overall structure, and the IDN itself offering **data analytics** about common user interactions. Because creating an IDN requires extensive testing and problem-solving, it's not a job for the thin-skinned. Time spent defending your flawed design strategy is time wasted. Also, arguing against negative feedback tends to have a chilling effect, silencing those who might otherwise offer helpful notes. So, check your ego at the door. Doing so will allow you to problem-solve much faster and efficiently.

Assessment

If the IDN is being created as part of a teaching assignment, I recommend foregoing the old-school "skill 'n' drill" approach to education. That outdated and ineffectual technique involves front-loading tons of information for several weeks or even months before finally testing the students (if they're still awake) on what they have somehow managed to retain.

A far better approach related to IDN creation involves drip-feeding assessment at key touchpoints. This type of **formative** feedback can guide students fostering progress by helping them identify strengths and weaknesses as they continue to refine their work. Final assessment can be tied to a single **summative** mark for the finished output, or it can be linked to a series of formative marks adding up to a single **cumulative** mark. The latter approach affords opportunities to assess progress along a developmental trajectory.

The key to providing helpful formative feedback is offering focused, constructive, and consistent notes. All assignment criteria should be clearly defined at the outset of the project.

Examples of successful previous projects are helpful. Also, at every touchpoint, student-creators should be told both what's working and what can be improved. They also need guidance on how they can enhance the quality of their work.

As IDNs are creative projects instructors should try to avoid offering overly subjective value judgments based on personal biases. If you don't like the horror genre, that doesn't mean a blood and guts story can't succeed on its own gory terms. The most useful creative criticisms tend to focus on the more objective aspects of design and storytelling, that is, identifying moments where the narrative is overly expositional, or suggesting ways that user choices can be clarified.

BTW: If you supervise a project that requires the students to do a bit of coding, you'll notice a nice added benefit. The creative team will have to proofread their coding with extreme care, or it simply won't work. Hopefully, this transferable skill with carry over to the copy editing of their writing assignments as well. ;)

Sensitive Content

If your IDN includes material that might be triggering—such as violence, eating disorders, suicide, bullying, animal cruelty, racial slurs, or abuse, be sure to include a content warning before the story begins. Also, when designing your IDN, bear in mind that this is a highly immersive medium that allows users to step into the shoes of a person experiencing a traumatic event. This can create empathy, but if creators don't exercise restraint, the depiction itself can be traumatizing. For example, an IDN that portrays the challenges a young woman must navigate to safely enjoy a night out can raise awareness about this topic. But if the IDN includes a first-person POV recreation of a sexual assault, it risks being perceived as insensitive, exploitative, or even harmful to the user.

Accessibility

Now that you have a sense of the topography this book explores, a word about navigating it with disabled users and creators in mind. As IDNs are highly immersive projects they are an effective means of promoting empathy about disabilities. The interactive VR experience *Notes on Blindness* (Digital Productions Arte 2025) and the Choose Your Own Adventure game *Deafverse* (2025) place users in the bodies and minds of disabled characters allowing them to see (and not see), hear (and not hear) the world in new ways. But what about users who are already disabled and want to experience the pleasure of engaging with an IDN? Physical locations aren't the only spaces with accessibility challenges. Virtual spaces can also present barriers to participation. This is why it's best to create your IDN with accessibility in mind by following Web Content Analysis Guidelines (WCAG 2024). Here are a few tips that will make your interface more accessible:

- Use a platform that supports accessibility features.
- Keep the language simple and straightforward, avoiding jargon.
- Include clear navigation and signposting.
- Add descriptive text for all interactive elements.
- Use strongly contrasting colors, especially between text and backgrounds.
- Include alternative audio and textual signposting, including descriptions.
- Allow users to navigate interactive elements with keyboard only.

- Have visual feedback appear when the cursor hovers over interactive elements.
- Include alternative input methods like voice commands.
- Include captions for all audio and video content.
- Include clear indications of user's progress through the story.
- Employ a flexible layout that adapts to different screen sizes and devices.
- User test with screen readers to identify accessibility issues.

If you are a disabled user interested in exploring projects that weren't designed with accessibility in mind, there are several tools that can help you accomplish this. Blind and visually impaired users may find useful tools online, such as Non-Visual Desktop Access (NVDA 2024). You can also try an online interpreter like *Parchment* (2024), which works well with most popular Windows screen readers.

These tools make IDNs more accessible for disabled users, but many disabled IDN creators are also seeking tools to help make their storytelling ambitions a reality. Fortunately, most development platforms are accessible to creators using screen readers. For parser projects, platforms such as *Dialog* (2024) and *Inform 6* (2024) offer features that support disabled creators. For choice-based projects, disabled creators should seek out platforms that feature a more Graphical User Interface (GUI) approach such as *GNOME Shell* (2024) and *Cinnamon* (2024).

Types of Interactive Stories

To round out this introduction to IDNs, here is a survey of interactive storytelling through the ages. This hyper-speed overview touches on a wide variety of interactive storytelling from the earliest analog games to some of today's bleeding-edge creations. This is followed by a section zeroing in on the types of IDN being discussed in detail throughout this book.

Arguably, all games and sports involving human interaction are capable of yielding sequences of dramatic action that a player or audience might recognize as a story. Narrowing our focus to modes where storytelling is the core purpose of the interactivity, there are still many different forms to consider. This is both the curse and the blessing of interactive storytelling: the idea that there isn't a single, universally accepted structure or design approach that a creator can master.

With that in mind, this section casts a wide net, discussing several forms of interactive stories, which can be broadly defined as any narrative—fiction or nonfiction—that an audience can interact with. The pages that follow start with a discussion of **analog** forms: stories that unfold in the real world and involve physical objects and human beings taking on tasks and/or adopting fictional personae. The discussion then moves on to the **digital** realm, focusing on many different types of IDN projects with virtual settings and simulated characters. This narrows the focus, but only slightly. Finally, the discussion locks into the main IDN form explored in this book: the **Single-Player**, **Choice-Based**, **Interactive Digital Narrative (SCIDN)**, which is defined as a kind of creative cornerstone yielding insights into all other modes of IDN creation. More on that in a moment, but first, a quick overview of interactive storytelling.

Analog Forms

A great way to start thinking about interaction design is to play an old-school board game and take note of the different rules of engagement. Most analog forms focus primarily on gameplay at the expense of storytelling. But even a game with narrative elements that are incidental or nonexistent can serve as a model to enhance your IDN. Pick an analog game, then search online for its digital counterpart. If the design structure has migrated into the digital realm, feel free to incorporate interactive mechanics that seem most useful to the design of your IDN. Common analog games include Dice (2024), Cards (2024), Deck Building (2024), Tile Based (2024), Abstract Strategy (2024), Trick Taking Games (2024), Klondike (2024), Toys (2024), Tableau Building (2024), Flicking, and Roll 'n' Write Games (2024).

Role-Playing

You're Batman. I'm Dracula. The couch is a spaceship. Okay, we're ready to role-play! Whether role-playing utilize game pieces, game controllers, or Viking helmets it always involves getting immersed in the perspective of a specific character in a particular story world. Some popular analog permutations include: Tabletop Role-Playing Game (2024), Tactical RPG, Social Deduction (2024), Charades (2024), and Live-Action Role-Playing (LARP) (2024).

With a digital Role-Playing Game (RPG) (2024), Action Role-playing Game (2024), or Massively Multiplayer Online Role-Play Game (2024), the user assumes a particular persona when navigating through a **virtual world**, that is, becoming fire juggler in an online munitions factory. Games of this type include *Dues Ex* (2024), *Final Fantasy* (2024), and *Mass Effect* (2024). Creators interested in producing their own RPG can check out handy platforms like *RPG Maker MZ* (2024).

Interactive Book (Choose Your Path, Choose Your Own Adventure)

These inventive little tomes demonstrate that reading doesn't have to be a passive experience. Every few paragraphs, they offer an array of narrative choices. Each choice directs you to a specific section, delineated by a page number, where you can discover the consequences of the option you've selected. If you like exercising your thumbs as much as your eyes when reading, interactive books reward multiple playthroughs, yielding different narrative detours and outcomes. Some early examples of the form include *Fighting Fantasy* (2024), *Lone Wolf* (2024), and the works of Edward Packard (2024). Writers such as Julio Cortázar (2024) and Svend

Åge Madsen (2024) have produced more experimental forms (2024). Some digital choose-your-path games include *4x4 Archipelago* (Trzaska 2021) and *80 Days* (Humfrey 2014).

A digital offshoot of the interactive book is the **visual novel**. This type of IDN combines text with either static or animated illustrations, while featuring various levels of interactivity. A platform like *Visual Novel Maker* (2025) is very user-friendly, offering **drag-and-drop interfaces**, **built-in menus**, **state tracking**, and **customization options**. If some of these terms sound like gibberish, don't stress—they're all explained in the pages to come. Also, you can always consult the glossary when a techy term vaults over your head.

Interactive Cinema

Moving images and interactivity have been on a collision course for years. The first interactive **shooters** took the expression literally. They date back to the silent film era and the advent of cinematic shooting galleries, as discussed in *First-Person Shooter Games . . . In 1909?* (2019). These arcades allowed viewers to fire live bullets at moving on-screen images. Then, in 1967, there was the release of the first interactive film *Kinoautomat* (2024). At key points, the audience voted on a choice, which triggered the projectionist to play a particular reel. The 1980s saw the release of the first **interactive videos** on laser disc, that is, *Astron Belt* (2024). By the 1990s, **VHS board games** appeared with moving footage guiding user interaction with projects such as *Nightmare* (2024).

This led to the advent of the **Full Motion Video Game** (2024), essentially a bunch of pre-recorded mini movies—as opposed to today's vectors and 3D models—which the player shuttled between. Gradually, interactivity became incorporated into the footage itself, and players were able to select options that would alter the on-screen action, as with interactive narratives like *Minecraft: Story Mode* (2015).

An early example of **Multisensory Cinema** was Morton Heilig's *Sensorama* (2024), which gave rise to today's **4D films** (2024) with motion-enhanced seating and other multisensory technologies, such as olfactory stimulators. *Funky sweat socks, anyone?*

Interactive Theater (Immersive Theater)

Stage plays have incorporated audience participation for centuries. During theatrical **pantomimes** (2024), still popular in the UK, spectators are encouraged to interact with actors—cheering them, booing them, answering questions, and ducking objects thrown from the stage. To explore modern interactive theater productions, check out groups like *Punchdrunk* (2024) and *Blue Man Group* (2024). Their productions are deeply immersive allowing—and sometimes requiring—audience members to become part of the dramatic action.

Another way to transform a stage play into an interactive experience is to empower audience members to vote on key decisions by equipping them with clickers, or apps that let them influence the unfolding dramatic action as with *Shelley's Heart Theatrical Version* (Gyori 2018).

Site-Specific Theater (Collaborative Mixed Reality, Performance Art)

In the 1960s and 1970s, *The Living Theater* (2024) took their interactive performances into nontraditional spaces such as prisons and city streets. Pushing audience participation to a new level, they encouraged participants to shed their inhibitions—and often their clothes. The legacy of this radical performance style lives on in the work of groups like *Blast Theory* (2024) and *Secret Cinema* (2024). Grassroots variations on this type of production include flash mobs (2024), silent discos (2024), and Live-Action Role-Playing Games (2024).

Themed Entertainment (Amusement Park, Water Park)

In the Middles Ages, people would gather at fairs and fetes to dance, get drunk, throw darts (occasionally at each other), and watch puppet shows. These gatherings eventually evolved into other traditions like traveling shows, circuses, pleasure gardens, exhibitions, world fairs, sideshows, and freak shows. The entertainment was always interactive, often offensive, and sometimes included elements of storytelling, like when the carnival barker explained how the snake man fell in love with the bearded lady.

By the mid-nineteenth century, the modern amusement park (2024) was born. It featured steam-powered carousels, Ferris wheels, and roller coasters. Live events are a common feature of these recreational romping grounds, including tightrope walkers, hot air balloon rides, concerts, fireworks, and theatrical productions.

In recent years, amusement parks have made rides more immersive and multisensory. An example of this is the *Web Slingers* experience at Disneyland's Avengers Campus (Disney 2021), which uses **spatial computing** to simulate the experience of webs shooting out of visitors' wrists.

Escape Room

Set in all sorts of fictional locations—from prison cells to space stations—escape rooms are designed to frustrate players at every turn and, oddly enough, that's why people love them. Working in teams of two to ten, players have a limited time (usually forty-five to sixty minutes) to beat the game and break free. They do so by completing a series of **puzzles** that allow them to progress through different levels of gameplay and into various physical locations. If you manage to escape in a timely fashion, you might end up on a **leaderboard** and become the top record-holder for future teams to beat.

Video Game (Digital Game)

IDNs are distinct from video games because they are primarily narratives with elements of interactivity, as opposed to games embellished with **cutscenes** (short bits of moving footage). That said, video games have much to teach IDN creators, as they harness and drive interactivity in all sorts of inventive ways. Here are just a few of the types of video game interactivity you can draw on when designing your IDN: Action Game (2024), Adventure Game (2024), Action-Adventure Game (2024), Interactive Film (2024), Fighting Game (2024), Battle Royale Game (2024), Stealth Game (2024), Survival Game (2024), Rhythm Game (2024), 4X (2024), Auto Battler (2024), Multiplayer Online Battle Arena (2024), Tower Defense (2024), Computer Wargame (2024), Sports Video Game (2024), Platformer (2024), Puzzle Video Game (2024), Hidden Object Game (2024), Tile-Matching Game (2024), Incremental Game (2024), Strategy Video Game (2024), Racing Game (2024), Shooter Game (2024), Casual Game (2024), Sandbox Game, and Simulation Video Game (2024).

Scrolling Story

These are narratives you explore by scrolling left to right or top to bottom to unlock interactive elements. They are often peppered with hyperlinks and media files that may or may not autoplay, depending on their creators' predilections. Examples include *Hollow* (McMillion Sheldon 2013) and *Snowfall* (Branch 2012).

Real-Time Digital Collaboration

The act of creating an IDN can form the basis of a spontaneous collaborative experience. This type of storytelling combines techniques of freewriting and improv theater to produce works that are more about the collaborative process (Barác 2018) than any polished final product.

One mode of digital collaboration involves the creation of a **wiki novel** (Wikinovel .net 2025). This involves a group of people simultaneously working on a single shared document to produce a hopefully coherent work of fiction.

Game hackathons (2022) and **game jams** (2024) are events where creators gather and collaborate to produce interactive narratives within rigid time constraints. This can be a fun way to jump-start the creative process and engage in high-speed problem solving, **prototyping**, and **user testing**. It's also a good way to show off your talents while discovering the skills and interests of fellow specialists.

Collaborative role-playing stories are usually led by a story master (AKA dungeon master) who guides the players' progress through the story via various handy tricks such as **reskinning** (directing players to an unexplored part of the story) and **kicking in the door** (breaking a story lull by leaping forward or inventing a new plot twist).

Another way to collaborate on an interactive project is a round robin approach where individual creators take turns inventing collaborative experiences for multiple participants to engage with. In 2019, I participated in a project that connected creators from ten different universities under the heading *Secret Story Network* (2024). Over the course of a year, we engaged with a collaborative online experience designed by a different participant each month (Gyori & Zaluczkowska 2022). The project I dreamed up, *Divided Kingdom*, was a dystopian post-Brexit tale that had participants interacting via *WhatsApp* (2024) to create political policies after the Midlands of England broke away from the UK and became a separate country (Figure 0.3).

Figure 0.3 Real-time digital collaboration—*Divided Kingdom*, *c.* 2019. *Source*: Author.

Locative (Location-Aware Ambient, In-Stu) Storytelling

If you want to get your steps in while exploring an inactive narrative, this is the approach for you. It allows players to explore physical locations (a park, a cemetery, or your granny's attic) while using their phone to unlock story elements linked to specific landmarks. Some locative stories feature multimedia elements, such as *Shelley's Heart Locative Version* (Figure 0.4; Gyori 2018b), and some incorporate augmented reality interactions as with the work of ACM SIGCHI (Wanwan et al. 2023).

Locative platforms may be app-based or web-based. Both approaches have pros and cons. Apps take a moment to download and take up real estate on your phone, but they tend to be reliable and may not require an internet connection. Also, they don't gobble up too much data when activated. Web-based interfaces are easy to access, but they are less reliable than apps and may be data-gluttons, especially when multimedia elements like videos are being viewed.

Some locative interfaces involve scanning **QR codes** placed around a specific site. This requires permissions and upkeep, and the codes can also be vandalized and rendered unusable. On a positive note, this approach is extremely precise, so it's possible to place readable images only inches apart. Also, QR codes aren't the only patterns players can scan. If it isn't covered with vegetation, defaced, or corroded, any reasonably complex image—a historic plaque, painting, or inscribed gravestone—can potentially unlock narrative content.

Another approach to locative tracking involves a sat-nav interface that geo-locates your nodes, as with *Location API* (2024) and *StoryPlaces* (2025). This frees creators from having to install physical signs with QR codes or other patterns on-site. Instead, they drop a **geo-tag** in a specific location, and the platform does the rest. One downside: most geo-tags are only accurate within about a 10-meter range.

Figure 0.4 *Shelley's Heart Locative Version, c.* 2018.

Locative stories may be fictional like *Zombie Run* (2024) or factual like *Find a Bristol Tree on the Move* (2024) and *History Unwired: Venice* (Epstein 2005) or a bit of both like *Story City* (2024). They might also be a form of location-aware **gamification** like *Geocaching* (2024).

Audio-only locative experiences are a natural because they free the user to focus on the environment that they're walking through rather than fixating on a screen. Platforms such as *Echoes* (2024), *SonicMaps* (2024), and *Voice Map* (2024) specialize in this approach.

Projection Mapping

This mode of digital design is all about spectacle. Dynamic 2D and 3D images are projected onto objects, buildings, or theatrical stages. These techniques have even been used to light up Stonehenge (2018). Projection mapping technology isn't always interactive, but with touch sensors, it can respond to pressure, and with motion control sensors, it can track movements and react to gestures.

360-images

This mode of interaction involves exploring a still image captured as a 360-degree array, as with the immersive shots taken of *The World's Largest Cave* (Edström 2015).

Virtual Reality (VR)

Your basic VR interface is reasonably straightforward. Wearing a **VR headset** (face sucker), the player explores a 3D virtual environment by looking in different directions.

VR interactions can also be enabled by pointing a data-glove, pressing a button on a controller, or even triggering responses with your eye movements.

Some VR setups include **spatial audio** (SA; sounds coming from specific locations within the virtual environment). **Wearable VR** gear can provide haptic feedback, such as a vibrating controller or tightening data-glove. And for the truly adventurous, there's **teledildonics** (2024). These are virtual hookups orchestrated via networked electronic sex toys and form-fitting **data-suits** (vibrating tail plug optional). On the other end of the spectrum, you can shed everything but the VR headset and a fig leaf and utilize sensing technology to track your body movements, hand gestures, and audio commands.

VR stories come in multiple flavors: fictional story-experiences like *INVASION!* (Madagascar, 2016); documentaries like *Bear 71* (Mendes & Allison 2012), workspace simulators like *training for healthcare workers* (TAVR Operation 2023), museum installations like *Curious Alice* (Viveport 2025), and virtual performances like *Justin Bieber in the Metaverse* (Animatrik 2022).

Augmented Reality (AR)

AR superimposes 3D story elements onto physical space by making them appear on your phone screen. This means you can watch a virtual dinosaur dancing on an actual tabletop. When players are empowered to manipulate such images, AR becomes an interactive experience.

A variation on this is *Pokémon Go* (2025), which translates physical locations into graphic representations of actual streets and buildings that players can navigate through. In this way, it combines location-aware geo-sensing with an AR overlay of the environment.

Mixed Reality (MR)

MR is a technological **mashup** of VR and **RL (Real Life)**. In other words, it allows people to interact with virtual objects and characters while remaining anchored in the real world. A user may move through physical space wearing a headset displaying virtual imagery while interacting with physical objects that add sensory dimensions. For instance, they may approach what looks, sounds, and feels like crackling flames in a fireplace when they are walking toward a space heater sitting on a stereo speaker. Or they may hug a translucent space alien who is actually an actor in a suit covered with **motion control sensors** which are mapping this ethereal being onto their field of vision.

Extended Reality (XR)

Extended Reality (XR) is an umbrella term that encompasses the entire spectrum of immersive technologies. These include VR, AR, and MR, along with any future developments. XR may soon allow us to try on virtual outfits with the help of an avatar with our exact physical dimensions (What is XR? 2024).

With the help of AI, XR is enhancing the resolution of images taken by Mars satellites and rovers to construct a physical Mars-like environment on Earth (Sirin Orbital Systems 2022). These are just two examples of how it will continue changing our interactions with technology and physical environments as it continues to evolve.

Mobile Story

If you like your interactivity on the go, download any number of apps to play on your phone, tablet, game console, portable media player, graphing calculator, or any other handheld digital device. Mobile apps feature bite-sized stories players can engage with while eating, driving, doing laundry, and showering (possibly at the same time). Story snippets can range from three seconds to five minutes in length. Creators tend to favor simple, striking images that stand out despite the small screen—think a screaming human face rather than a 5,000-person battle scene. Mobile stories may be fictional simulations like *Indefinite: Interrogation Game* (Li 2020), curated nonfiction experiences like *Rider Spoke* (Giannachi et al. 2010) Educational Tools like *Tinybop* (2024), or Alternate Reality Games (2024) like *I Love Bees* (2024).

Multimedia Story (AKA Multimodal, Digital)

This is what happens when you create a story on a single platform using all types of media: videos, audio files, slideshows, illustrations, animations, haikus, and more. Some interactive multimedia narratives include *Roxham* (Huneault 2018) and *The Sounds of CDMX* (Reiss 2022).

Transmedia Story

This approach involves distributing a single story across multiple platforms, media, and formats, for example, giving each character their own **blog** or telling part of the story as a film, part as an IDN, and part as a comic book as with *Collapsus* (2010).

Target BACRIM, the news game prototype I worked on, included a transmedia feature where players could share their cellphone number and receive messages from a fictional character based on members of a real-life paramilitary group (Figures 0.5 and 0.6).

Figures 0.5 and 0.6 Transmedia messages—*Target BACRIM, c.* 2016.

Interactive AI

IDN creators are now making forays into the brave new world of AI by transforming our loyal AI companions—**Siri**, **Echo**, and **Alexa**—into collaborators and characters in interactive audio games like *Adventures for Siri* (Storch, 2023) and on platforms like *Voiceflow* (2024). There are also many popular AI chatbots (2024) that can be incorporated into your IDN. For more highly produced audio AI, check out interactive radio dramas like *Code Name Cygnus* (Myers 2017). IDN creators are also generating text-based AI narratives with platforms like *AI Dungeon* (Walton 2019) that allow players to interact with AI as fast as they can type. And AI-based interactive story generators, such as *Talefy* (2024), *Story AI* (2024), and *Storynest* (2024), are helping creators craft multimedia IDNs.

As AI is a rapidly developing field, the "Conclusion" section at the end of this book speculates about some of the ways this groundbreaking technology may influence IDNs in the years to come, so stay tuned, or leap ahead—your call.

Hypertext Fiction (Hyperfiction, Digi Fiction)

The granddaddy of all IDN projects is hypertext. It comes in four basic varieties that resonate with some of the interactive patterns discussed in Chapter 2. Paths. They are **Axial**: A straightforward structure where one node leads to the next in a linear fashion, as with *The Virtual Disappearance of Miriam* (Campbell & Bedford 2000). **Arborescent**: As the name suggests, this approach is all about branching, creating multiple pathways and potentially numerous different endings as with *My Boyfriend Came Back from the War* (Lialina 1996). **Networked**: bumping up the complexity even higher, this structure is more like a fungus than a tree, radically nonlinear with no clear beginning, middle, or end like *Patchwork Girl* (Jackson 1995). And **Layered**: this approach involves creating a page of text with multiple links to various multimedia enhancements as with *Glitter in the Dark* (Vio 2014).

Interactive Fiction (IF)

Hypertext eventually gave birth to a two-headed baby known as Interactive Fiction. Much ink—and perhaps a little blood—has been spilled over which is the superior form: **choice-based IF** or **parser-based IF**. Both approaches have their upsides.

In a choice-based story, you can bounce around in a highly **nonlinear** fashion. You can also move swiftly, which creates a sense of narrative momentum that is well-suited for conveying emotions and sustaining interest.

Parser stories, in contrast, tend to be more linear and involve engaging with a simulated world in a more focused and methodical manner. You influence the environment by unlocking information in different ways. Available options are hidden, which means slowing your roll and relying on memory or intuition to solve a puzzle or combine elements in a certain way.

Simply put, parsers are more "thinky," and choice-based games are more "feely."

Another key difference involves the two computer tools players use to navigate through the IDN: the keyboard and the mouse. Parser stories require the keyboard to type in specific words, whereas choice-based stories rely on the mouse to click on options that influence the story.

Fortunately, the World Wide Web is big enough for both choice-based and parser-based stories to peacefully coexist. Creators are encouraged to explore both forms and, when possible, find ways to combine them.

Parser-based IF

Most early forms of Interactive Fiction were parser-based. The approach consists of a set of routines that allow the game to understand relatively simple English language commands. It has been described as "a narrative at war with a crossword." The player must solve a series of word puzzles to advance through the narrative world. This may involve typing a verb into a designated space to trigger a character's action or a narrative event like *Pick Up the Phone Booth and Die* (Noyes 1996). Some people find parsers frustrating as they can involve a lot of trial-and-error interactions as the player types in different word-triggers which may or may not prove effective. There are, however, clever variants like *Counterfeit Monkey* (Short 2012) that playfully subvert the form. Also, it's possible to create projects that have some parser elements yet are not exclusively parser-driven.

Inform 7 (2024) and *Squiffy* (2024) are commonly used for parser-based IF. *TADS 3* (2024) has a rich simulation library which makes it a good choice as well. Most of these tools expect you to do some programming, so if you're not thrilled by that prospect, take a look at *ADRIFT* (2024) and *Quest* (2024) as they are less technically challenging. Other parsing tools include *ANTLR* (2024), *StoryDev* (2024), and *Parse Platform* (2024). And you can find dozens more on *GitHub* (2024). To create a multiplayer parser, check out *Guncho* (2024).

Choice-based IF

Although Choose Your Own Adventure stories have been around since the early 1980s, their digital counterparts didn't emerge until the birth of Twine in 2012. The advent of this choice-based platform allowed creators to break with text-only interfaces. Images, audio files, animated GIFs, and video footage could be incorporated, so a new, all-singing all-dancing type of IF—the IDN—emerged.

Choice-based narratives are like their textual counterparts, Choose Your Own Adventure stories, in many ways. Players are given a set of choices. Each decision sends them on a path where they encounter story elements and eventually another set of choices. Because there are no textual puzzles to solve, these narratives tend to hum along at a swift pace. Also, unlike most parsers, they can be created with only a rudimentary knowledge of coding—or no coding at all.

Examples of Twine narratives include *Birdland* (Hennessy 2015), *Ultra Business Tycoon III* (Porpentine 2013), *Queers in Love at the End of the World* (Anthropy 2013), *Choice of the Dragon* (Fabulich & Strong-Morse 2009), and *Howling Dogs* (Porpentine 2012b).

iDocs (Interactive Documentaries)

Not all IDN projects are flights of fancy. Some are based on actual people and situations. This may encourage creators to take a more journalistic approach, such as filming interviews and reenactments. Still, these elements can be woven into a story structure the player explores by unlocking key pieces of information at specific moments. These projects may be linear like *The Shirt on Your Back* (Poulton et al. 2014); nonlinear like *Warsaw Rising* (Grabowska 2019); data-driven like *If the Moon were Only 1 Pixel* (Worth 2014); or personalizable like *Do Not Track* (Gaylor 2015). Other examples of nonfiction IDN design include the psychology story-quiz *Refined Self* (Lizardry 2023) and the interactive textbook *Earth: A Primer* (Gingold 2015) which allows players to build volcanoes and paint with the wind.

The Scope of This Book

I have worked in many of the storytelling forms listed above, but no single IDN creator can articulate everything about this complex and constantly changing field. Even when the scope is narrowed to just choice-based digital narratives it's impossible to examine every example in the level of detail necessary to help creators produce every possible permutation using every existing platform and coding language, let alone teaching all the production techniques necessary to create every conceivable type of media asset, while explaining all the logistical, organizational, and interpersonal skills needed to shepherd such complicated projects to completion. It would take a whole shelf of books and perhaps a whole library to cover all that terrain. Writing this book has, therefore, involved narrowing the parameters of the discussion to home in on the key concepts creators need to grasp when delving into the evolving world of IDN.

The Single-Player Choice-Based Interactive Digital Narrative (SCIDN)

To keep the discussion as focused as possible, I've chosen to concentrate on one type of IDN, the Single-Player Choice-Based Interactive Digital Narrative (or SCIDN). This is a good starting place because it allows you to master the skills necessary to start thinking like an IDN designer. Also, if you're not working with a multimillion-dollar budget and a large team of highly skilled professionals the goals it sets out are achievable. What's more—if you're not into it—you don't have to do any coding. I am not coding-adverse. Coding is a great way to enhance or your work or even invent entirely new story platforms. The trouble is, there are as many approaches to coding as there are colors in the rainbow, and an equivalent number of books and tutorials that can support a much deeper dive into the topic than this slim volume could possibly offer.

In the pages ahead, there are references to other modes of interactive storytelling: parsers, multiplayer games, RPGs, and so on. You should feel free to borrow elements from these forms, importing them into your project as you see fit. That is the beauty of IDN design: there is no single correct approach, so please feel free to invent something new and highly original.

But enough about what this book doesn't do. Here is what it *does* to. First and foremost, it focuses on the fundamentals of IDN design. If you're interested in embellishing your IDN with multimedia elements it includes tips for shooting short films, photographing still images, recording audio files, making animated GIFs, cinemagraphs, slideshows, and so on. On the other hand, if you plan to take a more stripped-down approach, that is, creating a text-only IDN, feel free to skip over or skim this material. There's nothing wrong with keeping things simple. Some of the most formally inventive interactive stories are text-only narratives. Foregoing the challenging of producing media assets can free creators to focus on designing highly innovative narrative structures. You may also choose to split the difference, producing a few media assets that play to the strengths of your team's skills and resources, while also challenging yourself to design inventive narrative patterns. Whatever the approach, this book can help you achieve your intended aim.

Now a couple anecdotes that support this book's unconventional structure:

From the Trenches

Cautionary Tale—Online Teaching Discussion

At the beginning of the Covid-19 lockdown—like everyone teaching in higher ed—I was required to suddenly pivot to offering online instruction to my students. A group of well-meaning colleagues who'd been researching online learning for years hosted a four-hour Zoom meeting for those of us looking to negotiate this radical shift in our pedagogical practice. Through this marathon session, they shared a scrupulously researched analysis about online learning. While it was all top-notch scholarship, the focus involved analyzing online learning in relation to traditional teaching practices, considering its evolution and how learners are rewarded by engaging with this educational paradigm. The academics addressing us made a compelling case for how students benefit from the flexibility of **asynchronous** lectures, the elimination of travel time, and the stimulus of virtual learning environments. Still, there was something missing.

None of the people in the workshop needed to be convinced that online teaching was effective. Even if some of us had harbored doubts it didn't matter. We all had to move online whether we wanted to or not, so we didn't need to know why this was a good idea. What we needed were some tips on how to pull it off. The knowledge being shared in the workshop was well researched and perfectly valid, but in terms of helping us create online lesson plans, structure Zoom workshops, breakout sessions, and discussion boards, it was like trying to build a lifeboat with a microscope: the wrong tool for the job.

Academic scholarship traditionally places a premium on knowledge acquired through **post hoc** analysis—studying texts, conducting interviews, and engaging in participant observation. However, this is not the only way to acquire new knowledge.

Researchers are sometimes skeptical of practical knowledge gained through an **ad hoc** creative process. It is criticized for being too instrumental, focusing on *how* to do things rather than asking *why* things should be done. But of course, without the how, the why is irrelevant because nothing will ever be accomplished. A person in need of lifeboat receives little benefit from information about the value of lifeboats, their key characteristics, impacts over time, and correlation to other modes of sea travel. What they need are some clear instructions of how to make a lifeboat from the tools and materials at hand. That's why, when writing this book, I've kept two basic tenets in mind.

1. It's for readers who want to create a working IDN.
2. It needs to be as useful as possible.

Designing an IDN is like attempting to understand a game of three-dimensional chess; there are a lot of variables to track. The last thing you need when grappling with such complexity is a guide written in a rarefied style with lots of distracting digressions. Far more useful is clear, practical advice presented in the most straightforward manner possible. That is what I have attempted to provide.

There is nothing wrong with research that analyzes IDNs by discussing how this form of storytelling relates to other artistic traditions and theoretical concepts and examining ways in which the values and beliefs of players are influenced by engaging with it. These are all valuable contributions to scholarly discourse, but they have one drawback: reading them won't help you create an IDN.

To be clear: this book cannot *make* you an IDN creator, any more than reading a book about guitar playing would have made Jimi Hendrix the virtuoso he became. Hopefully, however, it will serve as a jumping-off point and a safety net as you embark on your journey of creative self-discovery.

Takeaways

- Make sure the tool is appropriate for the job.
- Answering "why" questions won't help you produce creative output.
- When offering practical advice on a complex project, use straightforward language and focus on developing useful skills.

Success Story: Machinima

When it comes to overseeing IDN projects the word "success" can mean different things. In terms of creating a multi-million-dollar interactive narrative with a team of highly skilled and well-paid professionals, success means making sure the graphics are flawless, and the interface is perfectly intuitive. On the other hand, when it comes to organizing a community outreach project involving amateur creatives with limited skills and experience, success means supporting the tentative steps of novices building story maps or operating cameras for the first time. This isn't about managing expectations; it's about rethinking the nature of success itself.

When the creative development of the participants is paramount, quality control is bound to take a hit. You should still try to keep production values as high as possible, but it may be necessary to adjust your priorities. Ask the most experienced person on hand to demonstrate how to achieve a particular goal, then step aside and give the beginners a shot. Even if the results are less than perfect it's important to foster a spirit of meaningful play. This gives rise to the moments of spontaneous brilliance that can only emerge when an enthusiastic amateur is given an opportunity to take the reins. This can happen in all sorts of surprising ways: a sixty-year-old woman struggling with an editing program is assisted by a twenty-year-old man who, in turn, gains insights from her mastery of storytelling, a shy student embraces the role of a badass superhero, an egocentric teen learns to share the spotlight with her collaborators. Little victories like these may not rival winning Oscars or BAFTAs, but in terms of enriching the lives of your participants, they are invaluable.

Another way of saying this is that success can be measured in terms of process as well as finished product. If the creative process affords deep learning, professional development, and emotional satisfaction, the project is a success, even if the final output includes a few glitches. Throughout this book, you will find suggestions for sidestepping rookie mistakes and improving production values, but there are also plenty of tips for keeping things fun and engaging for everyone involved. After all, the most important thing anyone will take away from designing and producing an IDN is the experience of making it.

When supervising projects with amateur creatives it's helpful to value enthusiastic engagement over polish. A good example of this ethos relates to the now-defunct Tribeca Flashpoint Media Arts Academy in downtown Chicago. I had the pleasure of working there from 2011 to 2014. We taught an array of disciplines including film directing, producing, screenwriting, animation, sound design and games design. And during the second year, we brought together students from different courses to collaborate on a single large project that challenged them to engage with cutting-edge production techniques such as projection mapping and Alternate Reality gaming. This wasn't the first time they'd collaborated with students from other disciplines. It all started on the first day of school with a twenty-four-hour project called "Machinima."

A **machinima** is a short film created by utilizing the real-time computer graphics of a video game. This was a kind of baptism by fire for our new students, their chance to work with people with different interests and skill sets, creating a multimedia project in just forty-eight hours. The participants were divided into teams of four to six, consisting of students from different disciplinary tracks. They were told the basics of Machinima creation and shown some examples of completed projects. Then it was time to get started.

At each step of the collaborative process the students were encouraged to take on different roles, often stepping outside of their comfort zones as they volunteered to work as scriptwriters, directors, voice actors, and video editors. Their first task involved collaborating on a five-minute script utilizing characters from a specific video game. Each team quickly picked a writer to take notes and craft a narrative from the ideas they were frantically spit balling as members of staff circulated between them and assisted with these brainstorming sessions.

Once the teams had a rough draft script various students volunteered to voice the characters. Then it was off to the audio department where they took turns in a sound booth recording dialogue and sound effects.

Next, the team went to the games department where staff taught them the mechanics of a particular video game. At this point, one of the team members took on the role of director, instructing the other team members who were working with game controllers to make their characters move around according to the blocking outlined within their script. This "performance" was captured as a video file.

Finally, the team moved on to the assembly phase, which involved editing the recorded dialogue onto the footage of the game characters. Music and sound effects were also added, and, in some cases, visual effects were included.

To be clear, the completed machinimas were not IDNs, but the process of creating them *was* intensely interactive, constituting a kind of two-day multimedia-bootcamp spanning multiple disciplinary domains. This collaborative experience culminated on the afternoon of the second day with all the staff and students gathering for a screening of about twenty five-minute projects. The results were always rough around the edges, but the enthusiasm of the participants—cheering, laughing, and heckling the screen—more than made up for this. If our goal had been creating high-gloss media outputs, the process would have been an utter disaster. But because our goal was giving the students a crash course in cross-disciplinary collaboration, a high-speed, hands-on tour of each key department in our school, and a chance to work alongside our expert staff, machinima was an unqualified success every time.

Takeaways

* When leading inexperienced teams, define success in terms of them acquiring expertise rather than producing flawless work.

- A baptism by fire can energize participants and quickly upskill them in multiple ways.
- A baptism by fire is a shortcut in terms of team bonding.

Key Tasks: Introduction

Task 1. Seed Book

Sketch out loose ideas that might inspire your IDN.

1   Plans

Welcome to the part of the process everyone is tempted to race through at 100 miles an hour, cutting every hairpin turn and skipping crucial steps. When approaching the planning stage, it helps to remember the Buddhist aphorism: "Done well is soon enough." Often, the difference between a top-notch IDN and something fatally flawed is effective prep work. Whether you're creating a project that is primarily text-, video-, still-, or audio-based, a well-thought-out plan is a must. So, take a breath, pump the brakes, and embrace the idea that preparation can also be a highly stimulating part of the creative process.

This chapter is divided into two sections: Facilitation Planning and Production Planning. The former focuses on big-picture issues related to organizing your overall creative initiative. The latter focuses on creating a specific IDN.

Facilitation Planning

Thinking through your big-picture needs involves asking a lot of "what if" questions. "What if fifty people agree to participate?" "What if only three turn up?" "What if we have high-end equipment?" "What if we don't?" "What if we're working with an all-volunteer army?" "What if things go sideways?" "And when they do, how will we respond?"

At this point in the creative process, anticipating potential trouble spots is one of the most important aspects of brainstorming. After all, preventing a forest fire is much easier than putting one out. And—if and when—the first flames burst into view, you need a strategy for quickly extinguishing them.

Scale

When working on a collaborative project, few things will capsize your canoe faster than bringing the wrong number of participants on board. For most projects, you should recruit at least four people, especially if they are young volunteers who may get squirrely and abandon ship. This can happen for all sorts of reasons: infighting, jealousy, insecurity, fear, or apathy (often fear in disguise).

The maximum number of participants is intimately tied to our next concern:

Support

Getting the correct ratio of facilitators to participants is crucial. If you're working with a large group of young participants, consider putting them in small teams and appointing a facilitator who is only a few years older than they are—but not too much older. For example, a college student could supervise a group of high school students. The participants will tend to look up to their team lead and want to impress them by acting more mature.

This approach will free up more seasoned (read: older) facilitators who are subject matter experts, such as writers, videographers, audio technicians, still photographers, video editors, and your facilitation lead. These experts can float between teams, offering guidance at key points.

A typical setup might include twenty participants divided into five teams of four, each with a facilitator acting as a team lead. Additionally, four to five experts would float between the teams.

Budget

As they say in the film world, "There's never enough money or time." When creating a homegrown IDN, chances are you will have very little of either. However, if you have access to a school or library, a few computers and smartphones, and some eager volunteers, you have everything you need to create a dynamic and playable IDN. Any additional cash or in-kind resources (fancy equipment, a green screen studio, etc.) is—as they say in the culinary world—gravy.

Crowdfunding

If you're eager to spring for high-end production values, you may need to raise some cash. But who would invest in an IDN created by a team of enthusiastic but inexperienced amateurs? Your rich uncle perhaps?

If you have the time—and supportive friends and relatives willing to subsidize your dream—crowdfunding might be worth considering. A successful crowdfunding campaign often involves providing donor incentives at different contribution levels (e.g., $100 gets a toy shark autographed by the production team).

Keep in mind that running a crowdfunding campaign requires marketing skills and multitasking abilities. It can also become a bit of a time sink and energy vampire if it starts stealing too much focus from your main goal: creating the IDN.

Platform

When selecting a platform to support your project, it helps to bear in mind factors like time scale, production goals, and functionality. Also, budget, time frame, and the skill level of the creators should weigh into your choice of platform. It's worth considering whether the platform is likely to have a long shelf life or might be about to fold. How secure is it against hacking? Does it offer technical support? Is it regularly updated to prevent bit rot, link rot, and hacking?

There are plenty of affordable and even free options but choose wisely based on your aims and the constraints of your project.

As I'm typing these words, I'm wary that some of the statements I'm making may have a short expiration date. Since digital technologies develop at breakneck speed, any platform-specific insights may swiftly become outdated. Still, I would be remiss if I didn't share some information about some of the more prominent IDN platforms at the time of this book's publication. Apologies to any future readers who will discover I wasn't able to perfectly predict which platforms and features would stand the test of time, and which would age out faster than your dad's favorite action hero.

To begin with, the following platforms will all support the creation of your Single-Player Choice-Based IDN: *Twine* (2024), *ChoiceScript* (2024), *inklewriter* (2024), *Raconteur* (2024), *EkoStudio* (2024), *Klynt* (2024), Bitsy (2024), *Downpour* (2024), and *StoryNexus* (2024).

Twine is the most popular, but some of its competitors offer features not available (or that you'd have to build) in Twine. *ChoiceScript*, *inklewriter*, and *StoryNexus* have all been made available in a partially functional way to attract amateur creators. Visit their websites to find tutorials that allow you to dive into their unique features. Note: Inkle is generally used as a prototyping tool for projects that are later imported into a more advanced program like *Unity*. *Seltani* (2024) is a platform that empowers creators to design multiplayer choice-based stories.

Another question to ask when picking the software to support your vision is: How creator-friendly is it? Platforms like *Texture* (2024) offer drag-and-drop interfaces. Others, like *Inform 7* (2024) require you to do some rudimentary coding. Some, like *Eko*, are open source. Others, like *Klynt*, charge a subscription fee. Some, like Twine, generate **embed codes** that can be posted anywhere. Others, like *BBC StoryFormer* (2024), only generate a **URL**.

Some other considerations you might bear in mind: *Inkle* adds text to the same node building your story a sentence at a time. *Inform 7* includes a parser editor. *StoryNexus* offers a branching editor. And *Tuesday* (2024) features a visual novel editor for manga makers.

If you have deep pockets and a large team, you might check out *Articy: Draft* (2024). You can even create a low-tech IDN using the interactive functions of *Google Drive* (2024), *PowerPoint* (Articulate 360, 2014), or *Keynote* (Byrne 2019).

Production Schedule

If you're working with amateur creatives, your participants may not possess vast reserves of patience. But if properly motivated, they may have an abundance of creative energy and enthusiasm. The key is tapping into the latter, which means working quickly and keeping the creative process fun. Here are three possible schedules for producing IDNs:

1. A seven-day schedule for community outreach projects.
2. A twelve-week schedule for a semester-long class.
3. An open-ended plan for solo creators.

Seven-Day Community Outreach Schedule

Seven days, working from 10 a.m. to 3 p.m., should be enough time for the entire production process from beginning to end. These sessions should be supplemented with some short (fifteen to thirty minutes) lectures. A typical breakdown involves dividing the process into thirds: two days for preproduction, two days for production, and two days for final assembly, plus one more day for last fixes and a screening.

Development
- **Day 1:** Introduction of project, brainstorming outline.
- **Day 2:** Path plotting, user testing, location scouting.

Production
- **Day 3:** Capture and create assets, nodes, and socials.
- **Day 4:** Capture and create assets, nodes, and socials.

Assembly
- **Day 5:** Edit assets, nodes, and socials. Assemble IDN.
- **Day 6:** Edit assets, nodes, and socials. Assemble IDN.
- **Day 7:** Final fixes, screening.

Note: If you are working with multiple creative teams generating several projects simultaneously, break down the schedule accordingly. For instance, if you have four teams, you might have each team spend half a day working with different experts, for example, making stop-motion media assets with an animator, working on nodes with a graphic designer, or creating socials with a marketing expert. This ensures each team engages with several modes of creative expression.

Twelve-Week Teaching Semester Schedule

This approach assumes teams will meet in two-hour workshop sessions over twelve weeks. These sessions should be supplemented with short lectures and assigned out-of-class readings from this book (pardon the shameless self-promotion). Student teams should also be expected to shoot, record, edit, and assemble much of their work out of class. Rough cuts and prototypes should be brought in toward the end of the semester for player testing and refinement.

Development
* **Week 1:** Introduction of project, viewing and reviewing examples, starting outline.
* **Week 2:** Discuss planning part 1. Continue outlining, prototyping, and user testing.
* **Weeks 3–4:** Discuss planning part 2. Pre-produce assets, nodes, and socials.

Production
* **Week 5:** Discuss interaction design. Produce assets, nodes, and socials.
* **Week 6:** Discuss filming techniques. Produce assets, nodes, and socials.
* **Week 7:** Discuss sound design. Produce assets, nodes, and socials.
* **Week 8:** Discuss social design. Produce assets, nodes, and socials.

Assembly
* **Week 9:** Edit assets, nodes, and socials. Assemble IDN. User test rough version.
* **Week 10:** Edit assets, nodes, and socials. Assemble IDN. User test fine version.
* **Week 11:** Edit assets, nodes, and socials. Assemble IDN. User test final version.
* **Week 12:** Final fixes, screening, feedback.

Solo Project Schedule

There is no such thing as a "typical solo project." A solo IDN is, by definition, an idiosyncratic undertaking that must conform to the resources, production timeline, talents, interests, and bandwidth of the individual creator. This is not to suggest that schedules and deadlines don't matter for solo artists. They are just as important as team schedules, but for different reasons. Rather than wrangling multiple participants, a solo artist must manage the wild and woolly aspirations of the greatest enigma of all—themself.

Creative lone wolves should be ambitious but realistic. And if you're relying on unpaid volunteers to assist with important roles, keep in mind they may vanish during the production process—often when you need them most. This is yet another reason scheduling and deadlines matter. The longer a project drags on, the more likely you are to lose key stakeholders.

PRO TIPS

* **Set deadlines and sub-deadlines and stick to them.** Keep people on task and accountable.
* **Practice version control.** Use shared documents and sheets for all important documents: production schedules, contact sheets, hot-lists, prop lists, and so on. This will ensure there aren't alternate drafts floating around. For instance, create your schedule as a *Google Drive* (2024) document with tables or a spreadsheet, give your team members editing permissions, and share the link with them. This will empower

your team to collectively refine their work while ensuring everyone has access to the latest versions of this important organizational tool.

- **Encourage left brain mojo.** If you are lucky enough to be working with someone who thinks like a producer, ask them to go to town on coordinating your project. This may involve creating contact lists, production schedules, postproduction workflows, budgets, equipment lists, wardrobe lists, prop lists, and so on.

On the other hand, if no one on your team seems cut out to become the organizational overlord, don't fret. For a simple "run and gun" operation you just need a single document that enumerates essential elements in any order. This should be modified based on the needs of your IDN. For instance, if you aren't creating filmed assets, you won't need some of the items in the list below:

- Production Schedule.
- Production facility address.
- Crew names and contact info.
- Cast names and contact info.
- Production gear: computers, software, cameras, tripods, microphones, and so on.
- Props, wardrobe, and set decoration.
- Shoot dates and times.
- Location addresses and contacts.

LANDMINE

- **Don't be too rigid or too loose.** Too much control freak energy can squeeze the joy out of any creative project. On the other hand, completely winging it can lead to wasted effort and missed opportunities. The trick is first drafting a solid plan and then finding clever ways to embellish it—or even deviate from it completely—in order to keep things fresh.

Icebreakers

After the initial introductions, when your participants and facilitators are first getting to know one another, a quick icebreaking activity can help everyone get better acquainted. For instance, each person can share two truths and one lie about themselves, and the group can try to identify the BS, or you can have the participants show two keys on their keychain and share a few sentences about the area the key represents. Icebreaking activities can be time-consuming, but they're a great way to help people feel more invested in the project and connected with one another.

Models

At the start of the production process, be sure to explain what an IDN is and review examples of the type of project you plan to create. If you decide to navigate through projects you've supervised in the past bear in mind that participants may be overly critical of work created by previous teams, so it can help to encourage them to focus on the positive as well.

LANDMINE

- **Self-love is blind.** Teams can also be overly generous about the quality of their own work mistaking every self-indulgent flourish and in-joke for a stroke of genius. It's important to encourage participants to apply critical thinking throughout the production process identifying both pros and cons when reviewing works created by other teams—and especially when critiquing their own creative outputs.

Upskilling

Your facilitators are sure to bring different talents and abilities to the project. You might have a professional photographer, sound designer, or animator in the mix. Upskilling sessions led by such experts can equip participants with the knowledge they need to successfully handle the tasks ahead. Once participants are introduced to the fundamentals, they will feel more confident stepping into challenging roles and using expensive equipment. Facilitators, in turn, will feel more comfortable allowing them to do so.

Guided Practice

Having skilled facilitators on hand can significantly enhance your production values. Also, if they're also supportive mentors, they can create valuable apprenticeship opportunities throughout the production process. The expert demonstrates how to perform a task, then allows the novice to try it, guiding them as they develop new skills.

PRO TIP

- **Don't seek the spotlight—be it.** Traditional "sage on the stage" teaching involves commanding everyone's attention and lecturing ad nauseam. In contrast, co-creating an IDN requires moments when the facilitator shifts the spotlight to the novice, casting a positive glow on their growing mastery. This approach fosters **intrinsic motivation**. Participants engage more enthusiastically when focused on personal development rather than external rewards. The key is catching participants doing something right and praising them in front of their peers. This gets them seeking to excel as they look for more opportunities to receive positive reinforcement and shine. Fortunately, encouragement is not a finite property that needs to be hoarded—it's a limitless resource for building commitment and goodwill.

Facilities

For the production office—where most of the planning, writing, and editing will take place—you'll need a centralized location with lockable doors. This will allow you to leave equipment and personal items unattended while capturing images and sounds elsewhere. For sets and locations, prioritize places where you can control the lighting and sound. (More on this in a moment.)

Catering

If you can't pay your team, at least feed them. When your budget is tight, small gestures—like snacks—can go a long way. At a bare minimum, have potato chips, cookies, water, and coffee on hand. If funds are tighter, you can ask participants to bring their own food, but if you have a little more to spend, providing one meal a day is a gesture everyone will appreciate.

LANDMINE

- **Remember food breaks.** Avoid working for more than four hours without giving participants a chance to eat. Team members burn energy quickly and need to refuel. Ideally, take a full hour for lunch. If you're feeling pressed for time due to a looming deadline, ask everyone if they're okay with cutting the break to thirty minutes. Additionally, be sure to provide occasional comfort breaks so participants and facilitators can stretch their legs, use the restroom, or grab a smoke if needed.

Production Planning

Once the facilitators have assembled the troops, laid the logistical groundwork, and—if necessary—divided participants into separate teams, it's time to plan the creation of the actual IDN.

Skill Inventory

Every team brings unique—and sometimes hidden—talents to the table. Discussing these skills is a great way to discover untapped creative potential. The key is playing to your team's strengths. Joe's a juggler? Great! Mary yodels? Fantastic! How about a dream sequence featuring a juggling yodeler? If you're fortunate enough to have an audio specialist on your team, you might create a story involving elaborate soundscapes. Realizing an intricate dramatic sequence, like a Martian invasion, is often easier to accomplish with audio than attempting to film something equally complex. On the other hand, if you have a professional cinematographer and a skilled editor in the mix, they might come up with creative solutions to visually depict the Martian invasion (Figure 1.1).

With some **Visual Effects (VFX)** wizardry, your team might also depict a man caught in a giant spiderweb (Figure 1.2).

Or a giant thumb crushing an unsuspecting victim (Figure 1.3).

Figure 1.1 Green screen composite, Martian Attack—*Next Level*, *c*. 2023.

Figure 1.2 Green screen composite, Spider Traps Dad—*Next Level*, c. 2023.

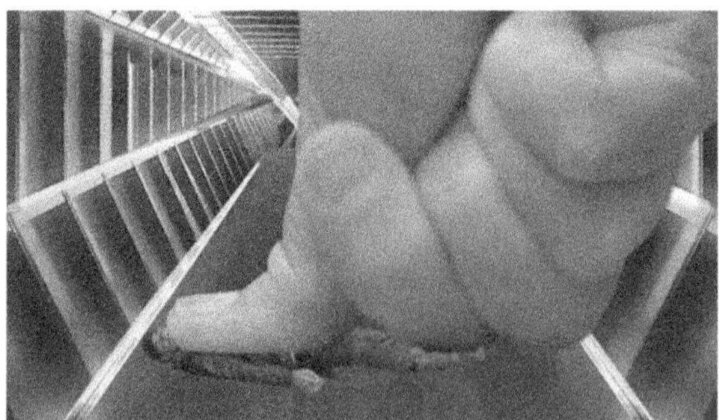

Figure 1.3 Green screen composite, Thumb Crush—*Next Level*, *c*. 2023.

Resource Inventory

Additional sources of inspiration are all the physical objects, locations, and clothing items at your disposal. You can take note of these by drafting a detailed resource list. Be sure to include everything—animal, vegetable, or mineral—that could possibly enhance the production of your IDN. Don't forget Aunt Kay's glow-in-the-dark bowling ball, Uncle Pete's stretch limo, or Cousin Darius' drone. Also, think about locations, set decoration, and live events you can crash—anything and everything that might enhance your project. Once you've taken stock of these odds and ends, scan the list to see if any story ideas jump out.

Experience Inventory

A rich source of comedy and drama is life itself, so consider drawing on the lived experiences of your participants. These can emerge from a brainstorming session where participants reflect on a prompt like:

- Describe a situation where you felt like a fish out of water.
- What's the hardest lesson you ever learned?
- Describe an accomplishment you're especially proud of.
- What's the most embarrassing thing you've ever done?
- What's the worst job you've ever had?

There's no need to meticulously catalog the anecdotes that emerge from these prompts. Instead, think of them as creative catalysts.

Brainstorming

During this process, facilitators should prompt participants to pitch ideas and build on them, considering many different narrative possibilities. As you're creating an interactive story, the more plot beats, the merrier. Have three ideas for an ending? Wunderbar! Include all of them. And along the way, ask yourself key questions:

- Is this a world people will want to play in? Why?
- How does interactivity make it awesome?
- Will players adopt a specific persona or play as themselves?
- How big will it be? How many characters, scenes, endings?
- What makes it replayable?
- How do the player's choices influence the plot?

The key is thinking like a designer. An IDN isn't merely a story; it's a **story world** containing many narrative possibilities that players can explore or ignore at will. Creating this kind of project means thinking through a variety of narrative options and carefully interweaving cause-and-effect sequences related to them. Design thinking also means examining the motives and expectations of players, considering what might inspire them to take a particular action, and finding ways to reward their engagement with consequences that enrich the process of exploring your IDN.

PRO TIPS

- **Celebrate divergent thinking**. What if the protagonist sprouts propeller ears and flies away? Embrace the unexpected. Each dramatic action and word of dialogue is a chance to do something surprising to keep your audience captivated.
- **Be a well, not a bucket.** Rather than hoarding your ideas like a finite resource, allow your creativity to be replenished by the infinitely deep subterranean springs of your unconscious and then share them generously.
- **Not all writing has to happen during brainstorming sessions.** A great way to turbocharge the creative process is to task participants with coming up with ideas outside of the group and recording them as notes, voice memos, or videos on their phones. The next time you convene, each participant can share their ideas with the group, and these plot points and character beats can be incorporated into your IDN.

Editorial

Chapter 3 discusses editing media assets, but there's another type of editing that isn't about combining produced elements; it's about establishing a clear vision for how those elements should be produced in the first place.

The **editorial guidelines** for an IDN may be proposed by a project lead, evolve democratically from a group discussion, or emerge from a mix of top-down and bottom-up approaches. Regardless of how these creative parameters emerge, they will serve to shape the production process moving forward. TV newsrooms have bullpens where reporters pitch ideas to editors. Publishing houses pair editors with individual authors to help them refine their manuscripts. And print journals have editors who focus on different beats and patches. In each of these cases, the editorial team shapes the tone, theme, and narrative point of view, ensuring the final output has a consistent and compelling voice.

Editorial decisions are the non-technical choices. It's important to focus on issues such as color grading and audio levels, but none of that will matter if the editorial content is lacking. Whether you are working on an IDN as a facilitator, a participant, or a solo creator, you are also consciously shaping and maintaining a specific editorial focus. Here are some of the concerns to bear in mind:

- **Interest**: Does the work hold our attention?
- **Relevance**: Does it matter?
- **Timeliness**: Is it topical?
- **Expiration**: How evergreen is the content?
- **Clarity**: Is it comprehensible?
- **Restraint**: Is the content potentially offensive or triggering? Or merely too obvious?
- **Legality**: Does it honor copyrights and avoid libel, invasion of privacy, and obscenity?
- **Ambition**: Does it challenge the creative team?
- **Originality**: Does it break new ground?
- **Sensitivity**: How does it portray vulnerable people?

LANDMINE

- **Avoid punching down.** If your participants are creating a narrative about a sensitive topic, character dynamics are key. If you're not careful, an interactive story can reinforce the negative behavior it means to critique. For instance, your team might create an anti-bullying IDN. But if the story mechanic allows players to heap verbal abuse on a character, the narrative will appear to promote and even celebrate bullying. A smarter, less problematic approach involves turning the tables on the bullying character and empowering players to challenge them in different ways, not by bullying them (as with a revenge narrative), but by allowing them to see the destructive impact of their antisocial behavior. The key is inverting the oppressive power dynamic rather than reinforcing its negative effects.

Story Concept

During the planning phase, you don't need to have every detail of your story mapped out. You might not have a clear sense of all the characters, scenes, or how things will end, but that's fine. You just need to identify a central premise that sparks ideas for you and/or your team.

One place to start is with a protagonist who has a specific intention: a goal they want to achieve or a flaw they need to overcome. This character may or may not be aware of the challenge(s) they face. Once you identify the biggest obstacle standing in their way—whether it's a human antagonist, social situation, physical barrier, or psychological block—you will have the makings of dramatic conflict. In other words, you'll have the beginning of a story.

Of course, one of the joys of interactive storytelling is that you can experiment with different types of story structures and forms. Eschewing the Hero's Journey (2024), you might reject the idea of creating a narrative driven by a goal-oriented protagonist and instead explore a stream-of-consciousness, multilinear, or looping approach. If so, have at it! Narrative rules are made to be broken, and there are other traditional narrative structures you can draw on including Scandinavian, Indian, West African, and Autochthonous Forms (Seager 2013), as well as Maureen Murdock's *The Heroine's Journey* (2024).

LANDMINE

- **Beware the unfocused premise.** This happens when you're not sure who your protagonist is, what they want, and what obstacles they must overcome to achieve their goal.

PRO TIP

- **Establish a shared vision.** And make sure everyone is rowing in the same direction.

Story Type

Before you can start plotting story beats, you must first decide the kind of IDN you want to produce. If you're interested in creating a fictional IDN, you'll need to think about issues such as **characters**, **plots**, **themes**, and **dramatic conflict**. To explore works of this kind visit the New Media Writing Prize (2024) or The Interactive Fiction Database (2024).

On the other hand, if you are interested in creating a nonfiction iDoc (Aston 2016), you'll need to stick to the facts and think more like journalists or documentarians. This will involve doing some research. You may also choose to shoot dramatizations AKA **dramatic reconstructions** (Murno 2018), **demonstrations** (Stewart 2020), and **interviews** (Fulltime Filmmaker 2022). You can find plenty of examples of iDocs at the MIT Docubase (2024). Also, consider checking out some data-driven interactive stories (Miller 2024).

Traditional Story Structures

Before moving on to a discussion of the unique challenges and opportunities inherent in interactive storytelling, here are a few words about the elements of traditional linear storytelling that can help inform the creation of your IDN. Whole books ten times thicker than this one have been dedicated to discussions of traditional narrative structure, so the best this section can offer is an extremely truncated barebones overview. Still, bearing in mind that a few old-school narrative tricks and tropes can come in handy when designing your nonlinear story.

Although your IDNs will feature detours, switchbacks, and digressions, it will still have plot twists, and character arcs. And although you can't predict the path a player will take through your narrative, you do know they will start at the beginning (Act I), proceed through the middle (Act II), and eventually arrive at some kind of ending, or endings (Act III).

Traditional narrative structure won't neatly map over the amoeba-like configuration of your IDN design, but it can still inform key plot points. For instance, in a traditional tale, the protagonist moves through a series of crossroads and makes key decisions at each of these junctures. When penning a novel or screenplay, the writer chooses for the character, but with an IDN, the player is empowered to make these dramatic choices. It's still helpful, however, to think in terms of those same crossroads. The difference is, you can offer a few options and allow the player to decide how they—in the role of the protagonist—wish to proceed.

Some key story elements related to traditional story structure are:

- **Protagonist(s):** Who is the story about? How are they unique, complex, flawed, or gifted?
- **Want:** What the protagonist desires.
- **Need:** The achievement that will complete their character arc.
- **Obstacle:** Antagonistic character, object, situations, or fear that generates dramatic conflict.
- **Narrative Question:** A hook in the form of a mystery that can only be solved by engaging with the story.
- **Stakes:** What happens if the goal isn't achieved? Why does this matter to the protagonist(s)?
- **Escalation (Rising Action):** Ratcheting up the tension as the story progresses.
- **Reflection (Falling Action):** Moments when the protagonist faces setbacks and takes stock of their situation.
- **Inciting Incident:** The player/protagonist picks an option that changes the status quo.
- **Midpoint Reversal:** The player/protagonist has an epiphany that changes their goal.
- **Climax:** The player/protagonist clashes with the antagonist.
- **Resolution:** The player/protagonist arrives at a new status quo.

Some traditional storytelling techniques include:

Subtext

This is an invitation for viewers to read between the lines. It can appear in dialogue when a flirty character delivers lines freighted with innuendo. It can also happen nonverbally, such as when a character's body language reveals they're anxious. Alternatively, subtext can involve a disconnect between dialogue and action, as when a character claims they're happy, but their posture suggests they're depressed or angry.

Suspense

This is all about the thrill of anticipation. For instance, we know someone is hiding in the closet. Will they jump out and attack the characters walking through the abandoned house? By slowing down time and focusing on each footstep, you keep the player/protagonist on the edge of their seat.

Dramatic Irony

This is another way of maintaining narrative interest during the nonlinear exploration of your story world. For example, include a **Non-Player Character (NPC)** who is oblivious to an important plot point—such as a huge monster lurking in the cupboard. As the player explores the IDN, their narrative interest will be enhanced as they wait for the other shoe to drop and for the monster to be revealed, triggering the NPC to panic.

Gaming Structures

An IDN that seems more game-like will have a lot of player choices and shorter cutscenes. However, creating something with extensive real-time gameplay requires a sophisticated developing platform like *Unity* (2024), *Unreal Engine* (2024), or *Godot* (2024). Even if you don't have the bandwidth, money, or skills to tackle that challenge you can borrow concepts from gaming to inform your interactive design, such as:

Ludic versus Narrative Pleasure

In terms of **User Experience (UX),** one thing every IDN has in common is a tension between two forms of enjoyment. **Ludic pleasure** is the rush we get from making interactive choices. It's the gaming impulse that gets us leaning in and steering the dramatic action. **Narrative pleasure**, in contrast, is the impulse that lets us kick back and go along for the ride.

The fundamental challenge of IDN design involves finding a way to switch between ludic and narrative pleasures at the right time in the right way so it feels natural to the flow of the story. Too much ludic, and your story becomes a video game. Too much narrative, and it morphs into a movie with a few interactive embellishments — or worse a website. As the field of IDN creation continues to evolve video games, such as *The Quarry* (2024), *The Last of Us* (2024), and *Uncharted* (2024) are finding inventive ways to become more story-driven. Meanwhile, digital narratives, like *The Walking Dead* (2024), and *Firewatch: Campo Santo* (2024), are finding ways to incorporate more player interaction. When designing your IDN always keep the ludic/narrative balance in mind to ensure your UX remains well-paced and engrossing.

LANDMINE

- **Avoid sluggish pacing.** This is a highly intuitive process. The key is to space out decision points so they don't disrupt the story flow too often or at irritating moments. Additionally, ensure they appear at key crossroads where the player can meaningfully influence the plot. What's more, an IDN shouldn't take too long to play. A total running time of five minutes is sufficient, especially for an episode of a mobile story.

Emergent Storytelling (Emergent Narrative, Procedural Narrative)

This term refers to any storyline that organically develops based on the player's choices as they navigate your story world. Some emergent stories are riveting; others are dull as dirt. That's why clever IDN design is crucial. While you can't predict exactly what a player will do, you can work to ensure that all the detours they explore are intriguing and, in some way, inform the plot or characterization, and ideally both.

Randomization (Aleatory Mechanics)

Adding an element of chance can make your IDN an unpredictable thrill ride. You might come up with the whole story with the help of an AI plot generator (2024) or incorporate some randomized mechanics into the narrative structure, for instance, games of chance that trigger dramatic actions: a toss of dice, a randomly selected card, or the spin of a roulette wheel. To get a sense of how this works, explore existing mechanics such as a list randomizer (2024), a random number generator (2024), or a wheel of names (2024). Each IDN can create its own rules related to randomization, that is, receiving an even number means the player's status changes, and they are able to access new information.

Menu

At key points during the story, players are offered an array of objectives, strategies, or tools. This can enhance UX by focusing the player's attention on certain elements while allowing them to ignore others. It also increases replayability, serving as the digital equivalent of a board game with a bonus deck that encourages players to achieve special objectives or unlock hidden abilities. Some story variations you might offer include

- **Complicating an event:** Add information, that is, two characters are divorced.
- **Linking moments:** Create an associative leap to show the significance of a related event.
- **Changing perspective:** Move the POV from one character to another.
- **Altering facts:** Change details, such as the color of the sky or the player's opinion of their pet goldfish.

Penalty

When a player fails to achieve a short- or long-term objective, they receive a penalty in the form of docked points, a setback, or a virtual kick in a sensitive body part.

Treasure Hunt

The more nonlinear your design, the more challenging it will be to maintain narrative interest. Players may feel they're wandering aimlessly without any sense of plot progression. Combat this by putting the player to work. Have them search the nooks and crannies of your story world, pointing and clicking on various objects to uncover clues, weapons, treasures, or even food and water on the surface of Mars.

Ticking Clock

This classic trope is a surefire way to ratchet up tension. For instance, the player might have thirty seconds to solve a riddle before a bomb explodes, or a scuba diver must collect three jewel-encrusted starfish before their tank runs out of oxygen.

Multiple Endings

This is an excellent way to incentivize replays. The player might die in one ending, become a famous movie star in another, and find true love in yet another. With clear signposting that highlights how key choices led to a particular result, players will feel compelled to restart the IDN and explore new pathways, hoping to arrive at a different finale.

Open World (Free Roam)

This game mechanic allows players to move in any direction they choose in real time. It requires advanced coding and a sophisticated design platform. An example of an open-world narrative is *The Witcher 3: Wild Hunt* (2024).

Sandbox (Sandpit)

This approach lets the player alter the design of the story. They can acquire tools that allow them to modify the world, change how they interact within it. They can invent entirely new games or even functioning computers all within the existing story world (Wickens 2022). The most successful example of a sandbox game is *Minecraft* (Persson, M. and Bergstein, J. [2011]).

Multiplayer

With some careful planning, single-player narratives can be altered to afford multiplayer interactions. One example of this is *Seltani* (Zarf 2013), an online environment for creating multiplayer, choice-based textual worlds.

Modding

This approach can apply to any interactive structure. It's a bit like music sampling meets fan fiction. It involves hijacking existing interactive stories and altering them to create something new and unique. Example: *Velvet Strike* (Schleiner, Leandre & Condon 2002).

Homebrew

If you're bored with the IDN platforms you're sampling online, you might employ a bit of larceny and a lot of ingenuity to formulate your own unique tech cocktail. The approach involves breaking into proprietary software and game consoles by exploiting vulnerabilities in those systems. Circumventing restrictions imposed by our corporate overlords allows rogue developers to invent new unofficial games and IDNs. The first homebrew creations involved revamping outdated first-generation consoles like the Magnavox Odyssey. This is how the homebrew game *Odball* [*sic*] (Console Mods, 2025) was cooked up. Recently, homebrew games have graduated to eighth and ninth-generation consoles like *PlayStation 5* (2024), *Nintendo Switch* (2024), and *X Box* (2024).

Personalization (Customization)

Whereas a high-end video game can allow characters to swap weapons, wardrobe, and even genitalia, chances are your humble little IDN doesn't have the processing power to handle such complex tasks. However, you can find ways of making the player experience feel a little less one-size-fits-all via simple forms of customization, that is, allowing players to engage with a quiz maker (2024), a badge maker (2024), or to pose for photo collages (2024) with your characters.

PRO TIPS

- **Let players customize their character's appearance.** As much as possible, let players alter the look of their character. This requires a platform with a state-tracking function, so key choices influence all subsequent interactions. The player may alter their character's gender, race, species, age, abilities, and so on, which may or may not influence the plot, depending on the type of story you're telling. Customization can also involve altering settings and adjusting or adding items such as weapons, tools, wardrobe, gills, blow-holes, wings, eyestalks, and so on.
- **Let players customize their character's behavior.** For instance, they can decide if the character utters a phrase with a smile or a sneer, or whether they shout a statement or whisper it. These adjustments influence their perception of the character and change the mood of the unfolding scene.

Mind Map

When designing your IDN, rather than dive in headfirst, consider dipping a toe in. A great way to do this is by sketching a mind map. This should not be confused with a story map, which will be discussed in Chapter 2.

A story map depicts a narrative pattern comprised of assets, nodes, and socials. In contrast, a mind map is a conceptual tool involving a much looser configuration of words and images clustered together with only one organizing principle. That structural consideration is a core concept written or drawn in the center of the mind map. Other images and words orbit this hub like satellites swirling in its gravitational field.

If someone on your team has artistic skills, have them take a crack at drawing your mind map. The key is keeping things whimsical, loose, and arbitrary to encourage intuitive leaps as participants consider the surprising ways different elements link together. Don't overthink things. This isn't a document for the literal-minded. It's a blob of grape jelly floating in zero gravity, congealing into something slightly coherent but mostly useful in terms of the tasty digressions it inspires.

Post-It (Sticky Note) Plan

Early in the brainstorming process, it's helpful to begin shifting from nonlinear spitballing to a more structured but still flexible approach. That's where the Post-it plan comes in. Jot every story idea on individual Post-it notes, and then—based on organizing principles such as theme, setting, or chronology—stick these notes on a wall in clusters.

As you experiment by moving story beats around, consider how they might play out in different sequences. What beat should be the dramatic climax? What beats work well clustered together? Should a particular beat function as foreshadowing or a flashback? Gradually, compelling patterns will start to emerge.

BTW: If you're not a fan of Post-it notes, there are other variants to this approach, including writing on whiteboards, butcher paper, or index cards.

Prototype

Once your project idea begins to gel, the next phase is creating a workable prototype. Paper prototyping can be achieved with a stack of index cards, or you can use any number of prototyping platforms, including PowerPoint and Keynote (using the hyperlink function). The trick is to iterate early and often and to ask a variety of people to test the interface. This will help you identify bugs before you go to the trouble of creating elaborate design elements you might have to scrap later.

Point of View

As stated in the introduction, this book will focus on the creation of single-player narratives (as opposed to multiplayer, which involves two or more players), but there are still choices to be made regarding the perspective of the PC.

First-Person POV

This involves capturing or rendering images in a character-specific POV style. The player sees what the character sees as they move through the story world. It is the most immersive approach and can be a powerful way of stimulating empathy, as the player experiences the world through the eyes of the character they have become, and the world responds to them accordingly.

Third-Person POV

The player sees an avatar or icon representing them navigating through the story world. This involves capturing or rendering images in a detached, fly-on-the-wall style. The strength of this approach lies in providing context. The player receives a lot of visual information, allowing for a clear understanding of how their character is interacting with the world.

Influence POV

In this perspective, the player is not tied to any character but instead has an influence over the story in general. This perspective is a common feature of real-time strategy and puzzle games such as *Tetris* (2024).

Note: For tips on how to film these different POVs, see Chapter 3. Assets.

LANDMINE

- **Avoid overly reflective sequences.** The past can't be altered, and the future is unwritten, so when designing narrative interactions, resist the urge to have your Player Character sit around reflecting on previous events or speculating about the future. Instead, make your story as immersive and experiential as possible. Parachute the PC into the center of high-stakes dramatic situations and get them engaging with the environment and other characters in real time.

Aesthetics

A memorable IDN often has a well-thought-out production design. This involves making key decisions during the preproduction process that may influence everything from the color of a character's jacket to how a location is lit to the type of font used for title sequences.

Like people, production aesthetics have distinct personalities: some are slick and polished, some are rough and ready, some have narrow comfort zones, and some are willing to try just about anything. When it comes to the overall look and sound of your IDN, there are two key things to keep in mind: **precision** and **consistency.**

- **Precision**: Determining the perfect aesthetic for your story.
- **Consistency**: Sticking to that aesthetic without excessive deviation.

Minimalism

A minimalist aesthetic may involve limiting your palette to a few striking colors, images, or sounds. It might also mean using only certain types of media assets, such as illustrations drawn in a distinctive style and enhanced with a recurring musical motif, paired with text in a sans serif font.

Pros
- Instantly iconic.

Cons
- May limit experimentation.
- May restrict your ability to portray certain narrative situations.

Maximalism

The everything-and-the-kitchen-sink approach involves incorporating all sorts of styles and media. It might randomly transition from a slideshow to a video file to an audio track to an animated GIF.

Pros
- Richly textured.
- Allows experimentation with different styles and forms.

Cons
- Purists may prefer a more constrained approach.
- The project can devolve into an ungainly hodgepodge.

PRO TIPS

- **Make your maximalism iconic.** When opting for this type of free-range aesthetic, keep other formal elements polished and cohesive. Striking compositions and distinct characters can help your creative choices feel less haphazard.
- **Match the media assets to the aesthetic.** If you're opting for a maximalist approach, present the player with a variety of formats immediately, and maintain this approach throughout. This ensures your design choices appear deliberate and consistent. Conversely, if you're going for minimalism, limit the types of assets you include. This choice could also be influenced by the skill sets of your team. For instance, if you have a talented illustrator and a gifted sound designer, you might commit to telling the story strictly through drawings and audio files.

Low-Fi

This approach is all about the power of cheese. It involves making the work look deliberately retro, poorly produced, and low-tech. This can be achieved by capturing shaky, out-of-focus shots, light flares, and dramatic zooms. You can also mix feedback and distortion into audio files and add other corny postproduction flourishes, such as film grain, freeze-frames, and dramatic stings during fight sequences.

Pros
- Extremely forgiving, as most production mistakes will seem deliberate.

Cons
- Can feel kitschy and old-fashioned rather than innovative.

Style Guide

An effective way to determine your project's aesthetic is to create an online style guide. *Pinterest* (2024) is a good platform for this, as it allows multiple team members to pin content to a single board. The style guide can help establish a unified and, hopefully, original approach when focusing on key questions such as:

- What font will you use throughout the IDN?
- What color scheme will you emphasize (earth tones, primary colors, pastels, or only red and black)?
- Will you create an eye-catching logo or certain iconic images?
- Will you compose a theme song? And if so, what will it sound like?
- What type of wardrobe, lighting, camera techniques, and acting styles will you favor?

PRO TIPS

- **Use the style guide as a stockpile.** Links to royalty-free sound effects, stills, and footage can be posted there. Later, during the assembly phase, they can be downloaded and used to enhance your IDN.
- **Include original prototype images.** In addition to preexisting materials, your style guide can include original mock-ups and rough drafts of nodes, assets, and socials. These can serve as models for the creation of future design elements.

Design Bible

Creators looking to formalize the somewhat free-form style guide may take the additional step of creating a design bible. As the name suggests, this document conveys a certain moral authority, defining what stylistic choices count as sacred or profane. Still, it doesn't have to be entirely inflexible. In fact, it's a great place to dream big and suggest ideas that may or may not actually materialize during the production process. For instance, the design bible for the *Shelley's Heart* Locative

Figure 1.4 Design bible page—*Shelley's Heart Locative Version*, *c*. 2018.

Version included plenty of ideas that were eventually realized, alongside others that proved too technically challenging to pull off (Figure 1.4).

Concept Art

The style guide and design bible are good places to showcase images and animatics (Barnhart 2024) of specific scenes. This concept art (Figure 1.5; 2024) can serve as a reference at key moments during the production process, informing decisions related to composition, wardrobe, lighting, media acquisition, and visual effects (VFX).

Figure 1.5 Concept art—*Shelley's Heart Locative Version*, *c*. 2018.

PRO TIP

- **Slow your roles.** Don't assign production roles until the team has started to flesh out the story concept. This approach has two advantages: 1. Once you have a sense of the type of IDN you're creating, you'll know which production roles need to be filled. 2. During the brainstorming process, participants will demonstrate specific skills and show interest in particular roles. This can help guide the decision-making process when assigning responsibilities.

Roles and Goals

When it's time to determine who will do what, you can divide roles based on the number of participants and their skill sets and interests. Aim for specialization, but don't be too prescriptive. After all, an inspired novice sometimes cares more about achieving excellence than a jaded professional. Also, a single role might be shared by multiple people, or one person might take on several roles. Regardless of how responsibilities are distributed, here are some key jobs your team may need to tackle depending on your approach:

- **Lead Facilitator**—Coordinates multiple teams.
- **Project Lead or Team Lead**—Oversees the production of a single IDN.
- **Artist/Illustrator**—Draws mind maps and illustrations.
- **Writer**—Creates the Post-it plan and story map.
- **Node Designer**—Creates nodes for your IDN.
- **IDN Editor**—Assembles your story pattern.
- **Prototyper**—Creates test versions of the IDN.
- **Beta Tester**—Tests prototypes and IDN, providing feedback based on these experiences.
- **Acquisitions Manager**—Gathers, clears, and coordinates third-party materials.
- **Director**—Oversees the filming of media assets.
- **Journalist**—Interviews iDoc subjects.
- **Actor**—Portrays fictional characters.
- **Cinematographer/Cameraman**—Shoots video footage or stills.
- **Audio Engineer**—Records sound.
- **Audio Mixer**—Edits sound.
- **Production Designer**—Coordinates all visuals, including wardrobe, sets, locations, and props.
- **Prop Master**—Procures and manages props.
- **Video Editor**—Assembles media assets.
- **Animator**—Creates animated sequences.
- **Composer**—Writes and performs the musical score.
- **Social Media Manager**—Promotes the project online and adds social elements to the IDN.
- **Media Manager (Data Wrangler)**—Backs up files and coordinates file sharing.

PRO TIPS

- **To build confidence, identify key roles early and reinforce them often.** Ask questions like: "Who has video editing experience?" And "Who wants to learn how to create an animated sequence?" Encouraging participants to claim an area of expertise, or seek a new skill will prompt them to think like specialists. This also ensures they take charge of quality control for their specific tasks.

- **Practice strategic communication.** Coordinate efforts with open and transparent discussions. Share big-picture concerns with everyone, but limit small-picture concerns to discussions with specialists.

From the Trenches

Success Story—Student iDoc

There once was a team of ambitious and talented IDN creators. I'll call them "Team Rock Star." They were part of an undergraduate journalism class I taught, and they had been tasked with creating an iDoc. This group had worked together during a previous semester, producing an impressive seven-minute documentary film, so they were already familiar with their individual and collective strengths. They had a skilled cameraman, an imaginative writer, a gifted video editor, and a director who generated plenty of strong ideas while enthusiastically supporting his teammates—a great quality in a leader.

Team Rock Star decided to focus their iDoc on haunted sites around Dorset County in Southern England. To capture a spooky ambience, they decided to shoot at multiple locations at night. Filming in low-light conditions is notoriously challenging, and they wanted to create a series of POV tracking shots where the player appears to drift into haunted locales surrounded by ominous sounds.

To achieve this effect, they checked out a gimbal camera and a pair of portable fluorescent light panels. Moving as a four-person unit, they navigated each murky location, with their director guiding the cinematographer, the cinematographer filming the scene, and two teammates flanking him with bright light panels. The result was a drifting visual that resembled the perspective of a ghost floating through darkened ruins.

Next, the team focused on sound design. They gathered royalty-free sound effects and ominous music, combining these elements with scripted voice-over, interview sound bites from experts (identified with title text), and the heavy breathing of a frightened spectator. This meticulous planning paid off, resulting in a richly atmospheric iDoc.

Team Rock Star also filmed interior locations, including an old theater supposedly inhabited by poltergeists. One of their most effective sequences involved the gimbal camera tracking along a gloomy theater aisle, slowly passing rows of chairs until, in the foreground, the seat of one chair suddenly popped up as if manipulated by an unseen spirit. This ghost was actually a team member lying on his back out of frame and pushing the seat up—a simple stunt but highly effective. During test runs, players consistently squealed with delight when they encountered this jump scare. Although Team Rock Star improvised this clever shot on location, they were building upon a well-thought-out production plan.

Takeaways

- Identify an idea everyone is excited about.
- Match roles to interests and expertise.
- Lead by honoring the skills of specialist stakeholders.
- Plan carefully.
- When a clever idea emerges on location, deviate from the plan.

Cautionary Tales—Student iDoc

"This has been my favorite class all semester," the prodigal student declared. "Sean," I'll call him, had skipped all the previous sessions. Was he struggling with mental health concerns? Nope. Had he been ill? Except for an attendance allergy, not really. Apparently, Sean just wasn't a fan of the restrictive classroom environment. Despite this, he claimed I was his "favorite teacher." I was almost flattered, but then I realized we had never met.

Still, Sean's bravado was impressive, so I was curious if it had helped yield a compelling—or at least semi-coherent—iDoc. Most of the other students taking the unit I was teaching had enthusiastically engaged. But Sean and his group of co-conspirators—let's call them "Team Chaos"—had been conspicuously absent all semester. Despite my best efforts to coax them onto campus, this rebel band had boldly committed to their policy of total educational abstinence.

Eventually, one member—"Cate," I'll call her—emailed me to explain they were "doing just fine." Despite the fact they had all missed every class session, she was confident of their ensuing success. She also confided that she had received some disappointing marks in previous units, so she was counting on me to rectify that injustice and give the team a high mark for their current off-the-grid efforts.

When I pressed Cate for details about her team's production plan, she confessed it had, thus far, consisted of watching a single PowerPoint lecture I'd posted online and kicking around a few ideas in a chat room. I again urged her and her fellow phantoms to come to class, but I received only another vague assurance that they had everything well in hand.

Four weeks later, Cate and another Team Chaos member—I'll call her "Zoe"— finally showed up for their first session. They informed me their group had yet to pick a topic, but they had narrowed it to three great ideas. In fact, they were excited to report that they had such cool concepts to choose from that, once they eventually picked one, the iDoc would practically write, shoot, edit, and assemble itself.

I urged them to pull the trigger and decide on a single topic as soon as possible so they could start researching it, but as I said this, I noticed their eyes fogging over. Later, when I circled back to see how they were doing, I discovered they had snuck out early.

Flash forward to the day of the in-class screening. For the first time, all four members of Team Chaos appeared, eager to showcase their iDoc. Although they still struggled to articulate its topic, they were proud of their streamlined production process. Here are some of the strategies they had employed:

- They chose a topic related to university life to avoid having to do any research.
- They cast themselves in lead roles to avoid interacting with others.
- They shot everything in a few hours in one member's apartment to avoid the entire preproduction process.
- They consumed actual alcohol on camera to add "realism."

As Sean anxiously boasted about the efficiency of this approach, I began to spot the first chinks in his Teflon armor. Then I pressed play, and the first shaky, poorly lit frames appeared. Within seconds, it became clear that—while making this iDoc must have been a lot of fun—watching it was painful. Misspelled graphics haphazardly appeared, linking incoherent scenes in an apparently arbitrary fashion. The on-set carousing had seemingly spilled into postproduction, resulting in a muddled and incoherent mess. Less than a minute into the screening, Team Chaos's excitement faded as they realized even their well-honed work avoidance skills could not save this labor of lethargy as it sank under the weight of their collective apathy.

Takeaways

- For better results, show up and do the work.
- Don't skip researching, writing, skill-building, communication, and editorial planning.
- Save the partying for the wrap party.

Key Tasks: Plans

Task 1. Skill Inventory

Download the Skill List Worksheet from our website, available at: https://www.blo omsburyonlineresources.com/creating-the-digital-interactive-story

This editable Excel file will allow you to add rows as necessary. Once you've opened it, list all the skills of project participants and facilitators including equipment they can provide and contact information. This will prove an invaluable organizational tool (Figure 1.6).

Figure 1.6 Skill list.

Task 2. Resource Inventory

This worksheet is where you can list all the things you can use and access when creating your IDN. These include props, wardrobe, set deck, vehicles, locations, live events, and more (Figure 1.7).

Figure 1.7 Resource list.

Task 3. Project Pitch

There is no template for this document, as it needs to reflect your unique vision. Just open a new Word doc and write a brief overview of the type of IDN you want to create. Be sure to address the following:

- Whether the project is fiction or nonfiction.
- The story concept.
- Key characters.
- Point of view.
- Target audience.
- Types of media you will include.

Task 4. Production Schedule

This downloadable worksheet can help you break down the flow of your production process. Key details to include

- Where you will be.
- When you will be there.
- What you will be doing.

Once you have filled out the Excel file, upload it to Google Drive and edit the sharing permissions (Figure 1.8). Use your own discretion about who should be granted editing permissions, but it should be visible to all members of your team. This will keep everyone on the same page—literally.

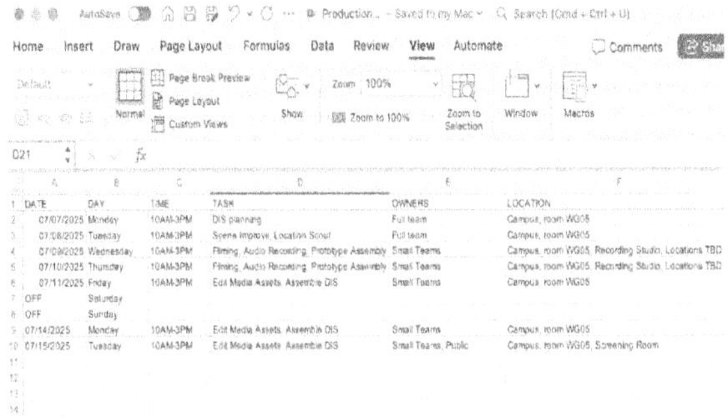

Figure 1.8 Production schedule.

Task 5. Contact Sheet

On this worksheet, list the names of facilitators, participants, and any additional personnel, along with their specific roles and goals. When assigning tasks, remember to play to the strengths of your team and consider that most participants will take on multiple roles (Figure 1.9).

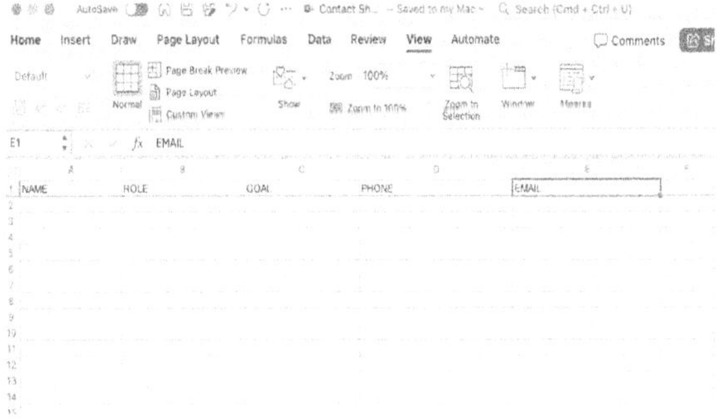

Figure 1.9 Contact sheet.

Task 6. Online Communication Hub

Be sure to create at least one central communication hub (e.g., Google Drive, WhatsApp, Microsoft Teams, Discord, Basecamp, or Slack). Here, you can include all members of your team and share editable production schedules, location addresses, prop lists, shot plans, story designs, and more.

Task 7. Style Guide

This is another hub where you can gather concept images and sounds, third-party media, and prototypes to inform and enable the production process or use in your final IDN. Pin elements to a shared board (Pinterest or Padlet) or place them in shared folders (Google Drive) for easy access.

2 Paths

One of the joys of traditional storytelling is playing God, deciding whether a character lives, dies, or gets probed by aliens. But when creating an IDN, the writer is demoted from deity to designer. Design thinking means surrendering some autonomy to the person navigating your story—the player—and allowing them to make choices that send them along specific narrative paths.

IDN paths come in two forms:

Unilinear **path:** Your classic one-way street. Like the passage of time, it marches on without ever turning back.

Bilinear **path:** Your classic two-way street. You arrive at a new destination but can also boomerang back to the previous one.

Each path branches from a **node**—an important IDN component discussed in depth in Chapter 4. For now, understand that a node is a type of digital landing strip containing information for the player to engage with. Each node displays one or more **points**—triggers that send the player down a particular path. An IDN is composed of multiple paths connecting to form a **pattern**. Here's how it all comes together:

- Nodes display points.
- Points link to paths.
- Paths weave together to form patterns.

The skeletal structure of your IDN is built from these components.

Now, let's kick things off by zooming into the smallest component.

Getting to the Points

Points are buttons that the player pushes to make things happen. A point can advance the story to the next node, leapfrog over it, or U-turn back to an earlier node. It can unlock a new perspective, take the player to a different time or place, reveal crucial information, or detonate a (fictional, hopefully) nuclear weapon.

Launch Point

Sometimes it's helpful to bring all players up to speed on key information before they navigate your IDN. For example, if players take on the role of a firefighter and must make a series of split-second decisions to save a puppy trapped in a burning building, this background information can be delivered through a short video.

A video lasting ten to twenty seconds can play before the player arrives at the home node, where their first decision will be made. The best way to trigger such a video is to have your IDN begin with a **launch node** featuring a single clickable **launch point.** Below is a diagram depicting a launch node with a launch point (Figure 2.1).

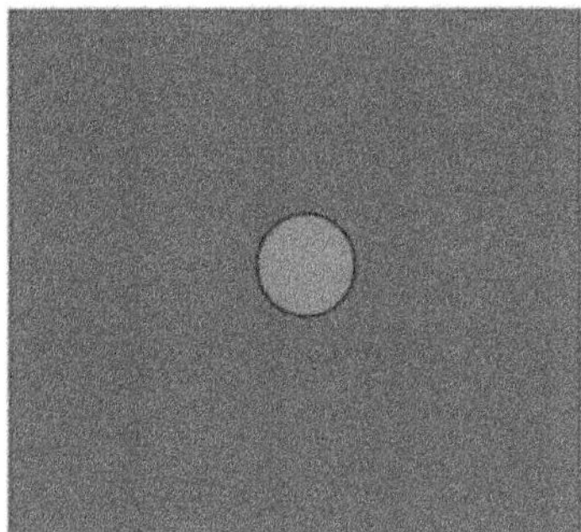

Figure 2.1 Launch node with launch point.

And here is an actual launch node with an actual launch point (Figure 2.2).

Figure 2.2 Launch node with launch point—*Shelley's Heart Locative Version*, *c*. 2018.

Clicking on the launch point makes the launch node vanish as a short **launch asset** plays. This sequence conveys crucial information to the player before ending as the player arrives at the **home node** (Figure 2.3).

Figure 2.3 Launch sequence.

Decision Point

This is an umbrella term for any choice made in an IDN that progresses the plot or unlocks additional content. Decision points come in various forms, corresponding to different types of choices. These include:

- **Entry points**
- **Action points**
- **POV points (Point of View)**
- **Location points**
- **Time points**

The diagram below represents a node with three decision points displayed (Figure 2.4).

Each of these points branches, via a different path, to one of three nodes. The following diagram depicts this (Figure 2.5):

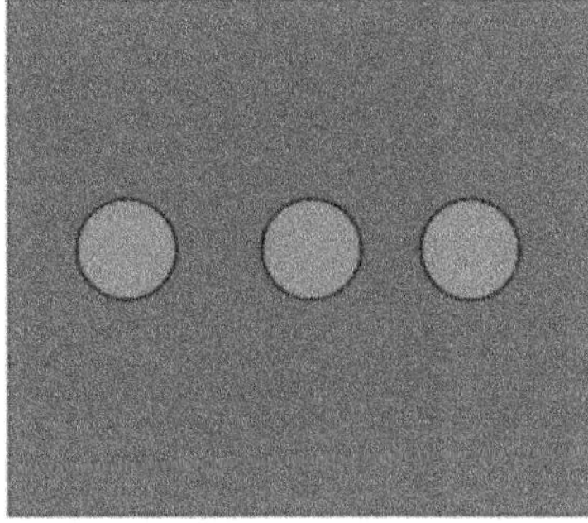

Figure 2.4 Node with three decision points.

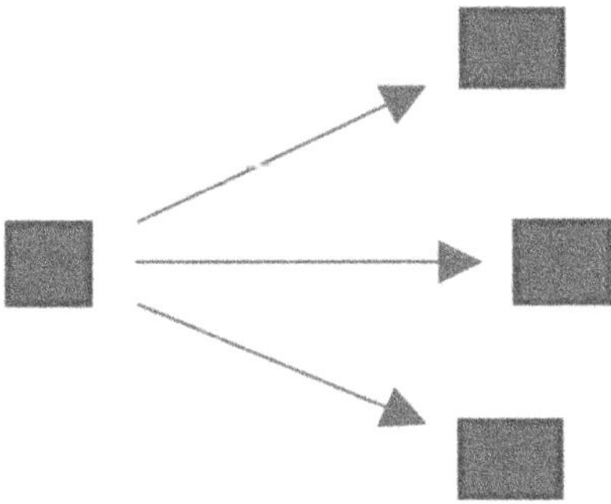

Figure 2.5 Decision points branching from a single node.

- **Foreground thematic concerns.** When creating decision points, think about the glue that holds plot and character together—namely, theme. What is your story about at the deepest level? If you're clear on this, it will be much easier to figure out the types of choices you want to offer players as they navigate your story world. Describe choices in terms of their emotional significance to the Player Character. For instance, instead of "stay" or "leave," you might write "confront your fears" or "follow your heart." This attaches feelings to the decisions offered. The player isn't just selecting random actions—they're making meaningful choices and experiencing happy, sad, painful, or thrilling consequences as a result.

LANDMINES

- **Avoid weak options.** When a decision point offers a boring choice, players will never select it—for example, choosing between "sword fight" and "take a nap."
- **Misleading or vague choices.** Beware of choices that can be interpreted in more than one way. For example, if a character is given the choice to "get what you deserve," it may not be clear whether this leads to a punishment or a reward. In some stories, such ambiguity may be the point, but try to avoid being unintentionally obscure.
- **Don't negate player agency.** If a player makes a choice, it should have meaningful consequences, influencing the story at the level of character or plot. Weak consequences are like empty calories—they leave players feeling hollow and unsatisfied. Also, avoid false choices, like when the player decides to reveal a secret to another character, only for that character to already know it. This cancels the impact of the player's decision and makes for a frustrating experience.

Entry Point

The entry point is the first crucial decision made by the player, often with major consequences for their overall experience. Think of it as the first big rabbit hole the player jumps into. Entry points may represent different perspectives, such as exploring the site of a plane crash in the role of a reporter, medic, or investigator (Figure 2.6). They might also represent different locations, times, topics, ideologies, or story genres. The key is that the entry point serves as the first significant jumping-off point, setting the player along a unique path.

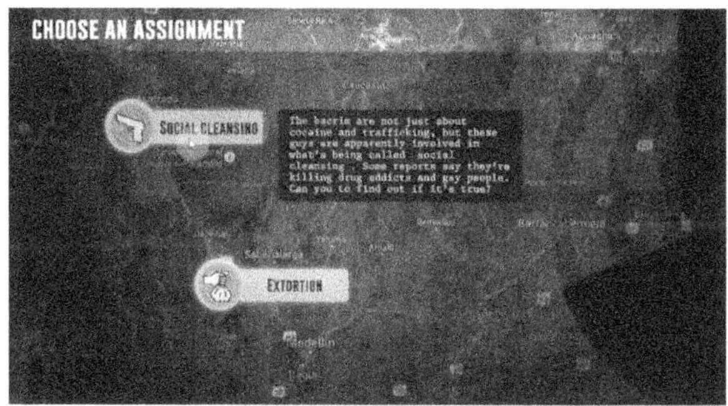

Figure 2.6 Entry points—*Target BACRIM*, c. 2017.

Action Point

This type of decision point triggers a specific narrative action. In a linear pattern, only one action is offered. In a branching pattern, two or more actions are offered (Figure 2.7). More on this in a moment.

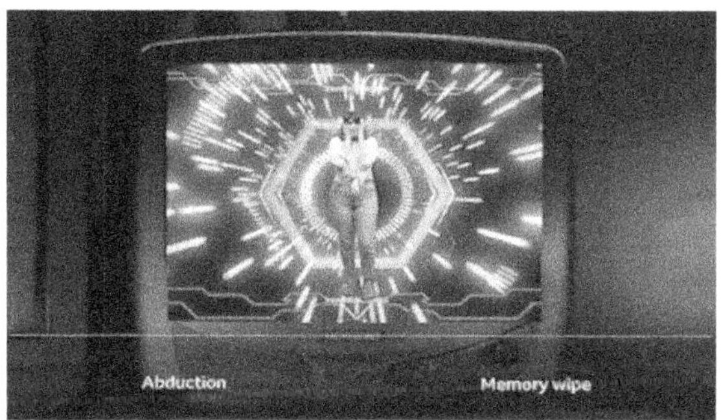

Figure 2.7 Two action points—*Next Level*, c. 2023.

Choke Point and Bottleneck

The art of interaction design comes down to two simple words: "managing complexity." Once your narrative starts branching, it will do so exponentially unless you can figure out how to rein things in. Enter: **choke points**, which work together to create a **bottleneck node** (Figure 2.8).

In a sense, choke points are decision points in disguise—two or more options that yield the same result. This is how the narrative can reduce the number of branches and, thus, the number of media assets you and/or your team need to produce to complete your IDN.

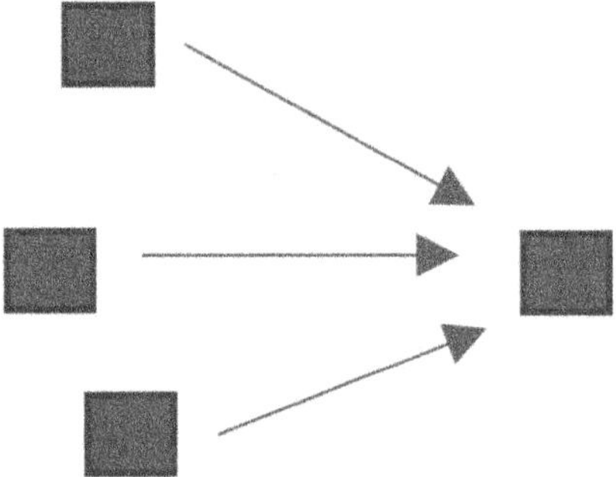

Figure 2.8 Choke points creating a bottleneck node.

Foldback

The term **foldback** refers to any path that folds back into the main story, but can also refer to a path that sends the player to an earlier point in the story, even the beginning. This design element is useful for avoiding frustrating redundancies and dead ends (Figure 2.9). It can be used to penalize a player who has made an incorrect choice by forcing them to take a step or two back and try again. It can also offer a second chance to a player who has made a fatal misstep that might otherwise end the IDN.

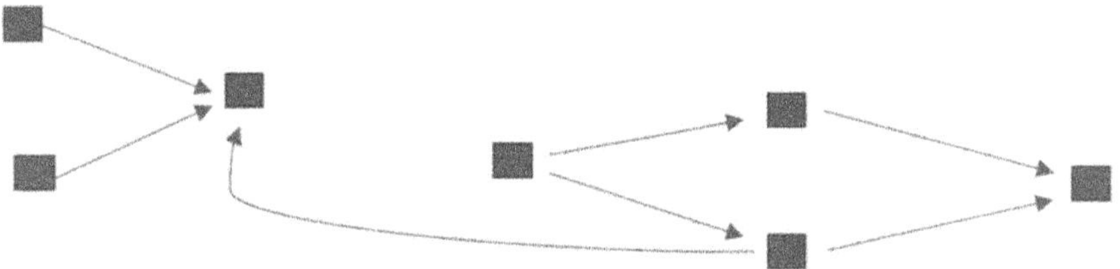

Figure 2.9 Foldback.

LANDMINE

- **Avoid narrative impasses.** This happens when the player hits a brick wall or is killed and must return to the start of the game. This can be quite frustrating.

Skip Point

Depending on how often you require players to move through sections they've previously encountered, you may wish to include skip points in key places. These buttons allow them to leap forward without waiting for a media asset to play from beginning to end (Figure 2.10). They are an excellent design tool for keeping the pace brisk and avoiding frustrating redundancies.

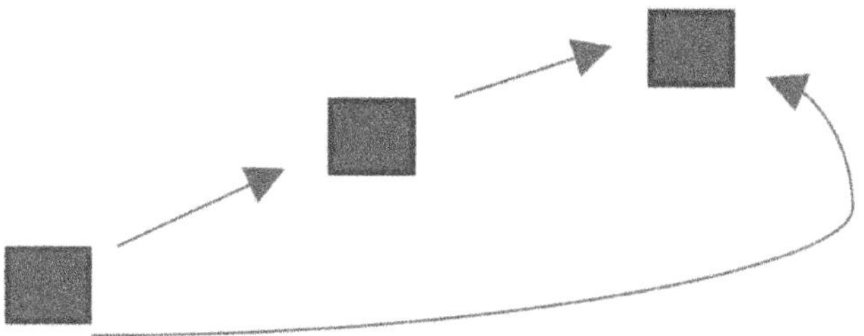

Figure 2.10 Skip point.

Home Return

An icon on every node, usually shaped like a small house, allows players to return to the home node at any point if the path they're exploring has grown too tedious or if they're interested in trying something different (Figure 2.11). Part of affording players a degree of agency is offering them an exit strategy at every turn.

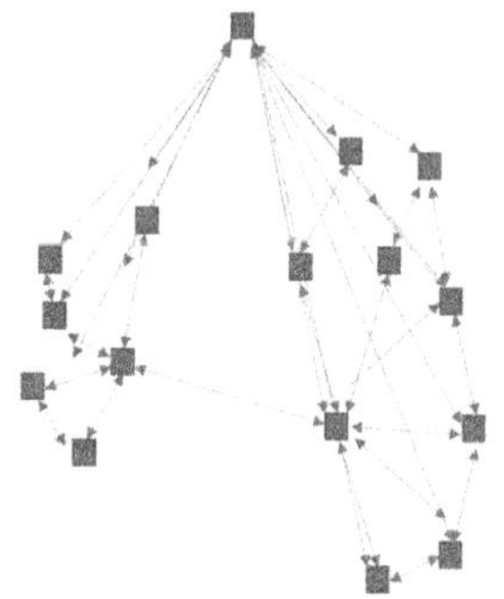

Figure 2.11 Home return.

Patterns

You can create an IDN based on any of the patterns discussed in this section, or you can invent a hybrid of multiple patterns. This may sound complicated, but the good news is humans have a natural ability to grasp the shape significance of complex configurations. We are the pattern-recognizing species par excellence. This helps us identify a face in a photograph or a letter in the alphabet. It also means we are susceptible to conspiracy theories and TV commercials that suggest drinking a certain beer will help us attract supermodels.

Pattern recognition is all about associating one thing with another. Written language, for instance, depends on our capacity to relate a specific word to an object or idea. This is why humans have a natural ability to think like IDN designers. Creating an IDN is, first and foremost, a process of thinking about patterns and how they interrelate.

Small Interactive Patterns

Game design researcher Jay Taylor-Laird (2018) identifies some small-scale interactive patterns, including:

Diamond

This pattern branches and quickly closes back in on itself. The branching elements don't have long-term consequences, but they can still influence the player's perception of the story by providing information that alters their point of view (Figure 2.12).

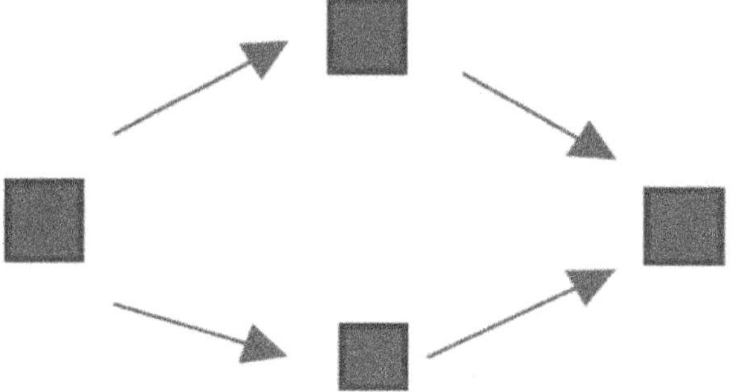

Figure 2.12 Diamond.

Loop

A foldback that involves repeatedly returning to a starting place is called a loop. This can be a helpful way to get players to reconsider choices, but if the player becomes stuck in a small or unchanging loop, it can become frustrating (Figure 2.13).

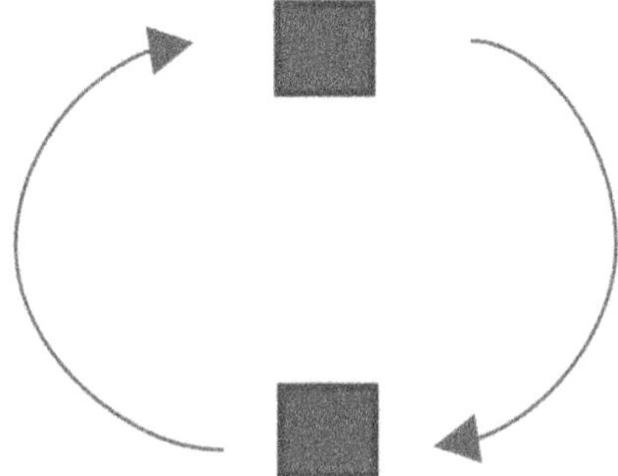

Figure 2.13 Loop.

Zipper

This pattern involves embarking on minor digressions that contain non-story information (Figure 2.14). Such beats offer contextual information related to the narrative (e.g., character descriptions and backstory) without influencing the actual plot. A more elaborate version of this is known as a "Fishbone" pattern. More on this in a moment.

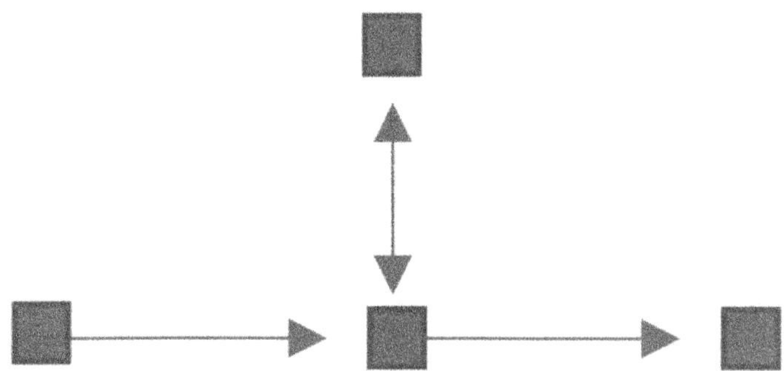

Figure 2.14 Zipper.

Lock and Key (Gating)

Not every node needs to be an open door. Lock-and-key patterns force the player to pause and think through issues related to the themes of your IDN (Figure 2.15). For instance, they might need to correctly answer a multiple-choice question before being allowed to move on. Or they might need to complete a puzzle, solve a riddle, or—as with a parser—fill in the missing word in a line of text. Gating slows the pace of your narrative but heightens the sense

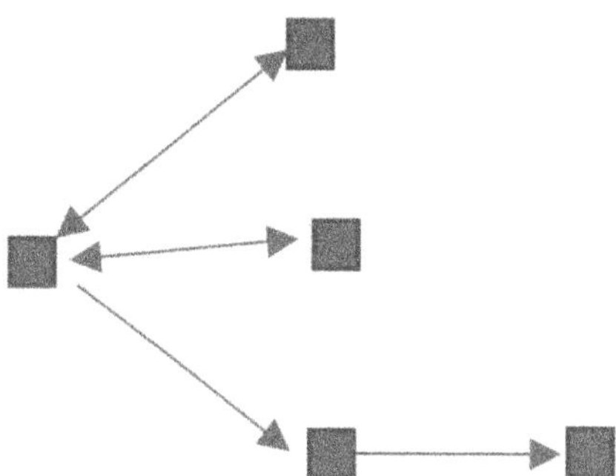

Figure 2.15 Lock and key.

of engagement and immersion as the player must effectively problem-solve before continuing.

Large Interactive Patterns

Game designer Florent Maurin (2014) identifies six large interactive patterns: **linear**, **fishbone**, **branching**, **concentric**, **parallel**, and **threaded**. The following pages define these terms and provide examples of each. I've also included three common variations on these common patterns. They are a **string of pearls** (a variation on linear) and **branching with bottlenecks** and **time cave** (two variations on branching).

PRO TIP

- **Pick and mix.** To enhance the originality of your design, pick two or three narrative patterns and graft them together. This can be done by sketching designs on paper or by digital prototyping with the platform of your choice. Hybrid designs are often the most inventive, so challenge yourself to mix things up right out of the gate.

Linear

The first pattern Maurin identifies is a structure right out of Aristotle's *Poetics*, featuring a fixed sequence of events with a beginning, middle, and end. The linear narrative is the least interactive structure, so navigating it is like crossing a river by jumping from rock to rock with no other paths available (Figure 2.16). The player can only head in one of two directions: forward or back. While this approach can frustrate players if overused, when incorporated in small doses, it allows the creator to briefly unleash their inner control freak, ensuring that key plot points are experienced by all players.

Pros

- Easy to generate.
- Easy to play.
- Provides more narrative control for the creator.

Figure 2.16 Linear.

Cons

- Players don't get to make dramatic choices, creating a mostly passive experience.
- Each player encounters the same story beats, making repeat playthroughs unappealing.

Linear IDN Example

The Boat (2015) is an interactive graphic novel based on the short story by the Vietnamese Australian writer Nam Le and illustrated by Matt Huynh. It's the story of a sixteen-year-old girl who crosses the sea alone after the fall of Saigon. The story utilizes linear storytelling via a scrolling mechanic. All players experience the same story. The only difference between one playthrough and another involves the pace of their progress through the story and which elements they spend more time focusing on.

A common variation on the linear form is:

String of Pearls (Rivers and Lakes)

This pattern is also highly constrained (Figure 2.17). The plot flows in a single, predictable direction. However, the central storyline is occasionally interrupted by moments when the player is free to explore a setting with some nonlinear choices—for example, arriving at a node that looks like a library and learning about various books by pointing and clicking on them.

Pros

- A strong central narrative.

Cons

- Highly linear, despite some interactivity, so the main storyline is fixed.
- Replays don't reveal new events or information.

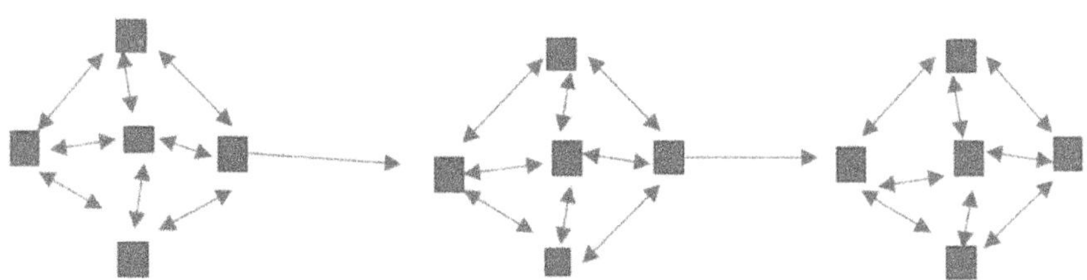

Figure 2.17 String of pearls.

String of Pearls IDN Example

This is the most common structure for video games. *The Legend of Zelda: Breath of the Wild* (2024), *Dark Souls* (2024), and many others follow the string of pearls pattern: linear **cutscenes** interrupted by periods of **free-roam** gameplay.

An example of an early Interactive Print Narrative with a string of pearls structure is *The Lost Temple: An Interactive Puzzle Book* (Knight & Harris 1999). The story's characters search for hidden treasure in a Mexican rainforest. This linear narrative is frequently interrupted by puzzles that players must solve before they can proceed.

Fishbone

Moving up a degree in complexity is the fishbone narrative (Figure 2.18). This approach allows the player to veer off and explore occasional tangents before returning to the main narrative strand. It's appealing to people who like to investigate the periphery of a story world—peeking behind the curtain of a room to discover the monsters lurking there or studying the marginalia scribbled on the pages of an ancient book.

Pros
- A compromise between straightforward narration and interaction.
- Authors may like the idea that all story beats are experienced in a single playthrough.

Cons
- Basically, a linear narrative with a lot of detours.
- Random exploration can undermine narrative interest, as the constant digressions can become distracting.
- Only highly motivated players will have the curiosity to browse through all the tangents.

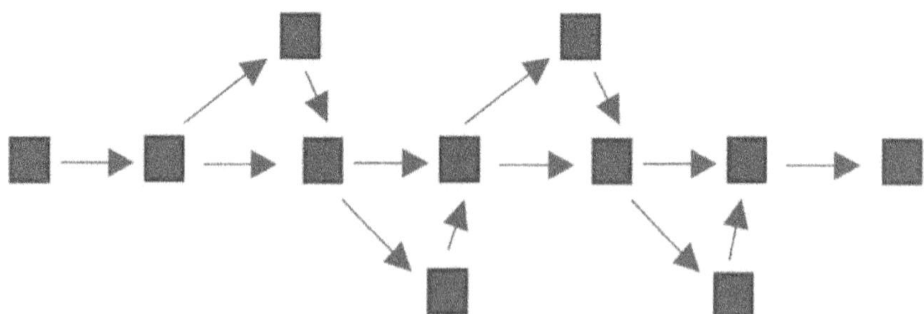

Figure 2.18 Fishbone.

Fishbone IDN Example

Like the television series *Lost* (2024), its video game spin-off *Lost: Via Domus* (2024)—
marketed as *Lost: The Video Game* in Europe—is packed with flashbacks and other
narrative sidebars that veer off temporarily before folding back into the main through
line. This is a classic fishbone structure. The TV show's executive producers, Damon
Lindelof and Carlton Cuse, came up with seven episodes following a timeline based
on the first seventy days portrayed in the series.

PRO TIP

- **Pick your "shoots."** This pattern is most effective when the narrative offshoots
  are placed at moments of falling action, when dramatic tension is reduced, and the
  player is feeling reflective.

Branching

The third narrative structure Maurin identifies is the most familiar to laypeople. The
branching narrative starts with a single node containing two or more decision points
(Figure 2.19). The player makes a choice, and the story branches in a particular
direction. This creates a greater sense of freedom for players but requires the design
team to produce many story assets and think through complex cause-and-effect
sequences.

Pros
- Potentially a very interactive structure.
- If players are provided with enough interesting choices, they can influence
  outcomes and explore topics in depth.

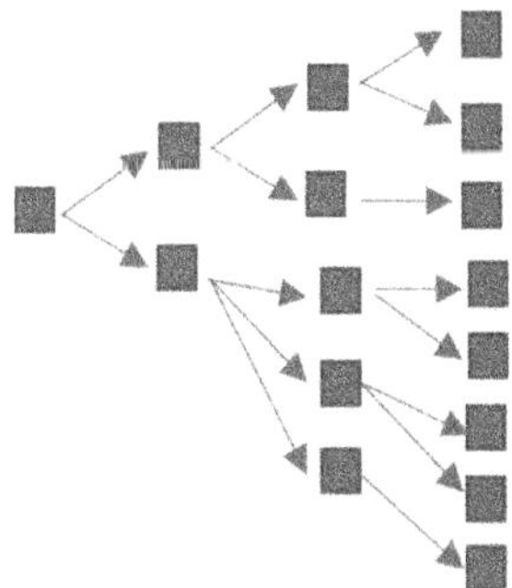

Figure 2.19 Branching.

Cons

- Mushrooming complexity brings the danger of production time sinks and ballooning budgets.
- Most players won't explore all the narrative possibilities.

Branching IDN Example

"Bandersnatch" (2024) is an interactive episode of the popular anthology series *Black Mirror*. The title refers to a mythical character from Lewis Carroll's *Through the Looking-Glass* (1871). This choice-based narrative follows a complex branching structure. At key points, it offers viewers opportunities to select how the action will unfold. Sometimes these decisions are trivial (picking a breakfast cereal). Sometimes they are monumental (deciding if a character will live or die).

> **LANDMINE**
>
> - Avoid meandering and/or confusing storylines that don't compel characters to make important dramatic choices tied to a clear goal.

The most common form of the branching pattern is:

Branching Bottleneck

In this approach, the story veers off in a bunch of directions, but the paths quickly fold back to join a central thread. This helps preserve the sanity of creators, as it means you don't have to cook up an infinite number of story nodes (Figure 2.20). If the platform allows for state tracking, early choices can have effects that echo through the story. This can help repeated playthroughs seem less redundant.

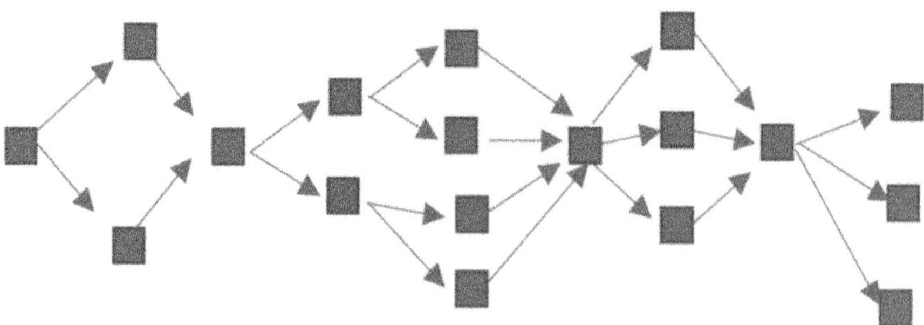

Figure 2.20 Branching bottleneck.

Pros

- It lets creators design a distinctive and manageable plot.

Cons

- Due to the bottlenecks, some of the same key events recur during replays.

Bottleneck Branching IDN Example

While *Bandersnatch*'s highly complex, big-budget design features more branching than bottlenecking, other interactive stories strike a more even balance between the two. The Japanese *bishōjo* (2024), or "cute girl game," *Long Live the Queen* (Hanako Games 2013), has a few branching elements but also focuses on a strong central through line. The main character is a sort of blank slate. This allows the player to craft her personality and future by making key decisions related to her education, wardrobe, and the décor of her bedroom.

A far less common variation on the branching pattern is:

Time Cave

The time cave is a branching sequence with little or no bottlenecking. It just grows and grows, tending to be broad rather than deep. In other words, there are tons of options and endings, but short playthroughs because the creators can't produce all the story nodes necessary to continue the story beyond a few key decision points. For instance, in the diagram below, it takes twenty nodes to give the player three levels of choices (Figure 2.21).

Pros

- Packed with unpredictable characters and bizarre outcomes.

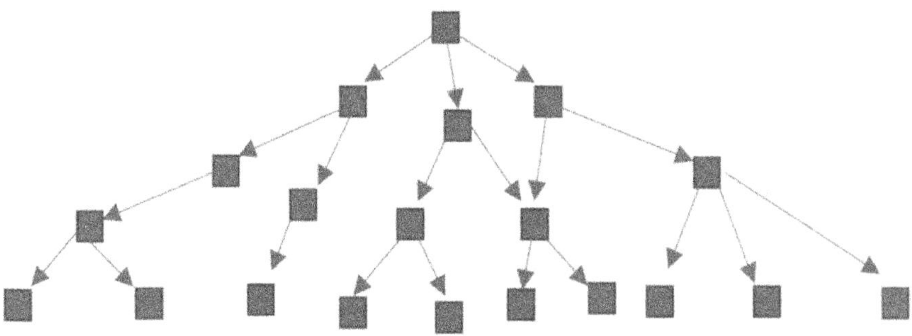

Figure 2.21 Time cave.

Cons

- So open-ended it can start to feel unmoored from reality.
- Loads of freedom, but players may struggle to make sense of all the wandering paths.

Time Cave IDN Example

Emily Short's text-based interactive fiction narrative *A Dark and Stormy Entry* (2013) is a kind of open-ended time cave that playfully rambles in all sorts of unpredictable directions, with no unifying narrative but multiple sub-stories that are never really finished. In this way, it reflects on the act of creative brainstorming. It ends when you give up or feel you have enough material to write your own story.

Concentric

Our next story structure is the most interactive (Figure 2.22). The concentric pattern cedes a great degree of control to the player. Classic point-and-click narratives employ this mode of storytelling. A rich array of choices is offered like options on a restaurant menu.

Pros

- Completely nonlinear, offering a high degree of player freedom.
- Opportunities for players to time travel and leap between locations.
- Good for clustering similar elements together.

Cons

- The author's perspective on the subject may be blurred or even disappear.
- Only highly motivated players will have the curiosity to browse through all the elements.

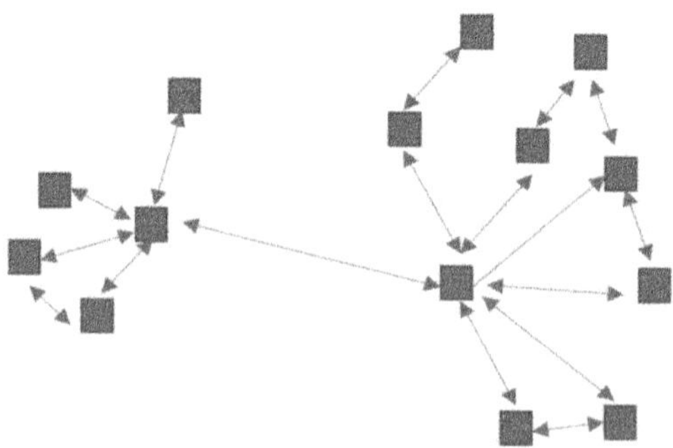

Figure 2.22 Concentric.

Concentric IDN Example

The American adventure video game *Myst* (2024) centers on a few key concentric settings. Players explore this story world by interacting with objects and solving puzzles to travel to different domains and eras. All this exploration helps them uncover the mysterious backstory of the game's characters and figure out who deserves their help.

PRO TIP

- **Motivate exploration.** To ensure players investigate more than a few choices, it helps to create a sense of urgency. One way to maintain narrative interest is the **treasure hunt** approach, where the player is tasked with solving a riddle or uncovering clues to achieve a positive outcome or avoid a negative one.

Parallel

The following narrative structure is two patterns in one (Figure 2.23). A parallel narrative is formed when a pair of linear stories are placed side by side and links are added where the player can travel between them.

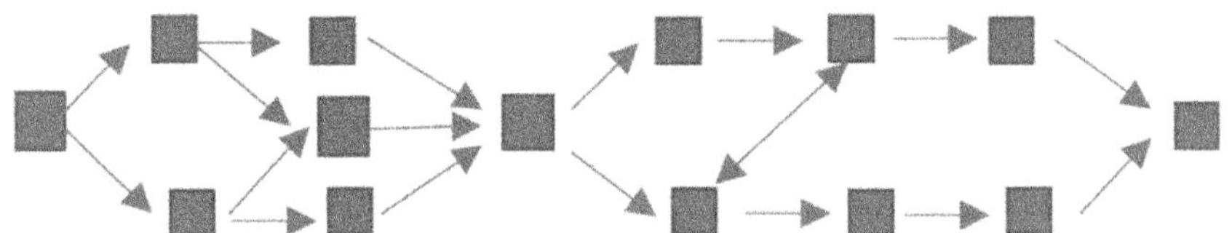

Figure 2.23 Parallel.

Pros
- Ability to juxtapose perspectives (crosscutting/parallel action).

Cons
- Essentially a pair of linear stories in disguise.
- Can disappoint players who want their choices to have meaningful consequences.

Parallel IDN Example

The now-defunct massive multiplayer online role-playing game *The Matrix Online* (2024), abbreviated as MxO, combined parallel story worlds. Players navigated between Zion, the last human city deep below the earth, and the computer-simulated world of the Matrix. In this way, the interactive story drew inspiration from the film that spawned it, featuring characters who were constantly navigating between a pair of juxtaposed realities.

An interactive documentary with a parallel narrative is *Gaza/Sderot* (Szalat, Ronez & Lotz 2008), which captures stories from the Palestinian city of Gaza and the Israeli village of Sderot, which are located less than a mile apart. It weaves together the stories of six residents from these two embattled locales, considering the different challenges they face.

PRO TIP

- **Compare and contrast.** These links are especially intriguing if they occur at moments when the two stories are either strongly similar or dissimilar.

Threaded (Multi-thread, Multilinear)

The final common interactive pattern is the threaded narrative (Figure 2.24). This approach merges elements of several previously discussed forms. Players explore intertwined threads that represent a variety of perspectives, locations, and/or eras. For instance, players might view the same car crash from three points of view: a paramedic, a cop, and a crash victim. They could also visit street markets in four cities—Singapore, Edinburgh, Rio, and Johannesburg—or give birth to a child in five different epochs: the Neolithic, the Classical, the Byzantine, the nineteenth century, and the contemporary. The narrative threads run parallel to one another and intersect at key moments, allowing players to cut between them. Each thread contains its own decision points and narrative trajectory.

Pros
- Many different stories can be told at once.
- Unique perspectives are juxtaposed.

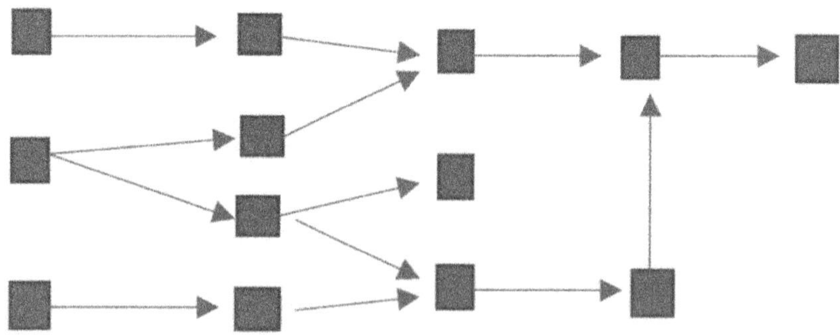

Figure 2.24 Threaded.

Cons

- Contains lots of information, which can be overwhelming.
- Requires a complex design.

Threaded IDN Example

You can experience the video game *Resident Evil 6* (2024) as one of multiple characters, each with their own storyline. These plots are unique but also intersect.

A community-based threaded narrative is the Irish IDN *Weird View* (Nisi & Haahr 2006). Combining hyperlinked structures and oral storytelling, this multi-branching tale captures nonfiction stories from the inhabitants of a terrace of houses in Dublin. These are supplemented with videos and photographs to create a collection of interwoven narrative strands.

PRO TIP

- **Portray competing realities.** When designing a threaded pattern, consider having characters see the same event in different ways based on their individual biases, much like the classic Japanese film *Rashomon* (Kurosawa 1950).

Other Interactive Patterns

I've covered the basics, but there are still some exotics left in our menagerie. These patterns are less common and tend to be embellishments upon, or combinations of, the patterns just discussed. Still, they have some intriguing features that are worth considering. Sam Kabo Ashwell writes about these additional patterns on his blog *These Heterogenous Tasks* (2015).

Gauntlet

The gauntlet is a fairly linear structure modified with complex tangents and foldbacks (Figure 2.25). Gauntlets tend to come in two flavors: playground or minefield. The latter has plenty of fun detours to explore, while the former is strewn with booby traps. Both have a central spine with stubby little branches that create opportunities for making good and bad choices, leading to positive or negative outcomes, such as winning the lottery or walking in front of a bus.

Pros

- Easy to create, as the main plot is a straightforward linear story.
- Players see all the important content.

Cons

- If there are multiple endings, they tend to be based on a final choice rather than state tracking of earlier choices.
- A minefield gauntlet can quickly seem frustrating and discouraging.

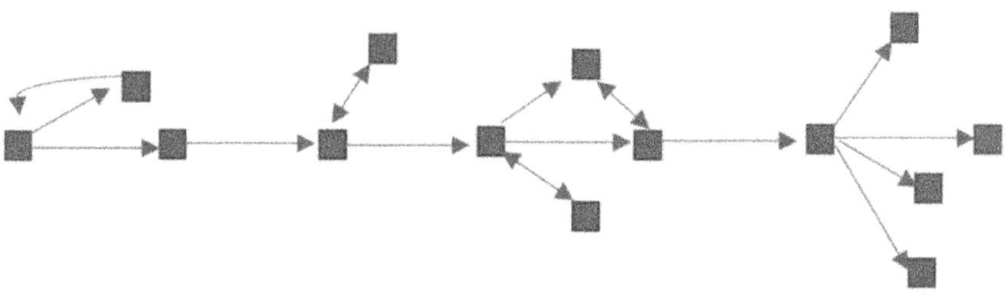

Figure 2.25 Gauntlet.

Gauntlet IDN Example

Megan Stevens' text adventure game *Our Boys in Uniform* (2013) features several stories about the Second World War, some factual and some fictional. Every page has several clickable links. If you select a link that's factual, you move forward. If you select a link that's false, you boomerang back to the start of the game. Thus, only by dialing up your BS detector can you successfully navigate this narrative obstacle course.

Quest

The quest structure is about the journey, not the destination, which makes it an appealing design for players who are happy to explore every corner of your story world. It's a collection of concentric patterns loosely linked by branching paths that players can navigate, often in more than one direction (Figure 2.26). The concentric bits are eddies swirling around the edge of the big river that is the central narrative. To motivate exploration, quests are designed as treasure hunts with a specific purpose in mind. Players gather information, skills, weapons, and/or tools by snooping around and investigating different areas.

Pros

- Allows a high degree of nonlinear exploration.
- Rewards multiple playthroughs, as there are lots of narrative options.

Cons

- Because the clustered sections are extended digressions, the flow of the central story is fragmented and episodic.

- There are distinct paths, but they tend to reconnect and arrive at a small number of endings, and sometimes just one.
- A quest must be quite large to be effective, so creators need the time and resources to create numerous nodes and/or assets.

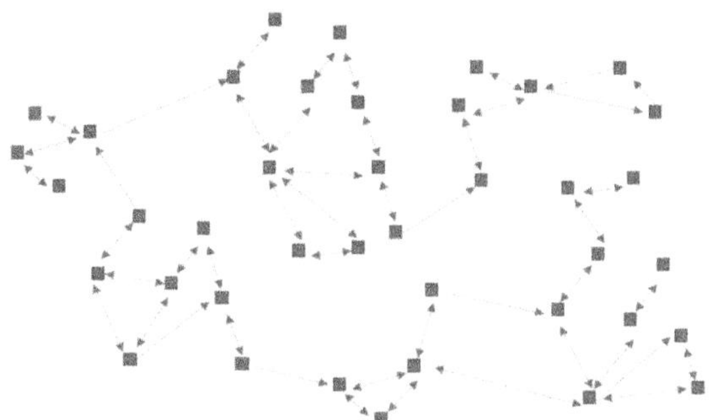

Figure 2.26 Quest.

Quest IDN Examples

The Elder Scrolls V: Skyrim has hundreds of quests and side quests for players to embark on. This highly complex action role-playing game allows players to hunt for all sorts of things, including skills, locations, tools, and the heads of defeated foes.

The Korean quest-based massively multiplayer online (MMO) game *LostArk* (2025) features three types of quests: dialogue, defeat/collection, and interactive. All of these keep players focused on accomplishing tasks rather than merely murdering opponents, although a bit of bloodlust is also rewarded.

Open Map

Even more than the quest, this pattern is a free-range experience (Figure 2.27). Its trademark feature is the absence of a preferred direction of travel. Think *Pac-Man* but with narrative nodes instead of digital breadcrumbs to swallow. The player can wander indefinitely through this structure, but there is always an escape route that allows them to reconnect with the main narrative.

Pros
- Can feel quite freeing as the player can explore the world extensively from any direction they choose.

Cons
- As the structure is radically nonlinear, any sense of narrative progression tends to seem haphazard and coincidental.

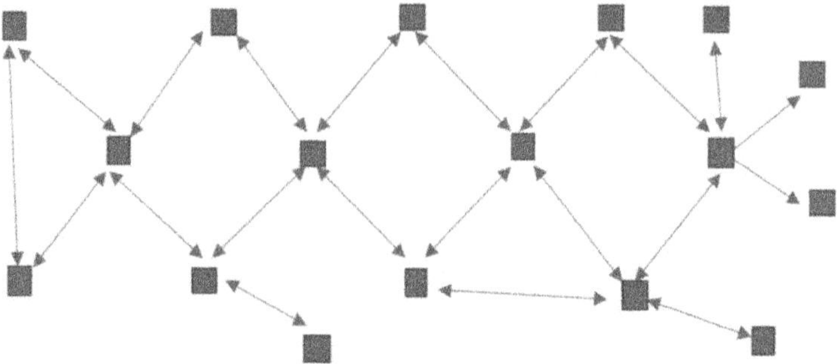

Figure 2.27 Open map.

Open Map IDN Example

Content warning: In the Twine game *Chemistry and Physics* (Sandel & VanEseltine 2013), an abusive boyfriend chases you into a locked laboratory. Once inside, you must run around in the darkness, hiding, distracting your attacker, and trying to escape. This disturbing open map mechanic reflects the terror of domestic abuse by trapping the player inside a kind of digital escape room.

Loop and Grow

The loop-and-grow pattern is a narrative merry-go-round, cycling through familiar territory over and over. With the help of state tracking, new options can be unlocked, and old options can be shut down with each cycle. This keeps things from getting too tedious.

Committing to a loop-and-grow structure means creating a story world that is deliberately confining, even claustrophobic (Figure 2.28). Often, the player is forced to engage in familiar activities in the same space repeatedly. A narrative conceit, such as getting caught in a time loop or being required to repeat a mundane task, may account for this degree of narrative redundancy. It's a bit like the film *Groundhog Day* (Ramis 1993), with fresh plot twists tied to each iteration of the loop.

Pros
- Puts all sorts of new and interesting spins on a familiar narrative world as it is explored over and over.
- Compelling surprises occur when a player's choice results in a radical variation on the previous loop.

Cons
- If there is too much narrative redundancy, the story can seem confining and stagnant.

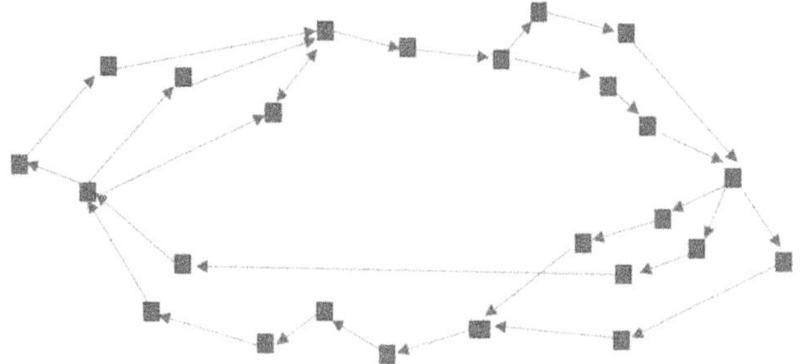

Figure 2.28 Loop and grow.

Loop-and-Grow IDN Example

In the spiraling Choose Your Own Adventure narrative *Trapped in Time* (Christiansen 2013), players cycle through a day in the life repeatedly, making choices by selecting which numbered sections to read next. You need to print out a PDF file to play this analog story-game. The document is divided into numbered paragraphs with clear instructions. Whenever you make a decision, you're told to turn to a specific paragraph. As you gain knowledge and items, you acquire the ability to add certain numbers to alter the dramatic action. If you stray a bit too far, the instructions remind you which page number you need to return to in order to get back on the main path.

Spoke and Hub

A common variation on the loop-and-grow structure is the spoke and hub (Figure 2.29). This pattern features major branches that flow to and from a central node or set of nodes. The player can move along each spoke as many times as they please.

Pros
- The spokes allow players to break up the redundancy of the looping pattern.

Cons
- Hopping in and out of the story at different points can be disorienting and disrupt a sense of narrative continuity.

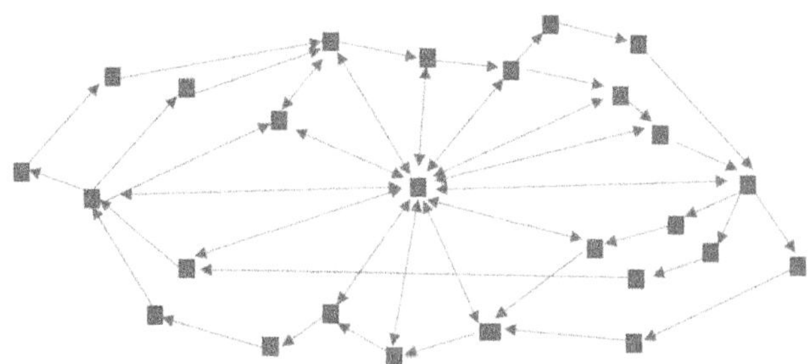

Figure 2.29 Spoke and hub.

Spoke and Hub IDN Example

In the tactical role-playing game *Planescape: Torment* (Henkel & Lee 2017), players navigate in and out of a dark city at the churning heart of the *Dungeons & Dragons* multiverse. The player chooses from various options located within a central **hub**. This sends them through a **spoke** to an outer hub, a process that continues until the player runs out of branching options and returns to the central hub, where they can select a different option before heading off again along another spoke.

Scripts, Who Needs 'Em?

In a moment, I'll discuss the story design of *Shelley's Heart Stage Version.* That project combined live-action performances with pre-recorded videos, so careful scripting was essential. But sometimes it's possible, even preferable, to improvise the dialogue incorporated into your IDN project.

IDN projects are often created on a microscopic budget with suffocating time constraints, utilizing amateur crews and nonprofessional actors. So why introduce the additional challenge of working without the security of a script? Well, because when producing stills, video, audio, drawings, and so on, under such conditions, drafting, refining, memorizing, rehearsing, and filming an actual script can feel a bit like roller skating in quicksand.

Does this mean you should totally wing it? Of course not. What you need is a flexible guide that lays out key dramatic beats, hence the . . .

Story Map

Unlike the free-form mind maps discussed in Chapter 1, a story map is a carefully constructed document where every node needs to be in the correct place (Figure 2.30). If the facilitators and participants understand the basic story flow, they should be able to improvise the short scenes that will serve as focal points along the narrative paths.

This is like the approach silent filmmakers used when shooting their one-reel productions. Often, dozens of scenes would be sketched out in the form of a skeletal outline, only a few pages long. The acting was largely improvised, and title cards were an afterthought drafted during the editing phase. In a similar sense, guiding titles and screen instructions can be added to your IDN during the final assembly phase. For more on this, see Chapter 4: Nodes.

To draft your story map, start with the basic spine of your narrative—the dramatic through line. This is the central plot, including a beginning, middle, and end. Once you've sketched this out, you will have a sense of the basic flow and can start to embellish with branches, foldbacks, bottlenecks, and alternate endings.

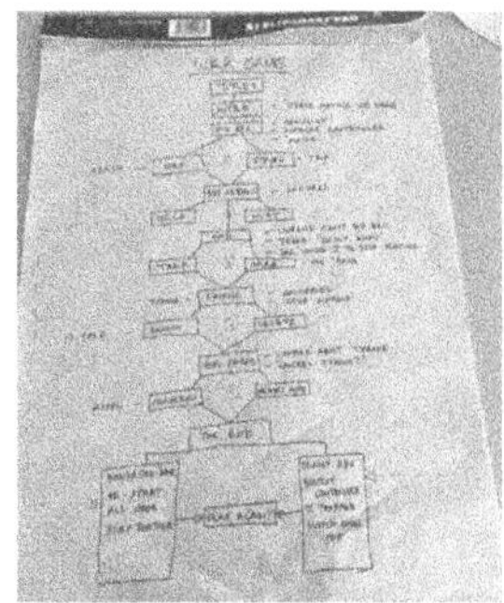

Figure 2.30 Story map, *Next Level*, *c*. 2023.

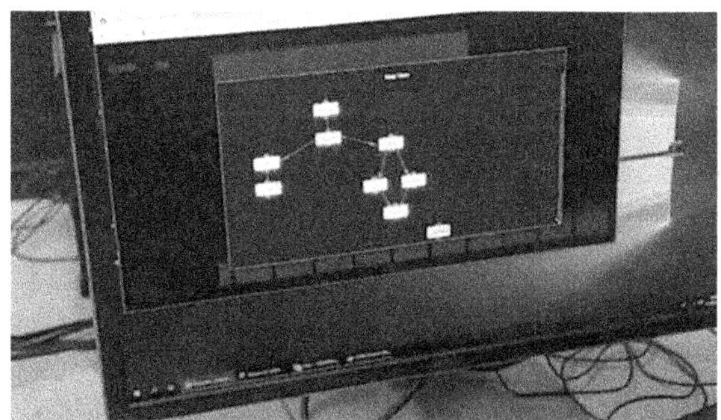

Figure 2.31 Story map in Genarrator, *c*. 2020.

When planning the story for *IDN Next Level,* we sketched out a simple story map on a large sheet of paper. I shot an image of this with my phone and occasionally referred to it during the shooting, which took place over two days. All dialogue, blocking, and camera work were created extemporaneously on location.

While this may not be the best recipe for crafting Oscar-worthy performances, if your main goal is to unleash the creativity of your participants in a spontaneous, high-energy fashion, working from an outline rather than a script may be your best bet.

You might sketch your story map on a piece of large paper, as above, or it can be created directly inside your IDN platform (Figure 2.31). When taking the latter approach, the nodes start out as empty shells with placeholder descriptions of what will occur when the player lands on that spot. Later, these can be modified with working decision points and playable media assets.

LANDMINE

- **Limit eleventh-hour rewrites.** One of the challenges of creating an IDN is that there are so many interconnected parts, even small changes late in the production process can have a ripple effect, forcing the team to radically reconfigure the story, throw out produced elements, and organize last-minute reshoots and reedits. This is why, when it comes to refining patterns, the outline and prototyping processes are vital. If you don't resolve story problems early, you will pay a steep price later. To avoid this type of eleventh-hour drama, IDN creators should obsessively outline, prototype, and user test to exterminate as many narrative bugs as possible.

PRO TIP

- **Blank slate protagonists are beautiful.** If you're writing a screenplay or a novel and create a main character who is just a "normal guy" with no flaws, interests, or dirty little secrets, you will put your audience to sleep. But when it comes to your IDN protagonist, boring is good. Because the player *is* the protagonist, you don't want their character to be too well-defined. Instead, give the player plenty of opportunities to define the character for themselves by making the kind of moral choices that determine who the protagonist is, what they value, and how they react under pressure.

From the Trenches

Cautionary Tale: Shelley's Heart Stage Version Opening Night

It's Saturday, November 25, 2017. The 100-seat Shelley Theatre in Boscombe, UK, is filled. The audience members have been given remote control clickers and, at key points, are prompted to vote on what the characters will do next. Based on the outcome of these votes, three live actors exchange dialogue with virtual ghosts appearing on video screens built into replicas of the Shelley Tomb and other grave markers from St. Peter's Churchyard in Bournemouth, UK.

As the action kicks off, the audience becomes invested in the plot, and everything is working perfectly. The actors are hitting their cues and performing convincingly with the on-screen characters. But then, suddenly, the audience goes rogue. Exploiting a previously unidentified design flaw, they start voting to skip crucial scenes.

Up to this point, we have tested the interface dozens of times with small groups of participants, but never with such a large crowd. Something about this new dynamic is tempting the audience to race past key story elements. The actors have no choice but to leapfrog past important dramatic sequences. As a result, the storyline grows increasingly fragmented. The cast manages to navigate through this somewhat disjointed plotline, arriving at the final scene and receiving a respectable round of applause. However, we learn an important—and very public—lesson about the value of working out all the kinks in your interaction design before opening night.

Takeaways

- Don't allow players to skip essential scenes.
- User test with a group the same size as your target audience.

Success Story: Shelley's Heart Stage Version Second Night

Opening night wasn't a complete disaster, but there were significant gaps in the storyline. To understand how we were able to fix those issues and recover for the second performance, it's necessary to go back to the birth of this complex transmedia project.

In 2015, I was in Copenhagen attending the 8th International Conference on Digital Storytelling. For two days, I'd been hearing about all sorts of mind-blowing interactive narratives when suddenly I cooked up the idea that became the genesis of *Shelley's Heart*.

I teach at Bournemouth University in Bournemouth, England. One of the most celebrated landmarks in that seaside community is a tomb in St. Peter's Churchyard where Mary Shelley is buried, along with the heart of her husband, Percy Shelley. The Shelleys were friends with other Romantic poets, including John Keats and Lord Byron.

As I sat in that lecture theater reflecting on the Shelley Tomb and the heart of Percy Shelley, I came up with the narrative that would form the basis of *Shelley's Heart*. It involved some modern-day doppelgängers of Mary Shelley, Lord Byron, and John Keats exploring St. Peter's Churchyard in search of the ghost of Percy Shelley, who, in turn, is searching for his missing heart.

The original plan was to create a location-aware narrative set in the actual churchyard. There would be a single path visitors could explore. At key locations, they would pause and unlock a particular scene in an unfolding drama. To add more interactivity, I came up with the idea of describing the same events from four different perspectives. Modern Mary, Modern John, and Modern Byron, along with Percy Shelley's ghost, would narrate each scene, and players would be able to shift between their POVs at will.

When I returned to Bournemouth, I scouted the churchyard and developed a path and a narrative outline. After that, I wrote the first draft of an unusual script, broken into a series of four-column **threaded** narrative scenes. Each column featured one character describing specific dramatic beats simultaneously to the other three (Figure 2.32).

Figure 2.32 Multilinear narrative—*Shelley's Heart Stage Version*, draft 1, *c*. 2016.

Once the script was written, some MA scriptwriting students were recruited, and we conducted an on-location **playthrough** in St. Peter's Churchyard. Different students were cast to play different characters and read their narration as we switched between perspectives.

After the playthrough, we met at a local coffee shop to debrief. I also had the participants fill out a survey sheet (see Chapter 4: Nodes).

All sorts of helpful feedback emerged from this process, including the insight that constantly leaping between the different perspectives was too disorienting. Additionally, the long reflective passages tended to slow the pacing and reduce the sense of dramatic conflict. To address these concerns, the next draft of the script featured what I called "fly-on-the-wall scenes." These were short sequences featuring only dialogue and action, with no character narration. They served to break up the story and make it less reflective and more dramatically compelling (Figure 2.33).

This modified approach ironed out some narrative kinks but there were other challenges to come. The next step in the development process was a script-in-hand **rehearsed reading** in the Winchester Theater-Pub with actors playing the characters on a small stage. To encourage audience participation, I created an online voting system. At key points, spectators were prompted to weigh in, and the character who got the most votes narrated the next section. In this way, the audience was helping to direct the unfolding action.

We ran a short rehearsal, and things went well (Figure 2.34). But on the night of the performance, an hour before showtime, an unexpected issue cropped up. The Winchester's Wi-Fi signal went out so the phone voting system stopped working. We called the pub's service provider and learned that some construction works had

Figure 2.33 Fly-on-the-wall scene—*Shelley's Heart Stage Version*, draft 2, *c*. 2016.

Figure 2.34 *Shelley's Heart Rehearsed Reading*, *c*. 2016.

taken out all internet connectivity within a five-block radius. As audience members started to filter in eager to participate in this new interactive play, much handwringing ensued. Fortunately, minutes before showtime, the internet was restored. After that, the performance went smoothly and was well-received.

Based on the success of this test performance, the historic Shelley Theater booked *Shelley's Heart* for two performances eight months later. Cue more handwringing. My locative story seemed to be morphing into a theatrical production, but how could I say no to debuting *Shelley's Heart* in a theater once owned by Mary Shelley's son, Percy Florence Shelley? The opportunity was too tempting to pass up (Figure 2.35).

I shook the funding trees and raised a bit of money but soon realized there was no way I could produce a theatrical production featuring the eleven characters in my still-evolving script. And there was an additional problem: mental bandwidth. Getting actors to memorize a full-length play is challenging enough, but an interactive play involves far more content. Each multi-narrative scene would require an actor to memorize an extended first-person aside. If only there was some way to address these logistical challenges without dumbing things down, slashing scenes, and cutting characters.

Then, like a lightning bolt striking Victor Frankenstein's lab, inspiration struck out of the blue. What if we pre-filmed all the ghost characters and had them appear on

Figure 2.35 Advert for *Shelley's Heart Stage Version* at the Shelley Theater, *c.* 2017.

Figure 2.36 Interactive theater set—*Shelley's Heart Stage Version*, *c.* 2017.

screens during the performance? These screens could be embedded into set pieces representing landmarks from St. Peter's Churchyard, including the Shelley Tomb, and the performers could interact with them! (Figure 2.36).

I hadn't abandoned my plans for producing the *Shelley's Heart* locative version. Instead, I leveraged interest in the theatrical version as a means of casting actors and creating media assets for the location-aware story. After all, every bit of footage we planned to shoot for the theater piece would eventually find its way into the locative version. The production process would be a win-win!

For the scenes with actors speaking, we needed to work in a controlled environment to avoid audio issues, so we shot those sequences in front of a green screen in a studio on the Bournemouth University campus (Figure 2.37).

Seeking to bring more depth and atmosphere to the production, we added two night shoots at St. Peter's Churchyard in Bournemouth town center. Our team captured both moving footage and static images to serve as the basis for looping **cinemagraphs** (Burg & Beck n.d.).

Stationary scenes were lit by fluorescent panels on stands. For live-action scenes, crew members raced around the churchyard backward, pointing the light panels at actors while trying to avoid tripping over tombstones—and our fleet-footed

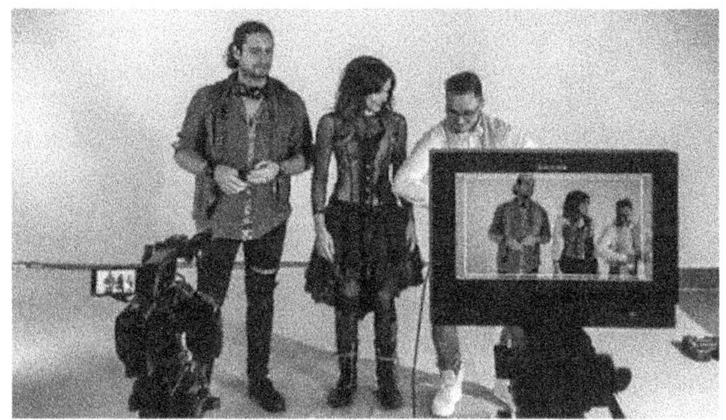

Figure 2.37 Green screen BTS—*Shelley's Heart*, c. 2017.

Figure 2.38 Location lighting—*Shelley's Heart*, c. 2017.

cinematographer, who was also jogging backward while filming everything with an HD camera mounted on a handheld gimbal (Figure 2.38).

Once the studio and location footage had been shot, I edited everything together, incorporating royalty-free backgrounds and visual effects. Then it was time to rehearse for the stage production.

To help our actors see where they were standing in relation to the characters on the projection screen behind them, a laptop linked to a large monitor was placed in front of them. This allowed them to face forward while still seeing what was happening over their shoulders—an invaluable aid for timing their interactions with the pre-recorded material and working out how to block each scene.

LANDMINE

- **Mixing live and pre-recorded performances is tricky.** It's tough for actors to exchange lines with filmed characters for several reasons. The timing can feel stiff, as there is no wiggle room to adjust the pacing. Improvisation

Figure 2.39 Rehearsal—*Shelley's Heart Stage Version*, c. 2017.

As the dates for the theatrical performance approached, we decided to promote the project with a **site-specific**, live-action interactive taster scene in St. Peter's Churchyard (Figure 2.40). To accomplish this, we rehearsed a twenty-minute section of the story in which Mary, John, and Byron head off in various directions and see different ghostly visions before meeting up again near the Shelley Tomb. On the day of this mini-performance, about thirty people turned up, and we advised them to follow whichever character intrigued them most. We also enhanced the experience with some audio cues and a few interactive prompts that triggered different responses from the actors.

The next evening, it was time for our big theatrical debut. Leery of depending on Wi-Fi signals after the internet outage that nearly derailed our rehearsed reading, I invested in some more reliable technology: small plastic clickers that operated via radio signals. We passed these out to audience members, and at key points during

Figure 2.40 *Shelley's Heart Site-Specific Taster*, c. 2017.

Figure 2.41 Interactive voting page—*Shelley's Heart Stage Version*, *c*. 2017.

Figure 2.42 Mary and on-screen monster—Shelley's Heart Stage Version, *c*. 2017.

the play, a voting graphic appeared on the multiple onstage screens. The audience could then vote to decide which character they wanted to hear from or what they wanted to happen next. While the votes tallied in real time, the actors watched from the wings. After a particular scene received the most votes, they took the stage and performed the appropriate dramatic actions (Figure 2.41).

Another technical challenge we had to address involved creating a large image at the back of the stage—something big enough for everyone in the theater to clearly see the on-screen characters and voting. We had two foreground screens built into set pieces, but an LED screen large enough to serve as a backdrop would have been too expensive to lease and too time-consuming and complex to set up. To solve this issue, we installed a projector in the back of the large set piece representing the Shelley Tomb and aimed it at a big screen at the back of the stage. This worked perfectly, allowing the live actors to interact with filmed characters (Figure 2.42).

And filmed objects (Figure 2.43).

But then there was the issue of lighting. From the rehearsed reading, we knew the stage lights would cause problems. When they hit the big screen, they drained the projected images of depth and color. Fortunately, some members of BU's tech team devised a clever workaround. With their guidance, we installed two large upright light bars, one on either side of the stage. At the start of each scene, we lit these

Figure 2.43 Mary and on-screen tomb—Shelley's Heart Stage Version, *c.* 2017.

Figure 2.44 *Shelley's Heart Stage Version*, *c.* 2017.

up, casting beams of light across the width of the stage. The light beams were just six feet wide—deep enough to illuminate the actors without hitting the screen and washing it out (Figure 2.44).

In terms of all these technical challenges, we still weren't out of the woods, but we were close. As I mentioned earlier, on opening night, there were some issues related to the story design. We fixed this after that performance by immediately removing the skip options appearing before any crucial scenes. This meant the second live performance was more coherent. The audience still had the ability to guide the dramatic action, but they could *not* skip past important moments.

Performing the piece to a large audience in a live setting also drew our attention to other challenges inherent in the production design. Pausing to tally votes tended to slow the dramatic pacing, and audience members who were outvoted didn't get to see their preferred options. On the plus side, the interface afforded the audience more agency than a traditional theater-going experience and added an element of unpredictability to the unfolding dramatic structure. So, overall, the second performance was a success, receiving an enthusiastic response from the audience.

Takeaways

- Test your project with readthroughs, rehearsed readings, and rehearsals.
- Listen to user feedback and refine the work.
- Use project deadlines, such as rehearsals and performances, to create forward momentum.
- Learn from unexpected issues that crop up and devise creative solutions.
- Anticipate logistical challenges and devise solutions for those as well.
- When things go sideways, swiftly identify the problem and fix it.

Key Tasks: Paths

Task 1. Story Map

Sketch out a story map on a sheet of paper that combines elements from two or more interactive narrative patterns. The design should be a good fit for the story idea.

Task 2. Paper Prototype

Use index cards to represent each node of your proposed interactive story and connect them via various points. Challenge yourselves to use different types of nodes, points, and patterns. Once your prototype is completed, user test it to identify problems and solve them, then revise your prototype and test it again. If you prefer to do digital prototyping, there are many free prototyping tools (Figma 2025) that can help you accomplish this, including a simple PowerPoint (Bloom 2016) presentation utilizing nonlinear hyperlinks.

3   Assets

A media asset is a special class of path. A typical path takes the player from one node to the next in a split second, but an asset provides an entertaining detour along the way. The cutscenes in a video game are a type of asset—media files that play out, revealing elements of story and exposition. It's possible to produce an IDN with no assets of any kind. In fact, some purists prefer text-only narratives and consider multimedia bells and whistles frivolous distractions or, worse, linear storytelling in disguise. The annoying thing is these killjoys are not entirely wrong. There is a risk to populating your IDN with media assets. If the story isn't particularly immersive and the interface isn't very interactive, the project can start to feel like a glorified website rather than an engaging story world.

On the other hand, if you include the right amount of immersion and interaction interwoven with some clever multimedia storytelling, you can ensure your IDN is both engaging and beautiful.

Types of Assets

One of the joys of creating an IDN is considering all the potential assets at your disposal. These include video files, still images, text panels, audio files, animations, and more. Assets can be ultra-short: a blaring alarm clock. Or much longer: a dramatic montage. They can be low-tech: a scribbled cartoon. Or high-tech: a 360-degree audio mix.

Assets can also feature modes of interactivity, offering choices embedded in their narrative structures (Figure 3.1). They can play as full-screen elements or appear in windows displayed on top of a node. They may also feature controls that allow players to stop, fast-forward, reverse, or skip. Once they've played, the player can be returned to the node that launched them or delivered to a different node.

Live-Action Video/Film

For many IDN creators, the default asset is a short film. Admit it: there's something thrilling about unleashing your inner Fellini and directing actors playing invented characters. But before you start creating shot plans for every sequence in your IDN, think about this: there's a reason student films are often embarrassing. There are so

Figure 3.1 Assets.

Figure 3.2 Location filming—*Shelley's Heart*, *c*. 2017.

many things that can go wrong. Even if the writing is brilliant and the acting inspired, the camerawork may be clumsy, or the sound may be muffled. Think your audience won't notice these issues? Think again.

Because film is the art form that most resembles lived experience, it is an inherently challenging medium. If the severed foot seems fake or the ancient prophet looks like a nineteen-year-old in a fake white beard, the spell is broken. Modern audiences have little tolerance for shoddy production values, bad acting, and stilted dialogue—all hallmarks of works created by budding auteurs.

But take heart, cineastes: if you want to include filmed assets in your IDN, lean into the challenges. Fight tooth and nail to make the work as impressive as possible. And when the inevitable flubbed line, out-of-focus shot, or cheesy special effect compromises your vision, take the hit, shake it off, and forge ahead. In the meantime, do whatever you can to keep your standards as high as possible. The film gods are fickle, but if you honor them, they will sometimes reward you with a glimmer of cinematic gold (Figure 3.2).

LANDMINE

- **Avoid railroading.** When producing assets for your IDN, keep things short and sweet so players don't get bored waiting for more decision points. Typically, assets such as video and audio files should have running times between five and thirty seconds.

PRO TIPS

- **Lots of assets mean lots of options.** Let's say your IDN contains twenty assets. During a single playthrough, a player might encounter 25 percent of these—that's just five. Keep in mind that the more assets you produce, the more interactive your IDN becomes. Rather than limiting your asset creation to a few slickly produced videos, consider generating dozens of low-tech assets, such as third-party stills punctuated with sound effects, or title pages with textual information. This will streamline your production process and free you up to offer a more diverse array of media content, including drawings, audio files, graphics, text, stop-motion animations, photo slideshows, and more. Even if some of the production values are less impressive, the user experience will be much richer due to the plentiful decision points and types of media on offer.
- **Phone it in.** Sometimes, images shot on a phone can be just as dramatically compelling as more highly produced sequences, lending a gritty realism to your project. For example, you might create an NPC who leaves several FaceTime messages for the player. No special lighting, microphone, or tripod required—just have the actor speak into their phone and leave a series of short messages in the portrait aspect ratio, which can be screen captured on the phone receiving them. These mini videos are easy to produce and can be quite impactful. The key is keeping things brief and having the actor deliver a compelling performance.

iDoc Assets

If your IDN is an iDoc, it can include images, audio, and footage captured in real-life situations, as well as interviews with people sharing their lived experiences. For the downloadable **news game** prototype *Target BACRIM*, we embedded interviews shot in Colombia with actual citizens, politicians, and members of a lethal paramilitary group. These interviews appeared in scenes where the Player Character interviews real people while searching for clues related to the disappearance of a fictional colleague, Morris Krammer (Figure 3.3).

Incorporating moving images into your iDoc is a simple and effective way to make it more dynamic and immersive. You can include a **demonstration** in the form of a demo video (Mansaray 2022) where an expert teaches players how to master a

Figure 3.3 Factual interview footage incorporated into fictional scene—*Target BACRIM, c.* 2016.

Figure 3.4 Dramatization—*Target BACRIM, c.* 2016.

particular skill, or you can include a **dramatization** (2024) related to an actual event (Figure 3.4).

Still and Slideshow

Sometimes a simple still image can pack a powerful punch, especially if it's paired with a sound effect or music sting. Or you can go for something more dynamic by embedding a slideshow comprised of multiple stills. These sequences can advance the plot, clarify backstory, or convey exposition. If you'd like them to autoplay and want to add some flashy production values, consider generating a short sequence with the help of a slideshow video template (2024). On the other hand, if you want players to read the slides at their own pace and trigger them at will, build them into your IDN as a sequence of interrelated nodes and consider linking them to sound effects.

Below are some images from an expositional slideshow featured in the *Shelley's Heart* desktop version (Figures 3.5 and 3.6; Gyori 2019b). They refer to Mary Shelley's father, William Godwin, and suggest how the scandals that plagued his unconventional wife, Mary Wollstonecraft, may have helped his daughter empathize with Victor Frankenstein's misunderstood creation.

Figure 3.5 Slideshow, Mary before—*Shelley's Heart Desktop Version*, c. 2019.

Figure 3.6 Slideshow, Mary after—*Shelley's Heart Desktop Version*, c. 2019.

Audio File

If you want to add bells and whistles, you need sounds. Audio files can be used to embellish images and videos. But audio-only assets are also a great way to enhance your IDN. In the example below, the player selects tracks from a playlist featuring quotes from the author Mary Shelley, read by an actor (Figure 3.7).

Figure 3.7 Quote playlist—*Shelley's Heart Desktop Version*, c. 2019.

Sim-Tool

With the help of sim-tools, your IDN can mimic the functionality of various devices, such as a television set, a movie screen, a wall mirror, or a cassette tape. These simulations are a combination of nodes and assets working together to mimic familiar media interfaces. For instance, a sim-tool can copy the functionality of your phone via fake voice memos, text messages, or notepad jottings. The trick is to create mock versions of these devices and simulations of their interfaces, peppering them throughout your narrative (Figures 3.8 and 3.9).

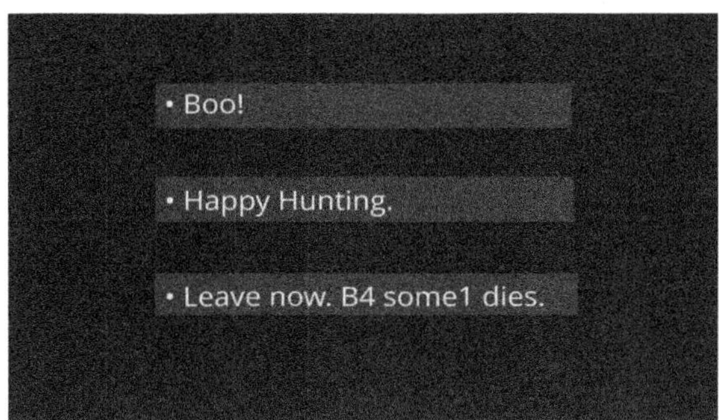

Figure 3.8 Sim-tool text message responses—*Shelley's Heart Desktop Version*, *c*. 2019.

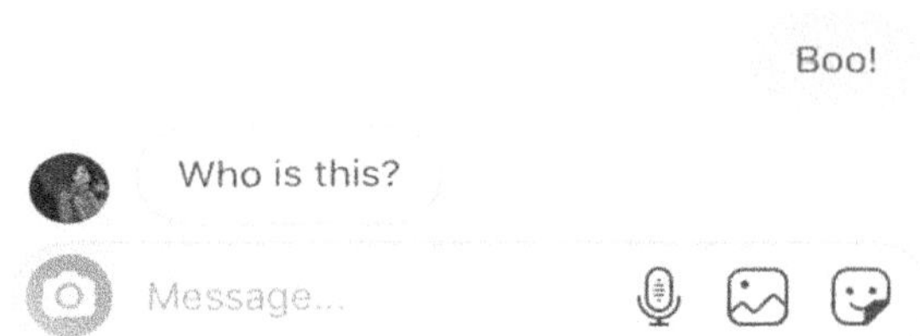

Figure 3.9 Sim-tool text message—*Shelley's Heart Desktop Version*, *c*. 2019.

PRO TIP

- **Text for Success.** The easiest way to replicate a POV visual of the player composing a text is to screen-capture your phone while typing a fake message. You can also screen-capture moments when an NPC responds to the player's text by sending a message from another device. Once you have this footage, consider enhancing it with sound effects, such as notification alarms, message sent swooshes, and digital typing sounds (Figure 3.10).

Figure 3.10 Sim-tool cassette tape—*Target BACRIM, c.* 2016.

Pseudo-Tool

Your IDN can also feature whimsical variations on existing tools that include strange, even supernatural, functions. These pseudo-tools might communicate with ghosts or read minds while enhancing your IDN with additional fictional plot points and/or factual information (Figures 3.11, 3.12, and 3.13).

Figure 3.11 Tag for pseudo-tool mind memo—*Shelley's Heart Locative Version, c.* 2018.

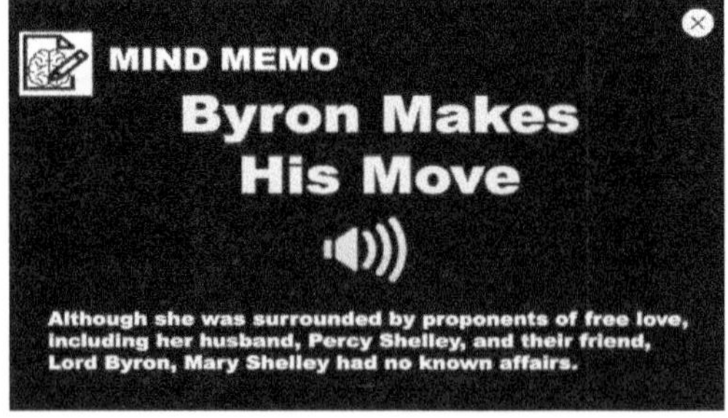

Figure 3.12 Pseudo-tool mind memo—*Shelley's Heart Locative Version, c.* 2018.

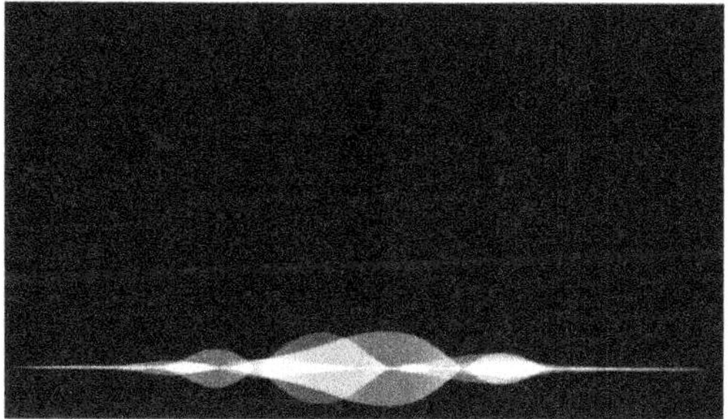

Figure 3.13 Pseudo-tool mind memo plays—*Shelley's Heart Locative Version*, *c.* 2018.

Sim-Plat

With embedded sim-plats, your IDN can also imitate the functions of various online platforms, such as fake Facebook pages, Instagram accounts, websites, or blogs.

Pseudo-Plat

Your IDN may also feature spoofs of existing web platforms with playful variations on their functionality. In keeping with its spooky graveyard theme, the *Shelley's Heart Desktop Version* features the following pseudo-plats: *BooTube, Instaghost, Deddit, Huffghost, Jitter, Spookify*, and *Soundshroud* (Figure 3.14).

Figure 3.14 Pseudo-plat, Soundshroud—*Shelley's Heart Desktop Version*, *c.* 2019.

Media Maker

It's also fun to show off a little by including multimedia elements that fool the player into thinking you have a massive budget, high-end production gear, and impressive coding skills. None of these are necessary if you avail yourself of the countless free platforms that allow you to create whizzy multimedia assets with minimal time or effort. These include:

- data visualization creator (Flourish 2024)
- character maker (Voki 2024)
- animated GIF maker (Ezgif 2024)
- graphic design tool (Vistacreate 2024)
- infographic creator (Canva 2024)
- map creator (MapHub 2024)
- logo maker (Logo Design 2024)
- text-to-speech converter (TTSMAKER 2024).

AI can also be your creative wingman. In terms of enhancing the writing process, consider *ChatGPT* (2024) and *Claude* (2024).

For visual assistance, check out image generators like *MidJourney* (2024), photo animators like *Simplified* (2024), and AI video creators like *CinemaFlow* (2024).

For audio simulations, consider AI voice generators like *Artlist* (2024), AI singing tools like *Kits.AI* (2024), and AI music makers like *Soundraw* (2024).

Quiz

One way to include a quiz in your IDN is to embed it with the help of an interactive widget. More on this in Chapter 5. Socials. But you can also bake quiz elements into the narrative itself in the form of a lock-and-key mechanic, which motivates exploration and discovery. This approach prompts the player to confirm something they've learned by exploring the narrative or making an educated guess about an unfamiliar topic. Whether they confirm what they already know or discover an interesting new fact, the quiz promotes active learning. This can be as simple as a multiple-choice question where a correct answer unlocks a new scene. For example, a text message might appear via a sim-tool as in *Shelley's Heart Desktop Version* (Figure 3.15).

This allows the player to click on the "QUIZ" icon, which causes a quiz node to appear (Figure 3.16).

This multiple-choice question requires the player to answer correctly before they can advance to the next portion of dramatic content. Selecting the wrong answer

Figure 3.15 Triggering quiz mechanic—*Shelley's Heart Desktop Version*, *c*. 2019.

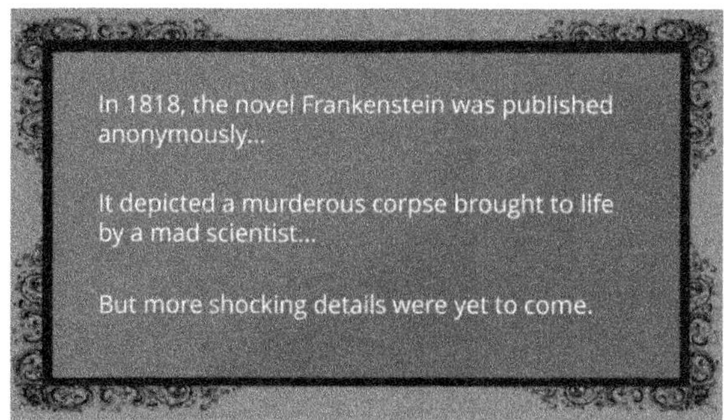

Figure 3.16 Quiz multiple-choice 2—*Shelley's Heart Desktop Version*, *c*. 2019.

turns the text red and triggers a loud buzzing sound. Selecting the correct answer turns the text green, triggers a pleasant ding, and makes a "SCENE" button appear, providing access to the scene node (Figure 3.17).

Another quiz mechanic allows players to repeatedly choose between the same two options. In the example below, various facts appear, and the player must decide whether the information refers to Mary Shelley or her mother, Mary Wollstonecraft (Figure 3.18).

LANDMINE

- **Don't quiz your story to death.** Be careful where you place a quiz as it requires the player to stop and think and can inhibit the dramatic flow of your IDN.

Figure 3.17 Quiz multiple-choice 3—*Shelley's Heart Desktop Version*, c. 2019.

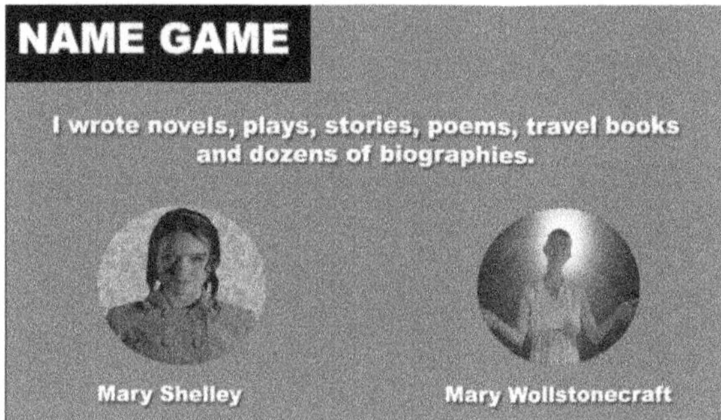

Figure 3.18 Quiz recurring choices—*Shelley's Heart Desktop Version*, c. 2019.

Puzzle

A puzzle can serve different functions in your IDN. Embedded within a single node, it can act as a lock-and-key mechanism. This gating function prevents players from advancing until the puzzle is solved. In the example below, the player needs to align images and texts related to three figures: Modern Mary, Mary Shelley, and Mary Wollstonecraft (Figure 3.19).

Figure 3.19 Puzzle lock and key—*Shelley's Heart Desktop Version*, c. 2019.

Alternatively, a puzzle can operate as a state-tracking device. For instance, at the end of each scene from the Shelley's Heart Locative Version, a piece is added to a puzzle related to that path. Once all ten scenes are complete, ten puzzle pieces are assembled, and the path is officially over (Figure 3.20).

Figure 3.20 Puzzle state tracking—*Shelley's Heart Locative Version*, *c.* 2018.

Filter

You can also offer players opportunities to alter media assets. For instance, activating a filter that alters an image, as shown in the example below (Figures 3.21 and 3.22).

Figure 3.21 "Fake Over" filter, before—*Shelley's Heart Desktop Version*, *c.* 2019.

Figure 3.22 "Fake Over" filter, after—*Shelley's Heart Desktop Version*, *c.* 2019.

Interactive Map

Another handy interactive element is a diagram tagged with information about a particular physical space, that is, a country, city, geological strata, anatomical region, and so on. This type of interactivity can be produced with the help of a map editor (StoryMaps 2024).

Note: Although interactive maps are sometimes called story maps, they shouldn't be confused with the story maps discussed in Chapter 2, *Paths.* Those are diagramming tools for plotting the nodes and paths that comprise your IDN, whereas interactive maps are images based on physical locations tagged with bits of information and assets (Figure 3.23).

Figure 3.23 Interactive map—*Target BACRIM, c.* 2016.

Producing Assets

If you are a big-time media professional with loads of experience, you've already mastered many of the skills discussed in this section. While you may benefit from some IDN-oriented twists on old techniques, feel free to scan the following pages selectively. On the other hand, if you don't have much production experience, or are just a bit rusty, and you still want to create some assets, this chapter will get you up to speed on the basics. Hopefully, it will also inspire you to experiment with some creative media-making techniques.

When it comes to producing the assets for an IDN, it helps to keep the final project in mind. This is where the style guide comes in handy, as it can keep you on track regarding the look and tone you're trying to achieve. Nothing screams bush league more than inconsistent production values. On the other hand, if the aesthetic is consistent, the audio quality high, and the images in focus, your final IDN will be something your team can take pride in sharing with the world.

PRO TIP

- **If you can't make it, fake it.** Avoid limiting your story concept based on production constraints. Instead, challenge your team to come up with the wildest ideas possible to see if you can figure out some way to portray them. If a meteorite filled with killer kittens is plummeting toward Earth, you probably don't have the budget to create a CGI sequence depicting this event, but you can shoot characters freaking out in response to it. To make the footage extra dramatic, you might film several actors from a tightly framed, radically canted, ultra-low angle. Then cue the screaming and arm flailing. You can add strobing visual overlays and crash sound effects in post, plus, of course, the evil meows of those killer kittens processed with audio effects to make them sound extra sinister.
- **Stills for stunts.** Consider shooting an on-camera stunt as a photographic montage. Don't know how to create a sequence where someone falls down a set of stairs without committing a health and safety violation? Try shooting photographs of an actor in different falling poses. Cut them together to form a quick stills montage paired with some crashing sound effects, and you've created a stylized stunt without breaking anyone's neck.

LANDMINE

- **Watch your gear.** In the field, avoid leaving equipment unsupervised.

Casting

Good news: Most people are big hams and love being on camera. Often, a key motivator for participants is the opportunity to take their star turn, so casting roles is usually easy. The trick is selecting the best person to play each part.

PRO TIPS

- **Cast to type.** With professional actors, it's sometimes interesting to cast someone against type so they can stretch creatively. With amateurs, casting to type is generally a safer bet. Have the party animal play the class clown, and the wallflower play the bookworm. If the role is close to their personality, it will be easier for them to stay in character and even improvise.
- **Shoot around shyness.** If participants are camera-shy but you need characters in shots, try shooting them from behind or focusing on body parts such as feet, hands, or a scowling mouth. This can create a mystique about a character we never see completely.

Recce (Location Scout)

The term "recce" comes from the military. It's short for "reconnaissance mission." It means venturing into unknown territory with a small group of people to gather intel. This handy concept has been co-opted by journalists and filmmakers, who usually scope out locations before shooting footage or recording audio in them.

Once you identify a location you want to use, have a good look around and consider how to best utilize the space. Don't forget common-sense concerns such as lighting, sound, foot traffic, and visual clutter. Also, think about what you're hoping to achieve in the particular space and what might enhance or detract from it. If you need to control the lighting, find a room where you can block out or limit natural light. If an actor will be positioned near a window, make sure the backlighting isn't turning them into a silhouette and confusing your camera's autofocus function. Will you need to close the blinds, tape them shut, or shoot from a different angle? If you need to record audio, find a relatively quiet location with a door you can close to block external noise.

Also, allow the recce to be part of your creative process. Use it to brainstorm about various aspects related to visual and audio storytelling, including blocking, camera movements, lighting, and more.

PRO TIPS

- **Shoot storyboard pictures during your recce.** If you plan to film a complex scene in a particular location, consider pulling out your phone and shooting still images of actors from specific camera angles that will comprise the sequence. You can later download them and assemble them as a photo storyboard to visualize how the shots will cut together. This can be a handy tool during the actual filming.
- **Consolidate locations.** If you have a tight schedule, be careful about venturing too far and wide during the shooting process. You might be able to shoot a scene in one corner of a room, then flip the camera around and shoot another scene in the opposite corner.

Set Pieces and Props

Your brainstorming sessions should identify key set pieces and props freely available to your team. However, there may be some additional production elements you need to acquire. If you have a small budget, appoint someone to be your **prop master** and have them do a bit of shopping at a costume supply store, hardware store, grocery store, and so on. Props include smaller items such as a bow and arrow, a toothbrush, and a giant rubber hand. Set pieces are larger items like a folding card table, a strobe light, and a fog machine.

Makeup

As with props and set pieces, you should be able to acquire a lot of makeup for free (Figure 3.24). Still, you may need to purchase some specialty items, such as gold face paint or devil horns. Usually, your prop master can also be the makeup and wardrobe master. If one of your cast members has visible blemishes, having some flesh-tone concealer on hand is helpful. Likewise, if a cast member tends to get shiny under the lights, keep a puff pad in a plastic bag filled with face powder. A couple of gentle pats, and the shine will vanish.

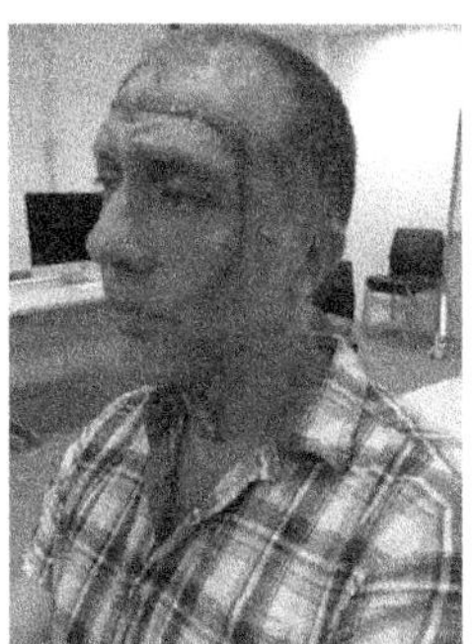

Figure 3.24 Makeup test—*Shelley's Heart, c.* 2016.

Wardrobe

Broadly defined, wardrobe includes anything your actors wear, such as clothes, shoes, jewelry, hats, and wigs. Be sure to get the correct sizes from your cast members before acquiring or purchasing any items for them. If they're supposed to wear earrings, check whether they have pierced ears or need clip-ons (Figure 3.25).

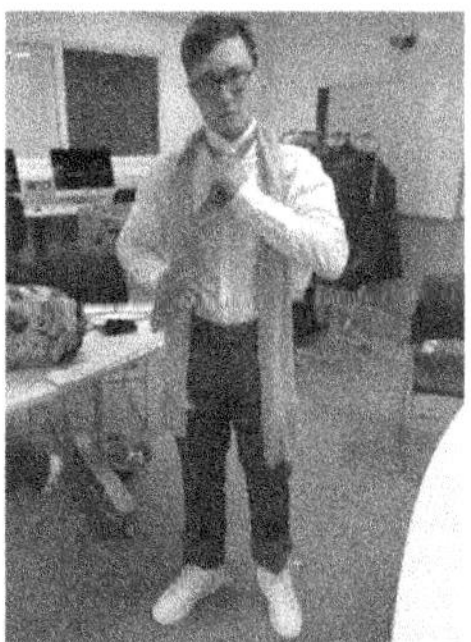

Figure 3.25 Wardrobe test—*Shelley's Heart, c.* 2016.

PRO TIPS

- **Spare wardrobe can avert disaster.** Have cast members bring an extra outfit to the first day of shooting. At the end of the day, have them change into this outfit and leave their "shooting wardrobe" with the team for safekeeping. The next day, when they return to act in more sequences or pose for additional photos, they can change back into the outfit they wore the previous day. This ensures that the footage and stills from both days will match.
- **Survey sizes.** If the cast requires special wardrobe, modify the shared contact list to include columns for their clothing, hat, and shoe sizes. Then give cast members editing permissions and a link to the shared document so they can fill in the information. This will save the wardrobe master the hassle of tracking these details piecemeal.
- **Offer options.** When gathering production elements (props, makeup, wardrobe), you may struggle to choose between multiple items. If the elements aren't too pricey or can be returned, consider acquiring more than one. This will provide a variety of options to choose from, another simple way to enhance your overall production values.

Kit

Use the best equipment you can for filming sequences. For some, this will be limited to a phone camera, but that can work just fine. The four most important pieces of equipment are:

1. **Two wireless lavalier microphones (2024).**
2. **A tripod (2024).**
3. **Two external storage drives (2024).**

These elements are relatively inexpensive and can improve your production quality exponentially. This is because the three most common production errors are:

Bad audio

Audiences can instantly tell when the audio has been recorded by an on-camera mic. The dialogue will be muffled as the sound of the actors' voices will compete with all the ambient sound cluttering up the echoey empty space between their mouths and the on-camera mic on the other side of the room, hence the need for wireless lavalier mics.

LANDMINES

- **Proximity is king.** The most common audio mistake involves a team that doesn't use external microphones—such as wireless lavaliers or a boom mic—and defaults to the on-camera microphone. A thousand-dollar microphone recording a person speaking on the opposite side of a room will sound far worse than a ten-dollar microphone clipped to the chest of the same person.
- **Delete extra audio tracks.** Even if your team properly mics the actors, your editor might still slip up in postproduction, forgetting to delete an extra audio track captured by the on-camera microphone. Often this will simultaneously play back with the clean audio, keeping it annoyingly muddy, so keep an eye out for bad audio tracks and mute or delete them.

Shaky shots

Your potential fan base will also lose faith if all the images are framed like a poorly shot home movie. This highlights the value of a good, steady tripod.

PRO TIP

- **Easy does it.** When shooting a pan or tilt shot with a tripod, move the camera slowly and smoothly. When the move is complete, gently stop the camera without jerking it, count to three, and then turn it off. This will provide you with smooth edit points.

Data loss

Be sure to purchase a couple of portable hard drives because nothing is worse than losing a day of shooting because someone forgot to back up the files and erased the camera card or deleted phone footage.

PRO TIP

- **Back up, back up, back up.** After every day of shooting, back up your media files on two hard drives and one computer connected to **the cloud**—minimum.

Special Equipment

If you're lucky enough to have access to some high-end goodies, go to town. Here are a few items that can improve your production values while giving your team some fun toys to geek out about. A slick 4K (2024) or 8K resolution (2024) camera (2024) is a great place to start. Everyone loves capturing a fluid tracking shot with a handheld gimbal (2024) or a *GoPro* (2024) mounted on handlebars, an opening door, or the 10-foot pole your ex won't touch you with. It's also fun to pilot a drone (2024) as it films an overhead shot of a beach. Other nice bits of kit include portable Zoom (2024) or Tascam (2024) recorders for capturing field audio. Portable chroma key (green screen) rigs (2024) are handy for capturing key components for visual effects shots in well-lit areas. An omnidirectional (360-degree) camera (2024) can allow you to shoot moving or still images that appear to surround the viewer. And a jib (2024) can allow the camera to swoop around in all sorts of interesting ways.

Framing

It's helpful to know how to frame shots to achieve specific effects. Along with framing, camera angles, camera movements, blocking, editing patterns, and pacing can all influence the dramatic and/or comedic impact of a filmed sequence. A sustained wide shot is a good way to maintain dramatic tension, as the unblinking camera locks onto an unfolding sequence. On the other hand, at key moments, it can be exciting to break things up with a variety of shots, including close-ups.

The lazy choice is always shooting home movie style—capturing a series of loose, handheld shots with little or no thought given to the dramatic impact of framing, camera movements, or blocking. This is the default for people who aren't used to thinking like filmmakers. Just pull the camera from your pocket, stand a few feet back from the action, point, and shoot. Yawn.

The good news is that, with a bit of planning, you can do something far more interesting.

Shot Plan

A well-thought-out shot plan inspires creators to capture a variety of images, from wide shots to macro close-ups and from tracking shots to static masters. This shouldn't become a straitjacket, forcing you to stick to a rigidly preconceived blueprint. Instead, think of your shot plan as a launchpad, allowing you to reach new creative heights.

So, what should you include? If you're baking a cake, you'll want to write down all the essential ingredients before heading to the store. The same approach applies to your shot list. Be sure to jot down everything you need to create a tasty scene. If the situation involves characters noticing a magic lamp, write down **"INSERT: LAMP."** This will remind you to capture a POV shot of this important story element that you can cut to during editing.

If it's a dialogue scene, you'll want a MASTER WIDE SHOT that captures all the dramatic action. Then, you'll want some OTS (OVER-THE-SHOULDER) shots of the speaking characters and CLOSE-UPS as well. This is where the shot plan differs from a grocery list. While you only need a single version of each ingredient for your cake recipe, when preparing to shoot a scene, you need to double and triple up on key sequences, shooting the same dialogue and action from multiple angles. This is called . . .

Coverage

Alfred Hitchcock famously shot very little coverage. But please bear this in mind: you're not Alfred Hitchcock. In other words, there's a <u>very</u> good chance you'll screw up and miss a shot, or shoot something wobbly, out of focus, with bad audio, or a weak performance. But that's the beauty of effective coverage, which involves shooting the same sequence of dramatic action from various angles. This is worth doing because a bit of well-planned redundancy can save your project when inevitable mistakes crop up. It also gives you options during the edit. For instance, you can cut to the CLOSE-UP when the protagonist whispers a dramatic line or go wide when they realize no one is listening to a word they're saying. If you want to make sure editing your assets is as exciting and creative as the rest of the production process, the key is to capture lots of coverage.

PRO TIP

- **Shoot out of sequence.** To maximize efficiency, shoot your film assets in the sequence that makes the most sense logistically. If your characters return to the same location repeatedly throughout your IDN, film all the shots related to this setting in one go. If you want to create a sense that time has passed between these scenes, have the cast change their wardrobe and possibly alter the lighting.
- **Work with a script supervisor.** They will ensure you don't forget to shoot anything, crossing out each item as it is completed and reminding you of what you need to film before moving the camera.
- **Capture B-roll.** Shoot plenty of cutaways of each location, including establishing shots, reaction shots, inserts, and general visuals.

Rookie Camera Mistakes

There are countless ways to screw up when filming, and more are being invented every day. Here are some of the greatest hits:

- **Shaky camera:** This happens when the camera operator doesn't secure the camera to the tripod effectively or doesn't bother with a tripod.
- **Blown-out lighting:** When a figure is filmed in front of a bright window, resulting in a silhouette.

- **Bad framing:** A figure placed in an odd position in the frame, such as tucked in a corner with an excessive amount of headroom above it.
- **Bad eyeline:** A figure looking in strange directions or self-consciously glancing into the camera lens.
- **Bad blocking:** A figure positioned awkwardly in relation to the camera, set, or other people—for instance, being pushed against a wall, standing too far from another character, or being uncomfortably close to the lens.
- **Out-of-focus shots:** This happens when the manual focus isn't adjusted properly, or when the autofocus locks onto a brighter element than the actor and focuses on that instead.

LANDMINE

- **Watch out for inconsistent aspect ratios.** If your team is shooting on phones and more than one person is capturing footage, a common mistake involves some footage being shot in the **landscape aspect ratio**, 16:9 (horizontal axis), and some being shot in the **portrait aspect ratio**, 9:16 (vertical axis). Another potential error involves two phones shooting in landscape but using different aspect ratios, such as 4:3 and 16:9. When such assets are combined in the same IDN or even the same edit, they look like a hodgepodge of mismatched elements. An exception might be videos meant to represent FaceTime conversations or video selfies, where shooting in portrait mode makes narrative sense. The key is carefully selecting the aspect ratio you want to use and sticking to it.

The Power of POV

Put some thought into the perspective you're shooting from. A third-person perspective includes an avatar character shot from behind to represent the player. In this approach, the player experiences an out-of-body sensation, seeing themselves interact with other characters from a perspective detached from the dramatic action.

In contrast, shooting from a first-person perspective turns the camera into the character's eyes. You might even have a character's arm enter the shot to knock on a door, shake a hand, grab a cup of coffee, or snatch up an engagement ring. This requires careful choreography but creates an immersive effect, drawing the player into the center of the dramatic action.

PRO TIP

- **GoPro a-go-go.** GoPro cameras work well for capturing a first-person POV. With a head strap or helmet mount, they can be strapped to your camera operator. This will allow your team to capture all sorts of compelling POV shots, for instance, you might shoot brief traveling shots as the Player Character arrives at the location where a node is set.

Lighting

There are two key aspects of cinematography: working with cameras and working with lights. The latter is sometimes called "painting with light," and for good reason. Effective lighting can be one of the most artistic aspects of capturing moving images.

Amateur filmmakers almost always rely exclusively on available light. This is a missed opportunity because controlling lighting is one of the simplest, cheapest, and most dramatic ways to create an emotionally compelling mood. Professional gaffers may illuminate a single location with dozens of lights, but there are many low-tech tricks that can achieve powerful dramatic effects. A strong single light source at a dramatic angle creates long, spooky shadows and sharp contrasts. A diffused overhead light produces a romantic dreamlike effect. A strong backlight can make a foreground character appear ominous or ethereal, silhouetting them against the background. You can also achieve interesting effects with gels (2024), gobos (2024), LED light panels (2024) and clever light plots (2024).

Recording Audio

When recording audio-only assets for your IDN, use a proper recording studio if possible. Studios typically feature carpeted floors, walls, and ceilings treated with sound baffles, and sealed doors and windows. All this helps reduce unwanted reverberation and blocks out exterior noise.

You don't need an expensive microphone to capture acceptable audio if you record in a well-insulated room and follow a few simple steps (Figure 3.26). Ensure the levels don't peak, keep performers at an appropriate distance from the microphone, and encourage them to wet their lips before speaking. This softens their pronunciation of the letter "p" and avoids annoying pops.

Figure 3.26 Audio recording—*Shelley's Heart, c*. 2016.

PRO TIP

- **Poor man's vocal booth**. If you're recording voice-over (VO) narration and can't afford a professional studio, here's a trick for capturing high-quality audio. Lay a chair on its back across a tabletop. Place a microphone underneath the seat, facing the same direction as the chair legs. Then, drape a thick blanket over the entire chair. Sit on a second chair and stick your head under the blanket, facing the microphone. You're now set to record quality audio. Bonus: You've also started building a pillow fort, perfect for when the adult world becomes too overwhelming.

LANDMINE

- **Outdoor scenes with indoor acoustics**. Studio acoustics often make it obvious when a voice has been recorded indoors. While adding reverb can help, the effect can feel artificial. For big moments, like a wolfman howling at the moon, recording outdoors may be your best option.

Field Audio

Another way to enhance your sound design is to capture field audio, also known as wild audio. Examples include keys unlocking a door, a window slamming shut, or a body hitting the ground.

LANDMINE

- **Listen for distractions**. When recording audio on location, with or without video, be mindful of distracting sounds. If you're inside, unplug appliances that give off an electrical hum and turn off loud fans or air conditioning. Whether inside or outside, pause the recording whenever you're interrupted by noises like honking horns, screeching tires, sirens, airplanes, barking dogs, or an angry old guy shouting profanities at the moon.

PRO TIP

- **Use a "dead cat" (2024).** This fluffy baffle fits over your boom mic and helps when recording outdoors as it prevents wind from distorting the audio.

Directing Actors

Method actors often ask, "What's my motivation?"—and it's a valid question. If the director answers clearly, the actor will know how to approach the scene. So, think about what each character is trying to accomplish in each scene and how this is generating dramatic conflict. If you can articulate these important details effectively — congratulations — you're a director!

PRO TIPS

- **The director is the first audience**. After key takes, give the actors feedback by starting with positive notes, highlighting choices that worked well, whether moving or funny. Then, if necessary, offer an "adjustment" to enhance the performance. You can also provide technical guidance — such as asking the actor to speak louder, slower, or faster — but avoid micromanaging their performance.
- **Encourage spontaneity**. Once you've captured a usable take, let the actors experiment. Allowing them to breathe life into a scene can make it feel more authentic.
- **Use visual dialogue aids.** If you're on a tight budget and shooting dialogue-heavy scenes, having the script on a **teleprompter** or **cue cards** can save time. This eliminates the need for actors to memorize every line. However, ensure the actors are familiar enough with the text so their delivery doesn't appear unnatural.

LANDMINES

- **Avoid menu-style direction**. Don't request emotions as if you're ordering from a menu, telling the actor to be "angry," "happy," or "sad." Instead, return to the character's motivation. Remind the actor what their character wants and what's standing in the way.
- **Resist line reads.** Avoid reciting dialogue the way you want the actor to perform it. This robs them of the opportunity to interpret the text in their own way.
- **Rushed productions**. Limited budgets often mean less time for rehearsing and filming. This can lead to rushed performances, which isn't ideal for the actors or the overall production.

Producing iDocs Assets

When designing an iDoc, creators should resist defaulting to a dry, just-the-facts approach and instead consider employing some of the traditional storytelling techniques discussed in Chapter 1: Plans. This type of **creative nonfiction** is ideal for an IDN design because it's highly immersive, allowing players to explore a specific narrative point of view.

Below are some techniques to make your iDoc more dynamic and creative. Unless you're creating a mockumentary, you may want to avoid familiar journalistic tropes, such as a piece to camera, a desk piece, or expository voice-over. One alternative is to conduct interviews.

Deconstructed Interview

One way to make an interview more interactive is to break it down into responses to specific questions. When all options are presented within a single node, there are both benefits and drawbacks.

Pros
- Allows the player to choose topics they find most interesting.

Cons
- Can create a brick wall of exposition that disrupts the player's immersion in the story.

LANDMINE

- **Avoid info dumps.** Don't front-load large amounts of exposition, as that will leave the player unmotivated to explore your IDN.

PRO TIP

- **Drip-feed exposition.** Present information in tantalizing, bite-sized pieces sprinkled throughout the story. Players will eagerly consume these to answer narrative questions.

POV Interview

If you plan to interview a subject matter expert, consider casting them as a character in your iDoc. Film them looking directly into the camera and providing useful bits of information. These can be scattered throughout your IDN, triggered by dramatic choices the player makes. For instance, if the player navigates through your story world in the role of a detective investigating a crime scene, they may choose to focus on various clues. This could trigger a subject matter expert—such as an actual police detective playing the role of a helpful colleague—to give advice on how to proceed.

Anonymous Interview

If an interview subject is confessing to a crime or discussing a highly sensitive topic, their identity should be anonymized (Figure 3.27). You can achieve this in several ways: blurring their image, cropping their head out of the shot, putting them behind a screen, covering their face, or filming them from behind or in silhouette.

Figure 3.27 Anonymized interview—*Target BACRIM, c.* 2016.

Cutting moving footage involves focusing on a linear sequence of action, but you may also enhance this process with techniques such as montage and parallel action. As with all forms of storytelling, the key to creating an effective edit is grabbing the viewer's attention and holding it via dramatic conflict, tight pacing, and spatial orientation.

You can find tutorials for all the major video editing platforms online. These include *Adobe Premiere Pro* (2024), *Adobe Premiere Rush* (2024), *Final Cut Pro* (2024), and *Avid* (2024), or you might use a free open-source editing program such as *DaVinci Resolve 19* (2024), or free browser-based editing platforms like *Clip Champ* (2025) or *Runway ML* (2025), which also feature many handy AI embellishments.

If you're mixing audio on a budget, you can opt for a free software platform like *Audacity* (2024). But if you have a bit more to spend, you might upgrade to *Adobe Audition* (2024). And if you have a big budget, you might spring for *Pro Tools* (2024) or *Logic Pro* (2024). With the right software, you can even create some 360-degree binaural audio mixing (Solano A. [2023]). Other handy postproduction tools can be accessed via the *Adobe Creative Cloud* (2024). These include *Photoshop* (2024), *Illustrator* (2024), and *InDesign* (2024).

Organizing Your Edit

Properly labeling your folders is the secret to a well-organized edit. Below is a suggested labeling approach for your folders and subfolders, but feel free to create your own variations. The key is for the labeling system to be logical and intuitive, and for your approach to be consistent.

Camera
- **Camera A**

  – Day 1
  – Day 2

- **Camera B**

    - Day 1
    - Day 2

Audio
- **Boom Audio**

    - Day 1
    - Day 2

- **Lav Audio**

    - Day 1
    - Day 2

Stock Images
- Footage
- Stills
- Graphics

Stock Audio
- SFX (Sound Effects)
- Music

LANDMINE

- **Avoid clustering.** This happens when multiple people gather around a computer to work on a single edit together. Worst-case scenario: the group starts voting on whether they approve of every single edit. Imagine attempting to write a poem with four people evaluating every syllable you jot down. What type of work would this produce? Clustering pours Super Glue on the wheels of progress and dumbs things down by subjecting each tiny decision to the homogenizing influence of groupthink, so please free your editor from the tyranny of the crowd and allow them to work in delicious reclusion!
- **Don't gather editing materials piecemeal.** A common editing mistake involves slamming on the brakes every few minutes to hunt down additional materials. For example, you need the sound effect of a crying baby, so you stop everything to search the internet until you find it. A minute later, you need the sound of screeching car brakes. Again, you stop everything and start searching. Once it's incorporated into your edit, you realize you need a doorbell ringing. You get the picture. This back-and-forth approach wastes a great deal of time.

PRO TIP

- **Divide and conquer.** Don't make a single editor do all the heavy lifting. Instead, delegate different editing tasks to different people. This will maximize efficiency while enhancing quality by unleashing highly focused individual expertise. An added bonus: it reduces clustering.
- **Harvest media.** By doing a bit of prep work, you can save a ton of time later. Make a list of all the additional third-party or original elements you need. Then gather them in folders titled **Sound Effects**, **Stills**, **Footage**, **GIFs**, and so on. This takes time upfront, but when you start assembling your IDN and your asset edits, you'll be able to work at lightning speed with all the needed materials at your fingertips.

(Free) Royalty-Free Media

When gathering third-party material to enhance your IDN, you want to know two things: Is it "free"? And is it "royalty-free"? "Free media" refers to any stock element you don't have to pay to download. If you have little to no budget, this is the option for you. "Royalty-free" refers to any material you can use without having to pay royalties to the creators.

If you are only sharing your IDN with friends and family, you won't need to worry about copyright violations. However, if you want the work to be public-facing, you should be clear about the usage rights. One way to do this is by performing searches on Google Images, selecting **Tools**, then **Usage Rights**, and opting for media with a **Creative Commons License**. Additionally, when visiting sites that offer stock media, such as the scores listed on *Blue Vertigo* (2024), check each item to see if there are licensing restrictions. When harvesting audio elements, check out *Freesound* (2024) for sound effects and *Free Music Archive* (2024) for music.

PRO TIP

- **Note credits.** If you are using media with an attribution license, note key details during the harvesting process (title, creator, license type). Open a Word document and make a list of these details. It's much easier to do this on an ongoing basis, so you don't have to go back later and struggle to figure out who should be credited for what.

Binaural Audio (360 Audio)

To make the *Shelley's Heart* locative version more immersive, our team utilized what was then a relatively new technology: binaural audio. This approach surrounds the listener with audio coming from multiple directions, allowing, for example, a ghost

Figure 3.28 Immersive audio play—*Mr. Illusion. c.* 2022.

to whisper in one of the listener's ears and then float around to whisper in the other.

The experience of working with *Bomo Audio* (2024) to create the 360-sound mix for *Shelley's Heart* inspired me to write the immersive audio play *Mr. Illusion* (Gyori 2023), a high-concept farce about the perils of modern masculinity (Figure 3.28). The story begins when a woman wakes one morning to realize she can read her husband's thoughts. Instead of hearing a single, predictable voice in his head, she is shocked to encounter a whole chorus of conflicting thoughts and feelings. Binaural audio was the ideal medium for achieving this effect.

Cinemagraph

If you want to create an IDN with an extended storyline but are working with limited resources, filming each scene may not be an option. One way to save money is to use more still images. However, stills can feel a bit, well . . . still. To keep things from seeming too static, you might consider creating cinemagraphs.

A cinemagraph is a photographic image where most of the scene remains stationary while the viewer's eye is drawn to a bit of seamlessly looping movement. When it comes to cinemagraphs, less is usually more. The cinemagraphs for *Shelley's Heart* feature subtle movements, such as a scarf swaying in the breeze, vape fumes drifting from a character's mouth, a candle flame flickering, and a shadow raising and lowering its arms behind a motionless figure (Figure 3.29).

LANDMINE

- **Beware of unsteady shots.** If you are shooting original footage to create a looping visual, be sure to use a tripod to avoid jump cuts caused by an unsteady camera frame.

Figure 3.29 Cinemagraph shadow moves—*Shelley's Heart*, c. 2017.

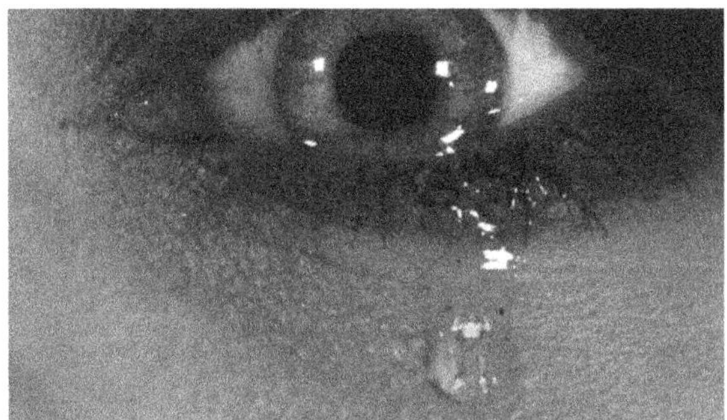

Figure 3.30 Macro shot cinemagraph with green screen—*Shelley's Heart Locative Version*, c. 2018.

Cinemagraphs can also be created as composite shots featuring visual effects. In the example below, the background is a macro close-up of a character's eye. The figure beneath the eye is an overhead shot of an actor lying on green screen fabric, moving his arms and legs. In postproduction, the green was keyed out, and foreground highlights were added to make it appear as if the actor were swimming inside a teardrop (Figure 3.30).

LANDMINES

- **Keep the green pristine.** When shooting green screen footage, make sure there are no shadows on the screen. If there are, you will see murky artifacts in your final shot. See online tutorials for guidance on how to key out the green.
- **Green screens and green clothes go together, a bit too well.** When working with a green screen, make sure the actors aren't wearing green clothing. You can also key out other colors, such as purple or blue. Avoid trying this with earth tones (brown, yellow, red, or pink), as they are too close to skin tones.

Animation

With a bit more budget and a team with the right skill set, you can generate original animated elements for your IDN. Animation is a slow, painstaking process, so make sure that every shot counts. Focus on big, dramatic moments that can't be depicted via traditional live-action filming. Additionally, recurring images, such as logos, are ideal to animate, as players will see them repeatedly, enhancing your overall production values (Figure 3.31).

Below, in a climactic moment from the Byron path, the pavement splits apart, and purple roses—Byron's color—burst upward, swaying back and forth (Figure 3.32).

Figure 3.31 Animation logo with heart beats—*Shelley's Heart*, c. 2018.

Figure 3.32 Animation with location footage, flowers break pavement—*Shelley's Heart*, c. 2018.

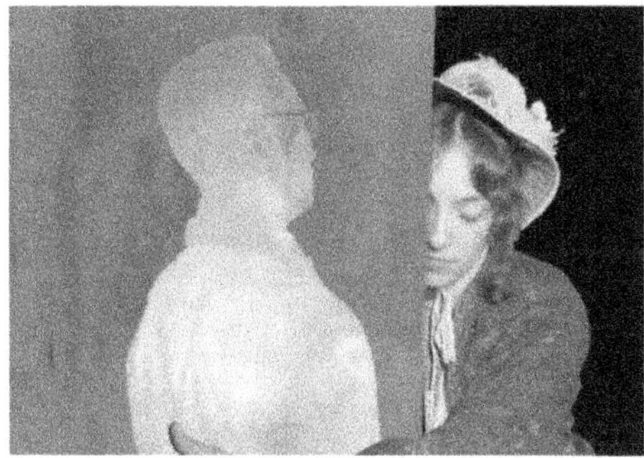

Figure 3.33 Animation with green screen composite, John frozen in ice—*Shelley's Heart,* **c. 2018.**

In a scene from the John path, John is frozen in a block of ice until Fanny Brawne's love causes it to melt and shatter into pieces (Figure 3.33).

Stop-Motion Animation

If you don't have the money or skills to create more elaborate animations, consider shooting them a frame at a time with a stationary camera. Stop-motion animations can be created with dolls, clay figures, or even bits of food dancing around on a plate to make a title sequence. Then there is the most popular stop-motion medium of all: *LEGO* (The JumiFilm 2024).

Animated GIFs

Another cost-effective approach to creating animations involves turning moving footage into animated GIFs. This can be done by uploading short video sequences into an animated GIF maker like *Ezgif* (2024). This allows you to generate short, looping sequences, which is how some of our favorite internet memes were created.

PRO TIPS

- **Make a seamless loop**. Animated GIFs are often marred by jarring jump cuts that occur when the moving image leaps back to its starting place. Here's a clever work-around to overcome this common flaw: Take a short piece of footage, such as a branch swaying from the bottom to the top of the picture frame. Duplicate it. Then attach it to the end of the original footage. Finally, reverse the duplicated section of footage. You have just created a looping video that shows the branch moving seamlessly up and down. Now, export it and turn it into an animated GIF.
- **Compress to ingest**. Your IDN may struggle to load animated GIF files that are too large. To prevent this, keep the sequences short and, if necessary, use a *GIF*

compressor (2024) to reduce their size. Some details will be lost, but this will keep your IDN interface from becoming laggy. If too much information is lost and the GIF becomes annoyingly grainy, strike a balance between image resolution and loading speed.

From the Trenches

Success Story—Target BACRIM: The Prototype

It's not possible to describe a project that never got past the pilot stage as an unqualified success. But there were moments while assembling the prototype of the *Target BACRIM* news game when everything clicked. A journalist and teaching colleague, Mat Charles, had been conducting fieldwork in Colombia for several years, focusing on a paramilitary group known as the BACRIM and people who had been impacted by their criminal enterprise. Mat had some compelling footage and a plan to structure it into an IDN. He asked if I would assist him in developing the project, and, intrigued by the concept, I agreed.

One of our early breakthroughs involved a story session where we wrote down a summary of each interview Mat had shot on a different Post-it note. There were dozens of these, which we stuck to a wall in three clusters based on different aspects of the BACRIM's illegal activities: "social cleansing," "criminal networks," and "extortion." See Figure 3.34.

We then came up with a narrative concept to tie the project together by inventing a character named Morris Kramer. According to our evolving story map, this fictional journalist had been investigating the BACRIM before mysteriously disappearing and leaving behind clues that could potentially reveal what had happened to him. The player of the IDN would step into the persona of a journalist who knew Kramer and hoped to track him down and possibly save him. This created a sense of dramatic stakes and a narrative goal compelling players to explore the material contained within the game.

Figure 3.34 Post-it plan—*Target BACRIM*, c. 2016.

We also created a mentor figure named "The Editor," who could guide the player through their adventure by providing bits of exposition at key moments.

The game would have multiple settings, including a small Colombian village and the BACRIM's jungle camp, but the main locale was Morris Kramer's last known residence—a hotel room filled with information related to his disappearance. This setting was a kind of home base the player would return to from time to time, but it wasn't static. It contained a bulletin board where bits of information could be added and removed. There was also a TV set that could play newscasts with important bits of exposition about the BACRIM and their victims.

As the story progressed, the appearance of the hotel room also changed, suggesting it had been ransacked and vandalized by the paramilitary thugs (Figures 3.35 and 3.36). In this way, the encroaching threat of the BACRIM was visually portrayed.

Another setting was the office of a local politician. This was based on an office space where an actual Colombian official had been interviewed by Mat (Figure 3.37). Much of *Target BACRIM* involved blurring the lines between reality and fantasy, hence our promo line: "When fact and fiction collide, how far will you go to uncover the truth?"

We wanted to ensure players could distinguish between Mat's factual reporting and my fictional embellishments, so we invented one of the project's key mechanics.

Figure 3.35 Hotel scene/level—*Target BACRIM, c.* 2016.

Figure 3.36 Altered hotel scene/level—*Target BACRIM, c.* 2016.

Figure 3.37 Office scene/level—*Target BACRIM, c.* 2016.

Figure 3.38 Sim-tool editing timeline in *Target BACRIM, c.* 2016.

While investigating Kramer's disappearance, the player constantly gathers clues that appear on a sim-tool mimicking the functionality of an editing timeline within the game. As the story develops, they make editorial choices, assembling a short video that includes footage of actual people who had been interviewed along with facts about the BACRIM. In other words, the primary game mechanic places the player in the role of a journalist engaged in assembling a video edit.

Our prototype succeeded in allowing players to combine actual production elements via an intuitive drag-and-drop interface. The ultimate objective became discovering what had happened to the fictional journalist, Morris Kramer, while completing a factual video exposé about the BACRIM (Figure 3.38).

Early on, we decided to create the IDN in Unity with the help of developers based in Colombia working in conjunction with tech-savvy colleagues in the UK. This allowed our team to create open-world environments, such as a small Colombian village where the player could wander in any direction (Figure 3.39).

The first mock-ups were promising, inspiring us to flesh out the narrative for the game. To achieve this, I created a PDF story map with clickable nodes that revealed details about specific scenes (Figure 3.40).

Mat also wrote a Criminal Networks Bible. It included information about the BACRIM and their nefarious activities, along with detailed profiles of the people he had interviewed. This was an invaluable resource as we continued to develop the story.

Figure 3.39 Free-roam open-world environment—*Target BACRIM, c.* 2016.

Figure 3.40 Story map extortion strand—*Target BACRIM, c.* 2016.

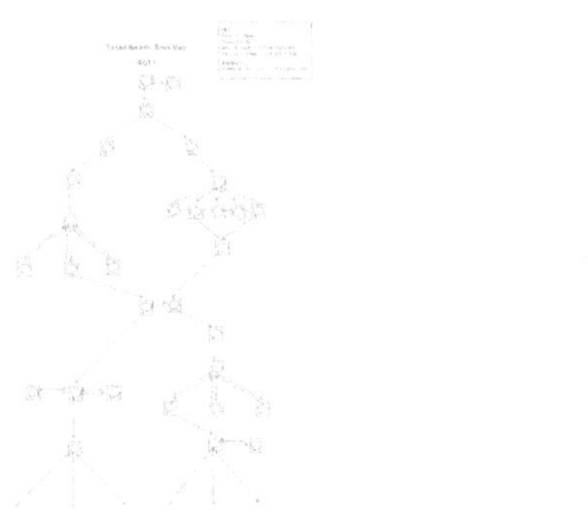

Figure 3.41 Interactive prototype in Twine—*Target BACRIM, c.* 2016.

The next step involved creating a digital prototype in Twine. This allowed us to navigate through the entire plot from start to finish, exploring every possible narrative choice and considering how different consequences influenced the player's enjoyment. This process helped us realize the amount of interview footage Mat had shot was far too much to fit into a single prototype, so we decided to focus on just one topic: extortion. Here is a section from the interactive Twine prototype (Figure 3.41).

Once the Twine prototype was complete, we focus grouped it with some teams of student-journalists, noting their feedback and drawing on it to make further refinements. This gave us enough confidence to begin producing a downloadable prototype in Unity. In a moment, we'll examine some of the setbacks that eventually scuttled *Target BACRIM*. But first, here's a recap of some key takeaways from these promising planning and prototyping stages.

Takeaways

- When creating an iDoc with fictional embellishments, make sure the player can distinguish between them and the facts.
- Create a compelling narrative goal that drives players to explore your topic.
- Promote critical thinking through a game mechanic that allows the player to assemble information in a meaningful way.
- Create a story map to plot how nodes and paths will be configured.
- Produce a digital interactive prototype to test narrative mechanics.

Cautionary Tale: Target BACRIM—The Prototype

As we continued to develop the mechanics for our nascent project, we wanted to enable more real-time gameplay—moments when avatars representing members of the BACRIM would confront the player, acting out the consequences of various narrative choices. To accomplish this, we reached out to some computer animation students and staff at Bournemouth University.

Flash forward to Mat and me dressed in blue Lycra suits dotted with electronic sensors on a production stage surrounded by thirteen motion capture cameras. Acting out the roles of two bloodthirsty BACRIM members, we performed the dramatic beats of some action sequences I had scripted. Although neither of us had previously worked as professional stuntmen or actors, I like to think we were suitably menacing. The playback allowed us to view the 3D action from any angle, which was exciting, so we wrapped the session confident we had captured some digital gold.

Unfortunately, in the weeks that followed, the student team post-producing our action sequences went rogue. Rather than following the scripted narrative, they improvised their own action sequences, which contained only minor nods to our meticulously plotted story elements. The images they created were eye-catching, and the character movements were dynamic, but there was no way to incorporate this material into our project (Figure 3.42). By the time the mo-cap materials were delivered, the students had moved on to other projects, and we'd run out of budget. As a result, we had no way to compel them to fix the material and deliver something closer to what we needed.

It wouldn't be fair to blame a single setback for preventing us from completing *Target BACRIM*. Mission creep ultimately got the best of us, along with the natural tension between topical journalism and the development of a highly ambitious interactive story. It didn't help that most of the people working on the project were

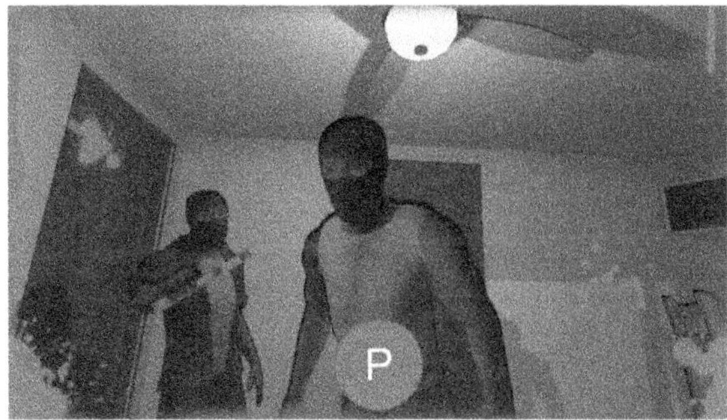

Figure 3.42 Motion capture characters—*Target BACRIM, c*. 2016.

unpaid volunteers with day jobs or academic studies distracting them—not to mention wildly varying levels of expertise and degrees of commitment. The revolving door of personnel created additional challenges, and ultimately, we simply ran out of time, money, people, and enthusiasm.

The final nail in the coffin was probably Father Time, who has a habit of marching on relentlessly. By the time we received the unusable mo-cap sequences, the interview footage Mat had shot in the jungles of Colombia was almost four years old and growing increasingly out of date. We were out of money and far from having a fully realized project. *Target BACRIM* languished for a few more months before eventually flatlining for good. A great deal of blood, sweat, and tears had gone into the project, but the main thing we had to show for our efforts was some hard-won wisdom about the types of things that can derail such an overly ambitious, time-sensitive undertaking.

Takeaways

- Beware the siren's song of mission creep. Don't bite off more than you can chew.
- Make sure volunteers are accountable for delivering promised outputs.
- Don't spend years creating a project centered on materials that will likely become outdated.
- Ensure you have enough funding to pay industry professionals to complete the project in a timely and professional manner.

Key Tasks: Assets

Task 1. Harvest Media

Gather all the third-party stock elements you plan to incorporate into your media assets and/or IDN. Seek media that is both free and royalty-free. Back these files up, saving them across multiple hard drives, computers, and the cloud.

Task 2. Shot Plan

The director and cinematographer/camera operator should review each section of the story map and create a shot plan. At a minimum, this should include coverage for a few scenes and at least one storyboard (Figure 3.43).

Figure 3.43 Shot plan example.

Task 3: Produce Assets

Shoot, record, and create videos, still images, and audio files.

Task 4: Edit Assets

Edit and compile videos, audio files, slideshows, cinemagraphs, animated GIFs, and other media for your final multimedia narrative.

Task 5: Organize Media Folders

Create a consistent folder system, backing up files on multiple hard drives, computers, and the cloud. Coordinate how files can be shared among team members.

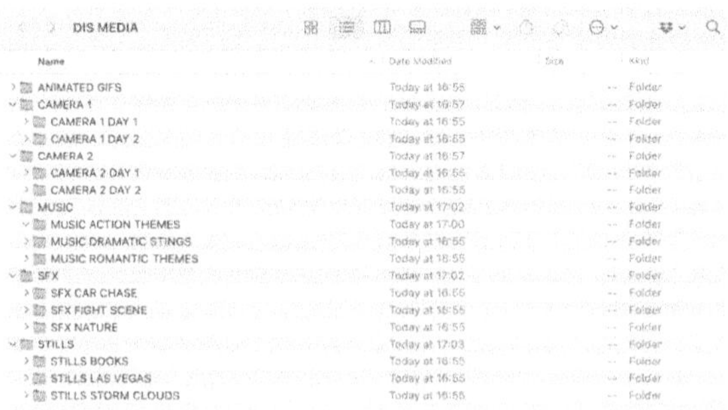

Figure 3.44 Media file folders.

4 Nodes

Unlike their digital cousins, web pages, nodes don't always display text. The only thing they absolutely must include is some sort of decision point(s) for the player to select. All nodes are static. They're landing strips where the player touches base and takes a breath before deciding how to proceed.

Though they come in all shapes and sizes, most nodes conform to standard website aspect ratios: 1:1 (perfect square), 4:3 (traditional TV screen), 16:9 (cinematic, landscape), or, for an IDN designed to be viewed on a mobile device, 9:16 or 2:3.

Intro Node

If you choose to create a media asset (video or audio file) that introduces your IDN to players, you will need to design an intro node to display the button that triggers it. Players will only see this once, as after the intro plays, the home node will become the central hub they return to from time to time. However, the intro node will be the first image they see, so if you want your IDN to make a powerful first impression, design it with care (Figure 4.1).

Figure 4.1 Intro node—*Shelley's Heart Desktop Version*, *c.* 2019.

Home Node

The home node displays important information about the IDN, including entry points and possibly instructions (Figure 4.2). The other nodes in your IDN will feature a home return icon, so players will likely circle back to the home node several times. This amount of traffic warrants well-composed imagery that rewards multiple viewings.

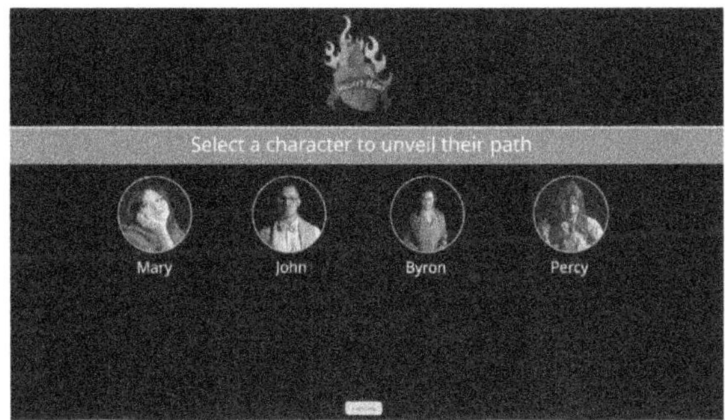

Figure 4.2 Home node—*Shelley's Heart Desktop Version*, *c.* 2019.

PRO TIP

* **High-profile nodes deserve high-end production values.** These are the nodes all players will see—perhaps repeatedly. The intro node, home node, and end node(s) will attract more attention than nodes buried deeper in the IDN that players may only see once, if at all. Since high-profile nodes receive more scrutiny, take care to make them as eye-catching as possible. Similar to a **splash page** in a comic book, they should feature an indelible image. One way to achieve this is to create a dynamic visual, such as an animated GIF, a cinemagraph, or a free loop video (2024), either from a third-party site or something you've created yourself. See Chapter 3: Assets for tips on shooting and editing steady, seamless looping footage.

Instruction Node

If the player would benefit from some guidance at the outset, consider adding an instruction node linked to the home page. Typically, this will open as a pop-up window, so when it is closed, the player will see they are still in the home node (Figure 4.3).

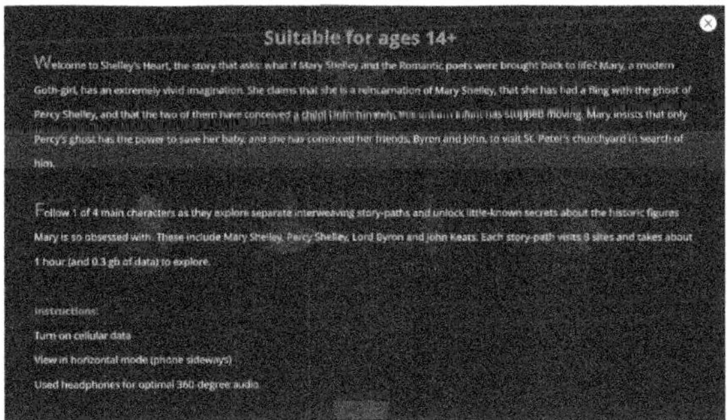

Figure 4.3 Instructions node—*Shelley's Heart Desktop Version*, *c.* 2019.

Landing Node

The term landing node is a catch-all phrase that applies to any node—except the intro node and home node—the player lands on after selecting a decision point. These nodes can be designed in various ways, depending on the aesthetic of your IDN. In addition to displaying decision points, they may include other elements such as a list of external links, an array of media assets, or a credit scroll (Figure 4.4).

Figure 4.4 Landing node—*Next Level, c*. 2023.

Grid Node

The grid node is a specific type of landing node with a patchwork structure that displays multiple images. These images may be static or dynamic. If clickable, they will link to other landing nodes or assets (Figure 4.5).

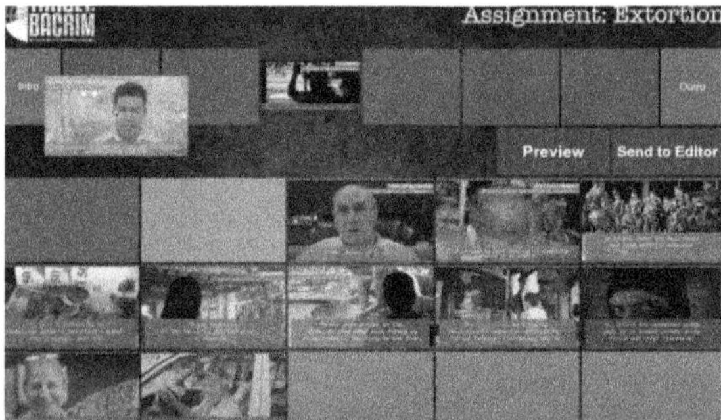

Figure 4.5 Grid view, editing timeline in *Target BACRIM, c.* 2016.

Pop-up Window

Not every decision point that the player presses must transport them to a different destination. In some instances, it might unlock a media element that appears as a window superimposed over the same node. This type of pop-up can reveal a still image, a video screen, an audio file, or a graphic containing text (Figures 4.6 and

Figure 4.6 Pop-up window, theater still—*Shelley's Heart Desktop Version*, *c*. 2019.

Figure 4.7 Pop-up window, editor video call—*Target BACRIM*, *c*. 2016.

4.7). It can also include overlays, such as a line of text appearing on top of a specific portion of a map to reveal statistical information. This design mechanic can also be used to playfully reveal hidden characters or objects, or to X-ray the belly of a character to show what they ate for breakfast.

Dialogue Tree (Conversation Tree)

This design mechanic occurs when the Player Character is interacting with an NPC. The PC is given dialogue options and selects from them, triggering different responses from the NPC. The two banter back and forth until the conversation ends. The dialogue tree can consist of multiple landing nodes or several pop-ups within a single node.

Interaction Design

The most important decisions you make when assembling your IDN involve the thrilling yet ephemeral concept of "love." You want the player to fall for your story world head over heels. So, at every turn, build a sense of mystery and reward choices with plot twists that feel both surprising and inevitable. Use all the storytelling tools at your disposal and spread them across your intertwined paths. This way—whatever direction the player wanders—they'll be rewarded with an enthralling tale. While there are no immutable laws for assembling an IDN, there are guidelines worth considering.

This section draws on principles from Donald Norman's book *The Design of Everyday Things* (2013). Norman's framework is popular with digital designers due to its focus on UX and its identification of six interaction design concepts: **affordance**, **constraint**, **visibility**, **mapping**, **feedback**, and **consistency**.

Affordance

This concept, rooted in the work of psychologist James J. Gibson (2024), refers to what the environment offers the individual. According to Norman, a design object with good affordances makes it easy for the user to discern how to engage with it. For example, a teapot has a handle that clearly affords lifting and a spout that affords pouring. In the digital realm, this is known as an "intuitive interface."

When editing your IDN, keep affordance at the forefront of your mind. When players are afforded narrative choices, they should have some sense of what's on offer. It's a balancing act. You want to entertain them with surprising outcomes, but choices that are too ambiguous with outcomes that feel arbitrary can negate emotional investment. In contrast, if choices lead to meaningful consequences, the player will feel emotionally engaged with your IDN.

Here are some affordances to consider during the assembly process:

- **Decision point**: Triggers an asset, pop-up, or a move to another node.
- **Modification point**: Alters some aspect of a node or asset.
- **Widget**: Allows players to engage with an interactive element, such as a game, quiz, survey, or poll.

PRO TIP

- **Break the binary.** Challenge yourself to offer more than two opposing choices. Instead of just "fight" or "flight," consider adding options like "problem-solve," giving players a wider array of affordances and thus a greater sense of agency.

LANDMINE

- **Avoid flawed consequences.** Choices that yield confusing results can frustrate players and undermine their sense of engagement.

Constraint

If an affordance is an open door, a constraint is a brick wall. It's a restriction the IDN design imposes on the user. As in life, there are often more obstacles than options for overcoming them. For example, you can choose whether to call in sick or go to work in the morning, but if you decide to show up, your paths to get there will be narrowly constrained. Also, you'll be expected to arrive at a certain time, engage in predetermined tasks, and wear pants.

In designing a virtual environment, the tension between affordances and constraints defines how open the system is. In a life simulation game like *The Sims* (2024), players can move around and alter their appearance at will, creating numerous affordances. Your IDN, however, will likely be far more constrained. This makes it especially important to keep your assets short and entertaining. Despite the medium's natural constraints, aim to offer as many affordances as possible.

Fortunately, constraints aren't inherently negative. They're the source of all dramatic tension, conflict, mystery, and suspense. The key is to use them strategically to tantalize, rather than frustrate. Some common IDN constraints include:

- **Barrier**: An obstacle blocking the player's progress.
- **Path**: A route defining the player's progress.
- **Frame**: Design limitations imposed by the aspect ratio of a node, asset, or pop-up.

PRO TIP

- **Create a morality system.** Design choices that compel players to make ethics-based decisions. This approach presents players with moral dilemmas and rewards or penalizes them based on their choices. Moral prohibitions act as constraints that define the values of the Player Character.

LANDMINES

- **Avoid puppeteering**: Don't make a character act without input from the player.
- **Avoid ventriloquism**: Don't make a character speak without input from the player.
- **Avoid unmotivated exploration**: Ensure players have compelling reasons to move through the story and make choices.

Visibility

Sometimes it pays to be conspicuous. That's what visibility is all about. It involves making the design of the IDN as clear and straightforward as possible. Unless your IDN is intentionally designed to be disorienting, ambiguous, or challenging to navigate, you should lay out elements in a way that draws attention to the most important features.

Ways to make key design features more visible include:

- **Intro sequence**: A short video that provides crucial exposition.
- **List**: Displays important information in sequence.
- **Hieratic scale**: Makes important elements larger than others.
- **Intensity**: Uses vivid colors or loud sounds to emphasize important elements.
- **Animation**: Highlights important elements by making them vibrate or flash.

Mapping

While visibility provides players with the lay of the land, mapping shows them how to explore it. Effective mapping relies on clear symbols and colors. For example, the plus and minus signs on the side of your phone symbolize the actions of increasing and decreasing the volume.

Examples of mapping modes include:

- **Icon**: Represents opportunities for engagement (e.g., the "home" symbol for returning to the main menu).
- **Menu**: Provides a range of options (e.g., play, fast-forward, reverse, stop).
- **Arrow**: Directs the player, indicating how to proceed.

LANDMINE

- **Beware of confusing signposting.** Colors and symbols have different meanings in different contexts and cultures. This creates an inherent tension between visibility and mapping. For instance, if you color-code three decision points as yellow, red, and green, players may interpret red as a constraint (stop) rather than an affordance (explore a new path).

Feedback

Designing for feedback ensures that the interface communicates the player's progress through the IDN. Without clear, consistent feedback, players can't tell if their actions are making a difference—it's like watering a seed that refuses to grow. Feedback can also indicate the degrees of impact created by specific actions, such as making sounds louder, images brighter, or mustaches creepier.

Methods for providing feedback include:

- **Progress bar**: Shows how much of the IDN the player has explored.
- **Status meter**: Tracks levels of various resources gained or lost, such as food, money, or love.

- **Message window**: Displays a text response from an NPC or the Narrator based on the player's choice. This can also prompt an additional action, such as responding to a multiple-choice question.
- **Scoreboard/Scorecard**: Tallies points for tasks completed or achievements earned.
- **Timer**: Displays time elapsed or remaining.

PRO TIPS

- **Make it bright, shiny, and fun.** Like Pavlov's dogs, humans love sensory stimuli, so provide plenty of multimodal feedback. For instance, when the player presses a button, it could change colors and emit a sound effect.
- **Include delayed impacts.** Choices don't always need to have immediate consequences. For example, instead of having the player's avatar punch another character in the face, they might spread a rumor, eavesdrop on a conversation, or send a scandalous text. These actions can create ripple effects with interesting belated consequences.

Consistency

This rule of thumb reminds us to make sure that form follows function. Consistency dictates that recurring elements in your IDN should conform to certain predictable patterns. For example, green buttons should always make things grow, while storm clouds should always symbolize trouble ahead.

Key elements to maintain consistency include:

- **Color palette**: Pick a few key colors. Also, match the hue to the tone of your story—for a bold action adventure, bright neon colors. For an ethereal romance, pastels. You might also color-code characters.
- **Motif**: Recurring visuals or sounds, such as images of the ocean or birds chirping.
- **Font**: The typeface you plan to use. If you vary fonts, do so consistently (e.g., the punk rock character's titles always appear in the punk rock font).
- **Sound design**: A recurring theme for your IDN or mini themes for specific characters, settings, or situations.
- **Graphic**: Charts, diagrams, infographics, or icons that convey information while adhering to a uniform aesthetic.
- **Logo**: An emblem representing your IDN or specific character(s).
- **Effects (FX)**: Modes of visual or audio manipulation used to create recurring looks and sounds.

Node Assembly

This section focuses on what happens when all the nodes come together to form your IDN. In the film world, this stage is called "postproduction," but in IDN creation, the process begins much earlier. Typically, creators start assembling their interactive narrative during the development stage, building off a crude prototype created within an IDN platform.

This phase involves ensuring all elements work together harmoniously. It's your opportunity to iron out the kinks, resolve story problems, and add new creative flourishes.

Rough Assembly

As media assets are created and edited, someone should continue assembling the IDN using your chosen interactive software platform. Each platform has unique functions and operating instructions, so it's important to familiarize yourself with them through online tutorials or guides.

The person responsible for this—the IDN editor—should have the most comprehensive overview of your story. They should constantly reference and modify the original story map, creating all necessary points and nodes to ensure an engaging and intuitive player experience.

This process requires organizing material in a way that allows players to navigate the IDN in various ways. As a result, the IDN editor must carefully think through multiple potential story paths.

Final Assembly

By keeping Donald Norman's six interactive design principles in mind, you can elevate the assembly process to the next level. Below are some additional tricks of the trade:

Exposition Title

During the silent film era, directors often shot scenes without knowing the exact words characters were meant to say (Figure 4.8). Actors were instructed to pantomime or improvise. While this approach usually conveyed the story effectively, filmmakers sometimes realized during the editing process that the audience needed more guidance. This is where exposition titles came in.

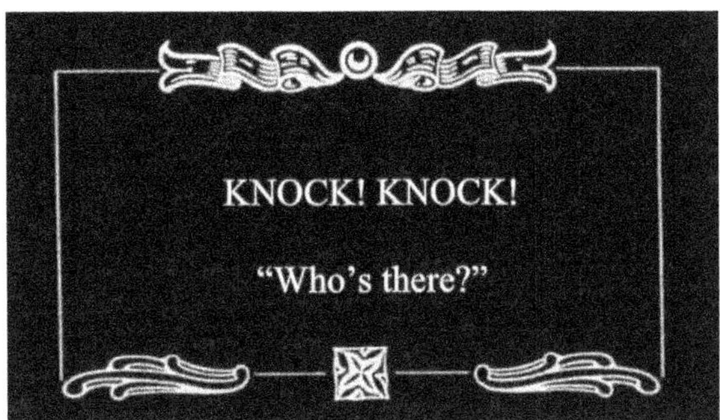

Figure 4.8 Title card.

Sometimes, the added title cards contained narration. Sometimes, they featured dialogue. But they always provided additional context, orienting viewers and advancing the plot. In the age of interactive storytelling, this old-fashioned technique has reemerged as a useful storytelling tool.

If your IDN is exclusively text-based, it is, in a sense, entirely composed of title cards. In other words, the story is driven solely by the written word. However, if your IDN is also supported by video or audio assets, you may occasionally find that a good old-fashioned title card is an excellent way to help players understand what's happening and how they should proceed. This bit of narrative connective tissue can fill in a missing plot beat, set up a scene, explain what's at stake, or provide some helpful backstory.

Like silent film title cards, IDN titles can be enhanced with photographic images, drawings, fancy fonts, music, and sound effects, but they can also include decision points, providing players with opportunities to make interactive choices.

LANDMINE

- **Beware of rushed titles.** A common mistake is including text that flashes on-screen for a few seconds and disappears before the player can read all the words. To avoid this, read the title out loud during the assembly process. Only after you've spoken each syllable aloud should you select the edit point. This ensures the player has enough time to read everything before the title card vanishes.

Location Title

Each new scene in the *Shelley's Heart* locative version begins with a high-contrast, black-and-white point-of-view Steadicam shot which drifts in close then freezes on a particular landmark. After that, the background dissolves, replaced by an animated GIF. As a musical theme plays, a title appears announcing the name of the location. This sequence serves to orient the player, confirming they are in the correct spot. It also acts as an audio-visual fanfare, signaling the start of a new scene (Figure 4.9).

Figure 4.9 Location title—*Shelley's Heart Locative Version, c.* 2017.

Tag

A tag is a special type of decision point that unlocks embellishments not directly influencing the plot. For example, a pop-up window might appear with expositional text.

In the locative and desktop versions of *Shelley's Heart,* tags unlock a variety of content. The letter "i" indicates information waiting to be shared. A quotation mark inside a speech bubble is linked to specific quotes from Romantic poets. A star icon signals extra footage, and a thought bubble with an exclamation mark flags an opportunity to eavesdrop on a particular character's thoughts (Figures 4.10, 4.11, 4.12, 4.13 and 4.14).

Figure 4.10 Various tags—*Shelley's Heart Locative Version, c.* 2018.

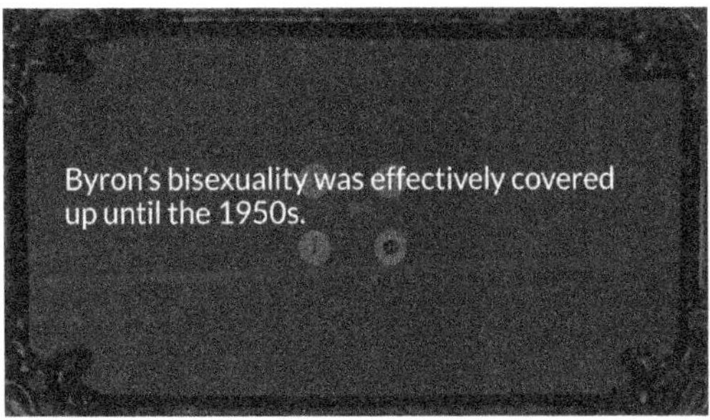

Figure 4.11 Tagged information—*Shelley's Heart Locative Version*, *c*. 2018.

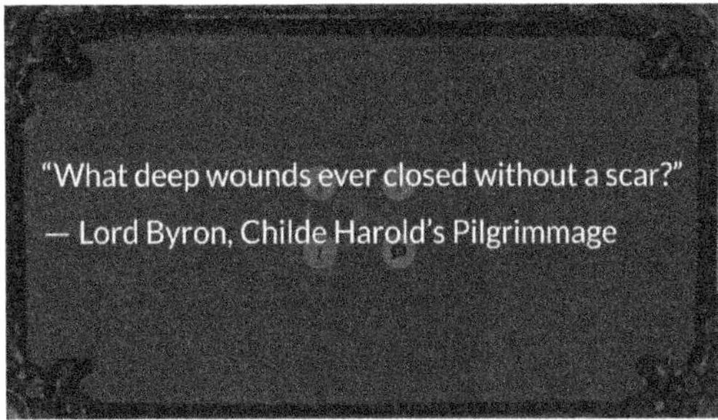

Figure 4.12 Tagged quote—*Shelley's Heart Locative Version*, *c*. 2018.

Figure 4.13 Tag to thoughts—*Shelley's Heart Locative Version*, *c*. 2018.

Figure 4.14 Byron's thoughts—*Shelley's Heart Locative Version*, *c*. 2018.

Copresence

In Real Life (IRL), copresence involves two or more things occurring simultaneously in the same place. But in Interactive Fiction, copresence can occur either simultaneously or **asynchronously** (at different times). Asynchronous copresence is sometimes referred to as "**Ambient Copresence**" (Appleton 2024). This approach involves players leaving their mark on an IDN so that it's experienced differently with each playthrough. In other words, the choices a player makes have a sustained impact on the story world, altering it so that the next player who explores it experiences something new.

One of the most famous examples of copresence is the massively multiplayer online role-playing game (MMORPG) *World of Warcraft* (2024), in which the interactions of players—both in real time and asynchronously—alter the experience of navigating through the narrative environment.

A more limited example of copresence was incorporated into the design of the *Shelley's Heart* locative version. Each path features one player choice that triggers a copresence effect on another path, altering the options available on the next playthrough. Our programmer was eager to implement this design strategy, and it works perfectly fine. The problem is, the player making the change and the player later experiencing the results are oblivious to what has happened. As a result, the sense of copresence is lost.

LANDMINE

- **Watch out for communal blind spots.** For copresence to have a meaningful impact on UX, players need to sense how their interactions are influencing others and how the choices others are making are influencing them.

Figure 4.15 Copresence cause, Byron Path—*Shelley's Heart Locative Version*, c. 2018.

Figure 4.16 Copresence effect, John Path—*Shelley's Heart Locative Version*, c. 2018.

Without this awareness, their engagement with the story world won't feel like a shared experience (Figures 4.15 and 4.16).

Assembly Mechanics

IDN platforms offer different types of assembly mechanics, offering various creative opportunities. Some common features include:

- **Drag and Drop**—Some platforms allow designers to drag media directly onto story nodes, while others require media to be imported.
- **Asset Editing**—Most IDN platforms allow designers to make minor adjustments to media assets after they're ingested, such as shortening a clip or cropping an image. More sophisticated tasks, such as adding visual effects or audio mixing, must be completed on other platforms before the asset is incorporated into the IDN.
- **Embedding**—Some platforms generate embed codes, while others don't. This is an important feature for designers who want their work displayed on a website.
- **State Tracking (Delayed Branching)**—This is a sophisticated mechanism that most open-source platforms don't offer. Key choices are remembered and reflected later without requiring entirely new narrative paths. Some of the variables that can be tracked include score, character reputation, skill level, items acquired or lost, time elapsed, and objectives achieved.

PRO TIP

- **Poor man's state tracking.** If the price point or learning curve of a platform with state-tracking capabilities is too steep, rudimentary forms of state tracking can still be implemented by relying on the player's memory or various analog aids. For example, if the player is navigating your story in the role of a pirate. Early on, they could be allowed to select one of two tools: a sword or a compass. If your platform isn't equipped to remember this choice, the player still can. Later, they might encounter decisions contingent on their earlier choice. If they picked the compass, they can navigate to an island or an iceberg in search of buried treasure. If they picked the sword, they could battle a sea monster or hack off a rival's wooden leg. If the options are stated clearly and the player remembers their earlier decision, this form of player-driven state tracking is achievable. To help players track multiple decisions, you could create a **stats scorecard**. Also—drawing on some old-school board game mechanics—you could incorporate instruction cards or game pieces into your IDN.

User Testing

The digital design mantra "fail early, fail often" simply means you shouldn't wait until the last minute to test your work. User testing involves having different users navigate your IDN and provide feedback.

Your first user test should occur during the paper prototyping stage. Later, when you assemble a barebones IDN, you'll conduct additional user testing. However, IDN creators often get so busy they forget to test the functionality of their work-in-progress—a big mistake. By occasionally pausing to make sure the design mechanics are working, you can avoid the hassle and frustration of producing flawed or useless nodes and assets by identifying elements that need to be altered or cut altogether.

Also, don't be precious about your work. Each time you pilot a new iteration, ask yourself: *How can it be better?* Don't be afraid to radically rethink your story. You're creating a project that involves producing narrative choices, so, as a creator, keep all options on the table. No idea should be so sacred that you won't consider cutting it, and no embellishment should sound so strange that you won't consider including it.

Another common mistake is only having people familiar with your project user test it. This creates blind spots because the testers already understand how the IDN is meant to function. A more helpful test subject may be someone completely unfamiliar with your work. Their response will be far more objective, and they are more likely to identify flaws that you and your team have overlooked.

Here are some different types of testers to consider recruiting:

1. **Core group**—Drawn from your team, focusing on story structure, interactivity, voice, dialogue, and visual storytelling.
2. **Fresh eyes**—People unfamiliar with your project, likely to discover bugs in the interactive mechanics and plot holes.
3. **Specialists**—Non-creative quality assurance (QA) experts who can analyze and measure key performance metrics, such as replayability, rewards, and recognition.

Figure 4.17 Survey—*Shelley's Heart Site-Specific Read Through*, c. 2016.

Always debrief testers and ask them key questions, such as:

- When were you most/least engaged?
- When did you connect emotionally—or fail to?
- Where would you like the story to move faster or slower?
- Where would you like fewer or more narrative options?
- What do you think of the dialogue?
- What shouldn't be changed?
- What could be improved? (Figure 4.17)

LANDMINES

- **Mission Creep (Death of a Thousand Cuts).** By its very nature, your IDN project involves generating a large number of narrative possibilities, which means producing a significant amount of content. Because of this, it can easily spiral out of control. The best way to combat this tendency is to nip it in the bud. During the story-mapping and prototyping phases, identify the elements you can live without and cut everything else.
- **Mission Drift.** Sometimes veering off course can be a process of discovery that helps you explore new creative frontiers. Other times, it's a pointless detour. In either case, it will cost time and resources and may result in some team members abandoning the project as it heads into increasingly unfamiliar territory. There are no hard and fast rules to distinguish between productive and unproductive detours. However, it may help to ask early on: *Is this new approach enhancing the central aim of the project, or could it be a fruitless distraction?* Identifying time-wasting rabbit holes early and often is a good way to avoid getting caught in the undertow of mission drift.

Cautionary Tales: Shelley's Heart Locative Version

After the debut of the *Shelley's Heart* stage version, one of our actors accepted a role in a film shooting in the United States. I had been planning to book the play into theaters along the south coast of England. However—because much of our multimedia theatrical production relied on filmed images of specific performers—I couldn't simply recast the role. For the show to go on, I would have had to reshoot most of the media elements as well.

I found the situation extremely frustrating, but in retrospect, it was probably for the best. What I didn't realize at the time was that attempting to produce and direct a theatrical run while simultaneously designing the new locative version of the project would have proven far too difficult. This became clear when I met with the creative technology staff member and student who had agreed to help with this next phase of the project, and they recommended rethinking the narrative completely.

For the stage version, it made sense for the whole audience to proceed along the same narrative path, but in a physical environment, there was no need for individual players to cluster together as if they were joined at the hip. I had four main characters, so why not give each of them a separate story path? (Figure 4.18)

The concept both intrigued and frightened me. Committing to it would mean significantly more development and production. The theatrical script could serve as the basis of the Mary path, but I would need to create three additional scripts for three additional paths. I would also have to produce and direct a substantial amount of new media content to flesh out these narrative strands. Annoyingly, the idea made too much sense to ignore, so I rolled up my sleeves and got to work, issuing a silent prayer of thanks that a theatrical run of the stage version was no longer a possibility. Now, I could focus exclusively on my original plan: creating a locative version of *Shelley's Heart* set in St. Peter's Churchyard.

Ultimately, this example of mission drift proved fruitful, but there were many moments along the way when I wondered if I should have shuttered the project after

Figure 4.18 Locative story map—*Shelley's Heart Locative Version*, c. 2018.

the two theatrical performances. To begin with, radically rethinking *Shelley's Heart* meant shaking the funding trees again and hoping a few more acorns would fall out. The new budget was minuscule. Still, it was enough to pay the actors and crew, and—through the university—I had access to some high-end camera equipment, so I decided to forge ahead. Even so, as I ventured back into the graveyard with the remaining cast and started shooting new material, I could sense additional challenges lurking in the shadows.

Here is a brief overview of some of the issues that plagued this phase of the production process. These roadblocks cropped up for different reasons: technological bugs, production blind spots, poor communication, lack of funds, ethical lapses, human error, and plain old dumb luck.

For example, during the audio mixing phase, our sound engineer became extremely ill and lost the hearing in one of his ears! Fortunately, he managed to work around this by angling his good ear toward different playback speakers at key moments to ensure the 360-degree sound worked effectively.

Another production challenge involved an MA student who became an "MIA student." This creative technology postgrad had linked the nodes to specific landmarks in the churchyard. However, before attaching the new media assets to these nodes—as he had agreed to do—he vanished like one of the ghosts in my story, never to be seen again. After my experience with *Target BACRIM,* I should have known better than to put so much faith in an unpaid student volunteer, but some lessons must be learned more than once.

Not knowing what else to do, I reached out to the staff member who had introduced me to the AWOL student. After some pleading, I convinced him to step in and tie up the loose ends the student had left dangling. Still, the hits kept coming. In the earliest planning stages, I'd been told the locative interface *Story Places* could play any media that would work on a website (Figure 4.19).

Typically, the platform only featured still images and text, but it could also play audio and video files—at least, in theory. Fast-forward two years. After I'd shot and edited all the media assets, I learned that the functionality for audio and video files had never been tested on *Story Places,* and there was a good chance that attempting to

Figure 4.19 Locative web platform—*Story Places, c.* 2018.

incorporate these elements wouldn't work. Suddenly, I could empathize with Percy Shelley—I felt my heart being ripped from my body. I had spent two years writing, shooting, and editing media assets, only to learn at the eleventh hour that they might not be compatible with the locative interface created to host them.

The next round of pleading included plenty of handwringing and some sleepless nights. Fortunately, after a few adjustments, the locative platform turned out to be perfectly compatible with our media assets, so the whole thing had been a false alarm. Insert sad trombone sound effect: *wah-wah.*

After that, everything went off without a hitch.

Kidding.

Another tech quirk involved the functionality of the locative version. This required a trade-off. The story nodes were created within the interactive platform *Klynt,* and when we uploaded even short videos, they took up too much space on *Story Places,* resulting in excruciatingly long buffering times. To get around this, we decided to host all the videos on YouTube and link them to *Klynt.* Because YouTube wouldn't allow the videos to autoplay over a mobile network, players were required to hit a play button each time a scene was unlocked. This development made the interface a bit inelegant, but it was the only way we could get the videos to play properly.

Having put out that fire, I assumed we were in the home stretch, but there was one more tech hurdle on the horizon. Unbeknownst to me, a lack of funding had begun to undermine the functionality of *Story Places.* As a result, some of the landmarks displayed by its GPS interface started appearing in the wrong places—for example, a location in the churchyard popping up inside the church.

By this point, my small team had been working feverishly to complete the *Shelley's Heart* locative version so it could be unveiled on Halloween night 2018 as part of a celebration commemorating the 200th anniversary of the publication of *Frankenstein.* This very public event was tied to a literary festival, and about 100 people were in attendance. Unfortunately, we didn't discover the functionality issues until shortly before the big debut.

I had no choice but to tell the attendees that some of the nodes weren't working properly, pointing them to a workaround where they could switch to "demo mode" and unlock scenes from any location in the churchyard. To say the launch was an unqualified success would be a stretch, but many people did explore the various paths for over an hour, unlocking scenes and getting better acquainted with Mary Shelley and the Romantic poets.

As of this writing, the *Shelley's Heart* locative version is still up and running in St. Peter's Churchyard. Most of the bugs have been worked out. It's still a bit laggy and fiddly in places, but overall, it functions effectively. That said, at least two of the physical landmarks it's geo-linked to look quite different. A large stump featured in the app has rotted away, and a map of the churchyard where another scene takes place has been vandalized beyond recognition. Such are the challenges of linking story nodes to landmarks that are likely to change over time.

As this is a cautionary reflection, I should probably list a few more drawbacks of the *Shelley's Heart* locative version. In retrospect, I feel there aren't enough narrative choices that influence the story at the level of plot and characterization. When developing the three additional story paths, I focused primarily on making each one a coherent narrative with lots of interactive embellishments. However, I should have created more intriguing narrative detours. There are alternate endings and some interesting digressions, but for the most part, the story paths are fairly "on the rails" narratives. Some of this comes down to my lack of experience in designing interactive locative stories, and some of it simply involves biting off more than I could chew.

What else? Well, at times, the ambiguity created by the ghostly doppelgängers and the actors playing multiple roles makes the plot a bit confusing. I should have had a lighter touch with that. Also, there are some overwritten sections and jokes that fall flat, and the scene where Percy goes hip-hop is pretty groan-worthy. All that's on me.

If I were to create *Shelley's Heart* all over again, I would probably take a completely different approach. Most likely, I would skip creating the stage version and opt to produce an audio-only locative version. That way, players could focus on the churchyard as they walked around and not have to look at their phones so much. I would also make the paths shorter, include fewer bells and whistles, and place greater emphasis on accessibility features. But enough about everything that went wrong. The next section will focus on the many things that went right! First, however . . .

Takeaways

- Roll with the punches and create workarounds.
- When necessary, shift focus from things you can't control to things you can.
- Don't count on unpaid students to complete crucial tasks—AGAIN!
- Test the functionality of any tech in advance to confirm it works as described.
- Don't depend on tech that may fall into disrepair if funding dries up.
- Make sure you have clear communication with all collaborators about important deliverables.

Success Stories: Shelley's Heart Locative Version

As I transitioned from the theatrical production to the locative version of *Shelley's Heart,* I was concerned about mission creep. Was I committing to a project beyond my resources and capabilities? As I've explained, there were many challenges to come, but there were also important breakthroughs that are worth sharing.

Changing from a single-branching narrative to a threaded narrative was both conceptually and logistically challenging. As the story maps evolved, it became clear that there were opportunities for the characters to move apart and come back together when their paths intersected at key points.

I learned other things as well. For instance, I discovered that locative scenes needed to be much shorter than theatrical scenes. An audience member sitting in a comfy chair is far more patient than a churchyard visitor standing on a patch of wet grass, possibly at night, possibly in the rain. The solution: cut, cut, cut. Scenes that were originally three minutes long were reduced to less than a minute and/or broken into multiple scenes.

Selecting scene sites for the story paths involved picking recognizable landmarks that were reasonably far apart. Keeping things accessible for the elderly and disabled meant avoiding any terrain that was too steep or uneven. Each of the four paths involved a bit of backtracking, but I tried to avoid too much meandering so players wouldn't find the experience becoming annoyingly redundant.

Producing assets for the three additional story paths meant creating new scenes and even new characters, which required casting additional actors and acquiring more wardrobe. The John path was enhanced with the addition of John Keats' fiancée, Fanny Brawne. William Godwin became a fierce antagonist within the Percy path, and Claire Clairmont (Mary's stepsister) was included in the Byron path. Also, all four characters would face a climactic clash with Mary's monster.

Part of the original story design was to make the characters as iconic as possible by assigning each a specific look and color. Mary was red. Byron was purple. John was yellow. Percy was blue. Each of the three modern-day characters encountered a ghostly doppelgänger played by the same actor and dressed in nineteenth-century garb that matched the color of their character's contemporary attire. This color coding extended to the story paths, where the production design for each path matched the color of the featured character.

Producing elements for the added paths created new cinematic opportunities, including shooting in the ocean with scuba gear and an underwater camera (Figure 4.20).

And filming high in the air with a drone (Figure 4.21).

We also captured more green screen footage (Figures 4.22 and 4.23).

Since each character had become the protagonist of their own path, I had to scrap my original plan to make the interface about shifting between character

Figure 4.20 Underwater shot—*Shelley's Heart Locative Version*, c. 2018.

Figure 4.21 Drone shot—*Shelley's Heart Locative Version*, c. 2018.

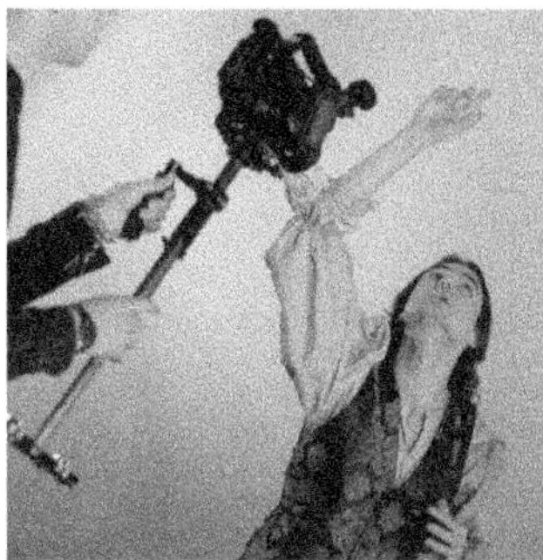

Figure 4.22 Green screen shot—*Shelley's Heart Locative Version*, c. 2018.

Figure 4.23 Green screen composite with VFX—*Shelley's Heart Locative Version*, c. 2018.

perspectives. Fly-on-the-wall scenes with clear dramatic action were foregrounded, while reflective scenes with characters sharing their thoughts became optional bonus material.

Committing to the multiple-path approach also involved rewriting the original decision points and creating new ones. Feedback from the theatrical production indicated that players wanted to make more meaningful choices, so I included more action-based options with clear dramatic consequences.

Figure 4.24 Theater footage with superimposed tag—*Shelley's Heart Locative Version*, *c.* 2018.

Figure 4.25 Locative welcome—*Shelley's Heart Locative Version*, *c.* 2018.

While researching Mary Shelley and the Romantic poets, I discovered all sorts of fascinating information. Sensing an opportunity to make *Shelley's Heart* an immersive educational tool, I incorporated these facts into the Locative Version in the form of short multiple-choice quizzes. These quizzes served as a lock-and-key mechanic, requiring players to pick the correct answer before they could access the next scene.

When assembling the IDN, I recalled that we had also filmed the first night of the theatrical production. The project's maximalist aesthetic made it possible to incorporate some of this footage as well. For some scenes, graphic elements and visual effects were superimposed over video of the theatrical performance, adding new textures to the multilayered multimedia tapestry (Figure 4.24).

Now that you know the thought process that went into designing *Shelley's Heart* Locative Version, let's take a closer look at its functionality. Here is a brief overview of how it works. The first thing the player encounters is a welcome page, where the basic premise of the project and the main characters are introduced (Figure 4.25).

Next comes an instruction node. When the player creates a new reading, an instruction page appears, explaining how the locative mechanic works (Figure 4.26).

After that, the player moves to the first landing node. The player sees an overhead map of the churchyard with four signposted areas. These represent entry points

Figure 4.26 Instruction node—*Shelley's Heart Locative Version*, c. 2018.

Figure 4.27 Locative entry points—*Shelley's Heart Locative Version*, c. 2018.

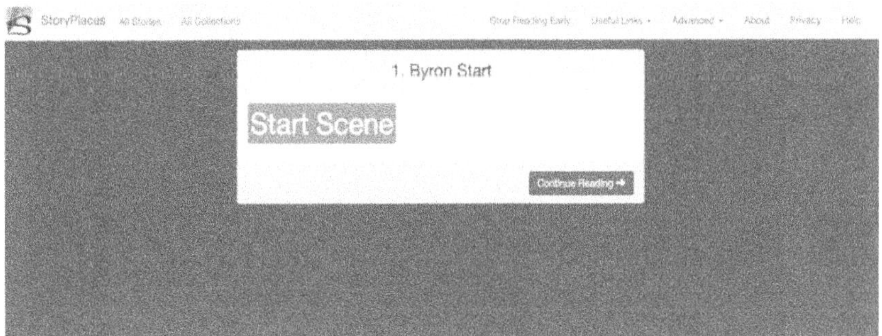

Figure 4.28 Locative scene start—*Shelley's Heart Locative Version*, c. 2018.

leading to the four story paths. As the player moves around the churchyard, a blue dot tracks their movements. When they get close enough to one of the signposts, it changes from red to green, indicating they are ready to enter one of the paths (Figure 4.27).

When the player clicks on the rectangle with the character's name, they access the first scene. Once they've done this, every subsequent option relates to the story path of the character they've selected (Figure 4.28).

After experiencing the scene, they return to its start page. If they click "Start Scene," the node repeats, but if they click "Continue Reading," they move on to the next locative map, which, in turn, unlocks the next node. Sometimes the map includes a single story-site for the player to locate, and sometimes it includes two or more sites that trigger different action points. In the example below, the player exploring the John path can interact with one of three characters. They choose who by moving toward the red signpost associated with their pick (Figure 4.29).

Eventually, the player visits ten sites in the churchyard, unlocks ten scenes, and explores dozens of added bonus elements. Finally, they arrive at the end of the path (Figure 4.30).

After the white-knuckle thrill ride of creating the *Shelley's Heart* Locative Version, you might assume I was ready to call it a day, but one more challenge still beckoned. Feedback from surveys linked to the Locative Version indicated players were interested in exploring the project from home as well. Thus, the *Shelley's Heart* Desktop Version was born.

This was originally conceptualized as a complete "respook," with all four paths being transformed to play in a fluid desktop interface. I was able to complete the Mary path, but the task proved so all-consuming that I ultimately decided to tap out and walk away without attempting to complete the other three.

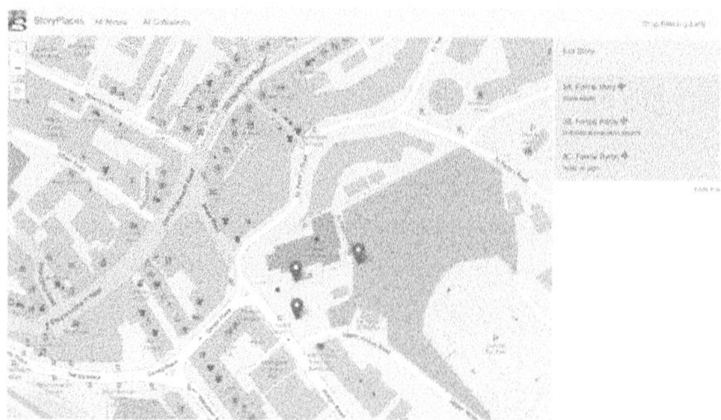

Figure 4.29 Locative decision points—*Shelley's Heart Locative Version*, c. 2018.

Figure 4.30 End of path—*Shelley's Heart Locative Version*, c. 1918.

Happily, the project ended on a high note. I prefer many of the features of the Desktop Version to the Locative Version (Figures 4.31 and 4.32). The YouTube videos were replaced with animated GIFs. This involved another trade-off: The quality and length of the moving images were reduced, but things loaded instantly, and those pesky play buttons vanished. Additionally, some whimsical new pseudo-tools and pseudo-platforms were added to enhance functionality. Some additional quizzes and puzzles were included, too.

Looking back at the creation of *Shelley's Heart* in all its iterations, I can't help but relate to Victor Frankenstein. I experienced the thrill of bringing a strange new creature to life, but at times, I also felt the horror of it rebelling against me. In the end, I've made my peace with the project's shortcomings, and I like to think that, overall, the pluses have outweighed the minuses. These days, I think of the *Shelley's Heart* Locative Version as a flawed little gem while marveling at the minor miracle that all the pieces eventually came together.

Are all those story elements flawless? Hardly. At the same time, many of the images we shot are striking, the interfaces are consistently inventive, and there are many moving scenes and lyrical turns of phrase. So, all things considered, I'm proud of what our tiny, underpaid, overworked team (see: Acknowledgments section) was able to accomplish with our microscopic budget, limited resources, crushing time

Figure 4.31 **Website with Desktop and Locative Versions, 2019.**

Figure 4.32 *Shelley's Heart Desktop Version*, **2019.**

constraints, and countless technical challenges. One thing I can say with absolute certainty is that I learned a great deal from bringing this unique mutant into the world, and I'm glad I've been able to share some of those lessons with you.

Takeaways

- Commit to the requirements of the medium.
- Respond to feedback.
- Go big or go home.
- Let different transmedia iterations infuse and inform each other.
- It ain't over till you're sick of it.

Key Tasks: Nodes

Task 1. Create Nodes

- Build each node following the design specifications outlined in this chapter.
- Ensure all required elements are correctly linked and structured for functionality.
- Test each node individually to verify performance and usability.

Task 2. Assemble Your IDN

- Integrate all the created nodes, media assets, and interactive components into the IDN.
- Maintain logical flow and consistency between elements.
- Create backup copies of the IDN at regular intervals to prevent data loss or corruption during the assembly process.

5 Socials

You've created your own self-contained interactive world—now it's time to connect it with the rest of the universe. That's where socials come in. According to media scholar Sandra Gaudenzi (2015), at the top end of the interactive spectrum are projects that act as platforms for users to express themselves and tell their own stories, creating a space for discussion. This chapter focuses on that type of interactivity. It's about cracking your insular IDN open and creating opportunities for connectivity and collaboration, transforming it from a closed system to an open system in two ways:

1. **Social media mechanics:** Embedding social elements inside your IDN.
2. **Social media marketing:** Connecting with platforms outside your IDN.

The common thread is that both approaches allow players to interact with each other. Here's a look at option one:

Social Media Mechanics

Bursting the hermetically sealed bubble of your story world has many advantages. It allows you to transform your IDN into a self-organizing, open-source system where stories can be embellished—or even fundamentally altered—by passionate superfans. In a more modest sense, it can mean creating a sense of copresence by allowing players to participate in polls, surveys, showcases, and other interactions where their contributions appear alongside those of their peers.

Permissions

User permissions are the rights given to users to access and perform actions on your IDN. At this point, we need to proceed with caution because whenever you allow the public to post comments, submit content, or edit existing elements, you are taking a risk. For instance, if you allow players to post anonymously or pseudonymously, you will likely be trolled with hate speech, pornography, violent imagery, and all sorts of other noxious nonsense. That's why a carefully thought-out approach to permissions is essential. The practices you put in place will depend on the sensitivity of the topics you are addressing, the breadth of your audience, and the amount of oversight your team can reasonably offer. Here are some permissions questions worth considering:

- What permissions will players receive (read-only or editing too)?
- How much interactivity will you allow (e.g., only voting, or comments too)?
- Will comments be gated (pre-screened) or non-gated?
- Will there be a flagging system for problematic content?
- Who will have access to a particular interactive element—select players or the public?
- How will the system notify the team of user activity?
- Is there someone willing, available, and responsible enough to effectively monitor and, if necessary, omit malicious user activity?

PRO TIP

- **Promote transparency.** To combat trolling, require players engaging with social media to share their names and contact information. This can also help with your marketing efforts, as you will be able to inform them of upcoming events or embellishments to your IDN.

iframe

If you are a brainiac coder, you can build any type of interaction you like directly into most IDNs. But for those who lack your programming mojo, it's helpful to embed an iFrame (2024)—also known as an inline frame. This tool allows you to display multimedia content within an HTML document. iFrames sometimes get a bad rap for slow loading speeds. Also, they don't allow content tracking for search engine optimization (SEO). However, they are commonly used for all sorts of things, including embedding Google Maps, videos, CAPTCHA security verifications, Facebook "Like" buttons, and PayPal payment forms. You can also use iFrames to embed polls, surveys, puzzles, games, forums, and comment areas into your IDN. Ultimately, whether you use an iFrame, an alternative like *AJAX* (2024), or choose to program the interactions yourself, there are many ways to make your IDN mechanics more social.

Widget

You can embed widgets acquired from other platforms that will bring additional forms of interactivity to your IDN. Depending on the platform you're working on, these can be inserted via embed codes, or the content can be mounted inside an iFrame (2024).

If you'd like to make your own widgets check out tools like the puzzle maker *PuzzleScript!* (2024), the digital book maker *Stepworks* (2024), the chatbot creator *Flowxo* (2024), the countdown clock creator *Countingdownto* (2024), the text-based game creator *ChoiceScript* (2024), and the aptly titled quiz maker, *Quiz Maker* (2024).

Multiplayer Collaboration

Want to unleash group genius at hyper-speed? Share an editable Google Drive document on a projection screen with a hundred people, ask them to post images and information about the Galápagos batfish, and then stand back to watch the magic unfold. You can capture the same type of enthusiastic engagement within your IDN. With the right curation practices, this approach can add a sense of excitement and unpredictability without offending players.

Wikis and other shared documents aren't just dumping grounds—they're proving grounds where editorial and gladiatorial elements converge. Users battle it out to determine which words will be cut, what title will be chosen, and which images will be prominently featured.

Is this a chaotic process?

Absolutely.

Is it effective?

Yes and no.

When it comes to long-form storytelling, a **wiki novel** has yet to hit the bestseller list. This is because works of art created without some form of editorial oversight quickly become unfocused. As the old saying goes, "What's a camel? A horse drawn by committee."

Nonetheless, by incorporating an editable wiki page, your IDN can prompt players to provide a backstory for a particular character, a juicy subplot, a dream sequence, or even a flashback. This type of guided enhancement can be exciting for players and designers alike, allowing in-story elements to evolve spontaneously—like little colonies of Shakespearean sea-monkeys.

Wikis aren't the only way to empower creative teamwork inside an IDN. Here are some other forms of multiplayer collaboration:

- **Cooperative problem-solving:** Players work together to solve puzzles or piece together story fragments. These tasks can require players to share knowledge across social platforms—for example, half the clue is found in the IDN, and the other half is showcased on Instagram.
- **Copresence features:** Players' usernames and progress can appear side by side, fostering a sense of community.
- **Third-party social tools:** Collaborative tools such as chat widgets, whiteboards, or hashtag-driven campaigns can be integrated. Examples for quizzes or collaborative brainstorming include *Mentimeter* (2025) and *Kahoot* (2025).

User-Generated Content (UGC)

Material created by users and uploaded to your IDN is referred to as UGC. This work can capture the creativity of enthusiastic fans in ways that surprise and delight IDN creators and players. Consider including galleries for fan art, videos, and music inspired by your project. For example, after completing a story sequence, players could be invited to view a **community wall** showcasing fan contributions. Platforms such as *Flickr* (2025) and *Notion* (2025) offer shareable and embeddable galleries with commenting features.

The downside of UGC is that it can sometimes look amateurish. While players can be encouraged to upload original drawings, music, or writings inspired by your IDN, it's helpful to have a process for vetting this material. After all, you've worked hard to maintain high production values despite countless challenges, so allowing strangers to submit content might feel daunting.

To address this, consider filtering UGC by implementing a ranking system (e.g., Tiermaker 2024) that allows players to vote on submissions. Typically, the best works rise to the top, while less-polished contributions fade into obscurity, preserving your aesthetic. Additionally, you can moderate the content by deleting hateful or inappropriate submissions and blocking users who attempt to post such material.

Here are some popular forms of UGenerated C to incorporate into your IDN:

- **Media additions:** User artwork, music, or videos that become part of the experience.
- **Story extensions:** Players submit alternate endings, fan fiction, dialogue, or subplots. Top submissions, as voted on by the community, can be incorporated into the main story arc.
- **Character contributions:** Users help design or develop characters for the story.
- **Fan spotlight page:** A dynamic section that showcases top contributions, updated regularly to celebrate standout work.

Crowdsourcing

Your IDN can also benefit from tapping into the collective intelligence of the crowd. Creators can crowdsource a task by encouraging players to create and submit content that aligns with specific themes or by inviting them to alter aspects of the IDN.

PRO TIP

- **Listen to new voices.** Getting players to share personal experiences is a great way to capture stories that haven't been told before. Create a safe space where participants feel comfortable discussing past traumas, encounters with discrimination, mental health challenges, and other sensitive topics. These personal anecdotes can be sent via voicemail or text to a gated area where they can be vetted by the team and then displayed within the IDN, keeping the sources anonymized. In this way, your project can draw on the lived experiences of a wide group of respondents.

Poll (Survey)

Humans love sharing opinions almost as much as debating the opinions of others. To harness these tendencies, invite players to weigh in on ideological, political, or cultural issues related to your IDN. For example, if your story centers on war, ask whether people are inherently violent or if humanity can evolve to become more peaceful. If your IDN explores fast fashion, query players on how individuals can make more sustainable purchasing choices.

You can engage players on these topics using embeddable platforms, including survey makers (Survey Monkey 2024), free online polls (2024), and various types of review management software systems (2024). Advanced story mechanics can even allow your IDN to change dynamically based on the feedback received. Here are some of the types of polls you might include

- **Opinion polls:** Players vote to share their views on a central theme of the IDN. Cumulative results reflect the community's overall stance on the topic.
- **Narrative polls:** Players vote on significant story decisions, shaping future storylines or unlocking alternate paths (e.g., "Who should the protagonist trust?").
- **Character polls:** Players influence a character's fate, traits, or status through their votes.

Internal Forum

Humans, like birds, exhibit flocking behaviors. But for us, the motivation lies in social learning and brainstorming in lively clusters. **Digital collaboration** has earned various labels: "convergence culture," "networked intelligence," and "decentralized knowledge." This phenomenon thrives in spaces where people gather to share information, solve problems, and generate ideas. Your IDN can harness the hive mind through tools such as forum maker (Forumotion.com 2024), comments host (2024), or live chat apps (Intercom 2024). These interfaces encourage players to pool their expertise and ideas, fostering a rich and interactive community within your IDN.

Leaderboard

While forums can foster a sense of community, leaderboards give players a chance to compete. These ranking systems highlight top scores and achievements, tapping into a primal motivational trigger: the desire to WIN!

Leaderboards can be generated using various development platforms, such as *Firebase* (2025), *GameMaker* (2025), and *Unity* (2024). If you're considering incorporating one—or several—leaderboards, here are some popular formats:

- **Scoreboard:** Displays players' cumulative scores numerically.
- **Progress bar:** Tracks players' advancement through the story.
- **Badges:** Icons awarded for specific achievements.
- **Resource bar:** Tracks quantities of tools, weapons, ammunition, skills, or life a player has gained or lost.
- **Internal spotlight:** Highlights top performers in high-traffic areas of your IDN, offering praise and recognition. You could even name a non-playable character (NPC) after one of these superstars.

Aggregation

When humans aren't flocking together, or flying apart, we enjoy feathering our nests. That's where aggregation comes into play. In addition to navigating media assets, players might want to enhance your IDN by bookmarking or embedding related assets they've discovered online. They can be empowered to curate this existing content if your project features an RSS feed generator (RSS.app 2024), a bookmarking tool (Instapaper 2024), and/or a playlist generator (2024).

Live Interaction Feeds

Few things get a player's pulse racing like live interaction with other players. One way to enable this is by designing livestreaming opportunities inside your IDN. Players can be encouraged to role-play as characters via platforms like *WhatsApp* (2024), *Zoom* (2025), *Kick* (2025), *TikTok Live* (2025), and many others. Creators can also embed hashtags into the narrative via platforms like *X API* (2025). They can also include a live comment stream via platforms like *X* (2025) or *Discord* (2025). Additionally, chat widgets such as Stream (2025) can be used to facilitate real-time conversations.

Additionally, a story master can prompt players to engage by asking them to speculate about a narrative mystery, such as guessing the fate of a missing character. This builds a sense of community by allowing players to share their thoughts and discuss how the story might progress.

Creators can also include collaborative scavenger hunts, where clues and Easter eggs are scattered throughout the IDN, coordinated using tools like *Discord Bots* (2025).

Balance

Adding effective social mechanics helps players feel intimately connected to your IDN, but if you go overboard, your project can start to seem like just another website with no compelling narrative drive or character development. Here are some tips for finding the right balance:

- **Prioritize storytelling:** Incorporate social features sparingly to support, rather than overshadow, the narrative.
- **Choose meaningful mechanics:** Select social tools that align with your IDN's tone and themes. For example, fan theories and collaborative puzzles might fit a gothic mystery, while polls may feel out of place.
- **Monitor engagement:** Use analytics to identify which features resonate with players and which should be reconsidered.

Social Media Marketing

Creating an IDN is only half the battle. The next challenge is ensuring people discover it. Leveraging social media allows you to connect with potential players who might otherwise miss your project. Successful social media campaigns can build excitement and attract a loyal fan base, ensuring your IDN's longevity.

PRO TIP

- **Empower the butterfly!** If you're lucky enough to have a social butterfly on your team, make them your Social Media Manager and encourage them to bring their community-building skills to your digital marketing campaign.

Hosting Your IDN

One way to increase visibility is by hosting your IDN on platforms dedicated to interactive narratives. Popular sites include:

- *The Interactive Fiction Archive* (2024)
- *Interactive Fiction Database* (2024)
- *Interactive Fiction Competition* (2024)
- *Itch* (2024)
- *Steam* (2024)
- *Docubase* (2024)
- *TellTale* (2024)
- *Choice of Games* (2024)
- *Game Developer* (2024)

Promotion

In addition to hosting your IDN on these platforms, consider creating your own website and driving traffic through clever marketing, publicity, and search engine optimization (SEO 2024). Since these efforts require time and expertise, you might want to partner with professionals who understand how to leverage both traditional and social media for maximum reach.

Permission Marketing (Pull Marketing)

Unlike email spamming—which is akin to a clumsy pick-up line at a bar—permission marketing (also called pull marketing) takes a more refined, targeted approach. This strategy invites interested parties to opt in to receive updates, promotional materials, or free content. Permission marketing can be implemented in several ways:

- Use Free HTML Email Templates (2024) to send updates to subscribers.
- Encourage potential players to follow you on various platforms,
- Collect contact information via *SignUp Sheets* (2024) embedded on your website or within your game.

This approach ensures your audience is genuinely interested in your content, making it more effective than indiscriminate, intrusive tactics.

LANDMINES

- **Unfocused marketing strategy.** Challenge yourself to be crystal clear on the single most compelling **value proposition** that makes your IDN compelling to potential players. What makes it unique and intriguing?
- **Fixating on one strategy.** Overcommitting to a single audience or marketing approach can limit your reach and hinder growth. Instead, explore multiple channels and marketing approaches to maximize engagement, *but always around your single focused value proposition.*

Social Media Platforms

The best place to start hyping your IDN is on the most popular social media platforms. Key options include *Facebook* (2024), *Instagram* (2024), *X* (2024), *Snapchat* (2024), *Pinterest* (2024), *YouTube* (2024), and *TikTok* (2024). These platforms are ideal for sharing teasers, trailers, and behind-the-scenes content. You can also use them to announce updates, showcase user contributions, and host interactive challenges.

To create eye-catching promotional materials, consider using tools like such as *Canva* (2024), *Snappa* (2025), and *Adobe Express* (2025). Scheduling tools such as *Hootsuite* (2025) and *Buffer* (2025) can help you strategically broadcast posts across multiple platforms at optimal times.

LANDMINE

- **Don't ghost yourself.** Keeping your social media accounts active is essential. Simply creating accounts for your project might garner some initial attention, but without regular updates, your channels will quickly lose momentum and become digital ghost towns. For example, for the Theatrical Version of *Shelley's Heart*, I failed to maintain an active presence, which resulted in limited engagement and only a handful of followers (Figures 5.1, 5.2, 5.3, and 5.4).

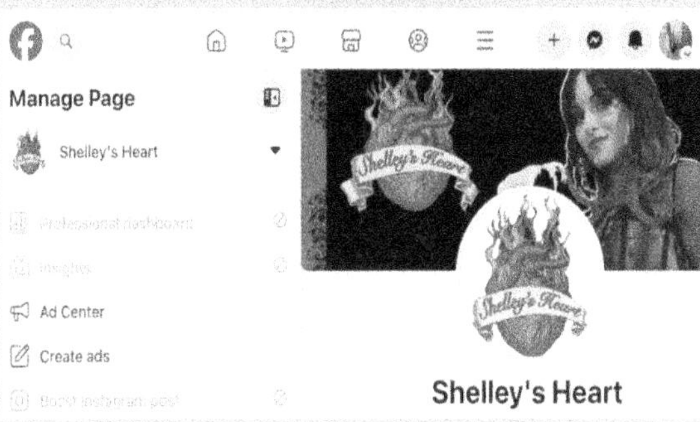

Figure 5.1 Facebook, *Shelley's Heart*, c. 2017.

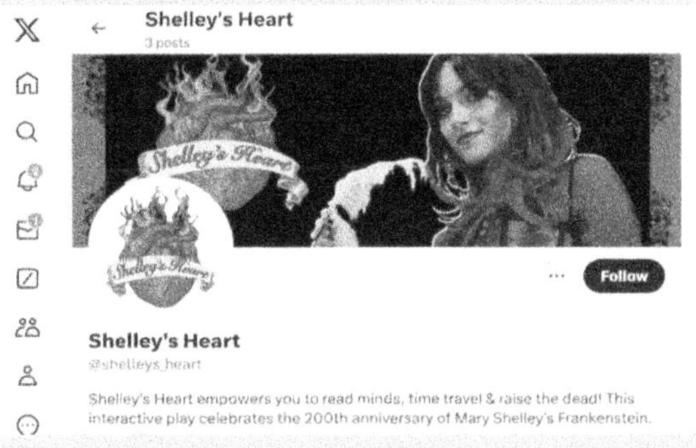

Figure 5.2 X, *Shelley's Heart*, c. 2017.

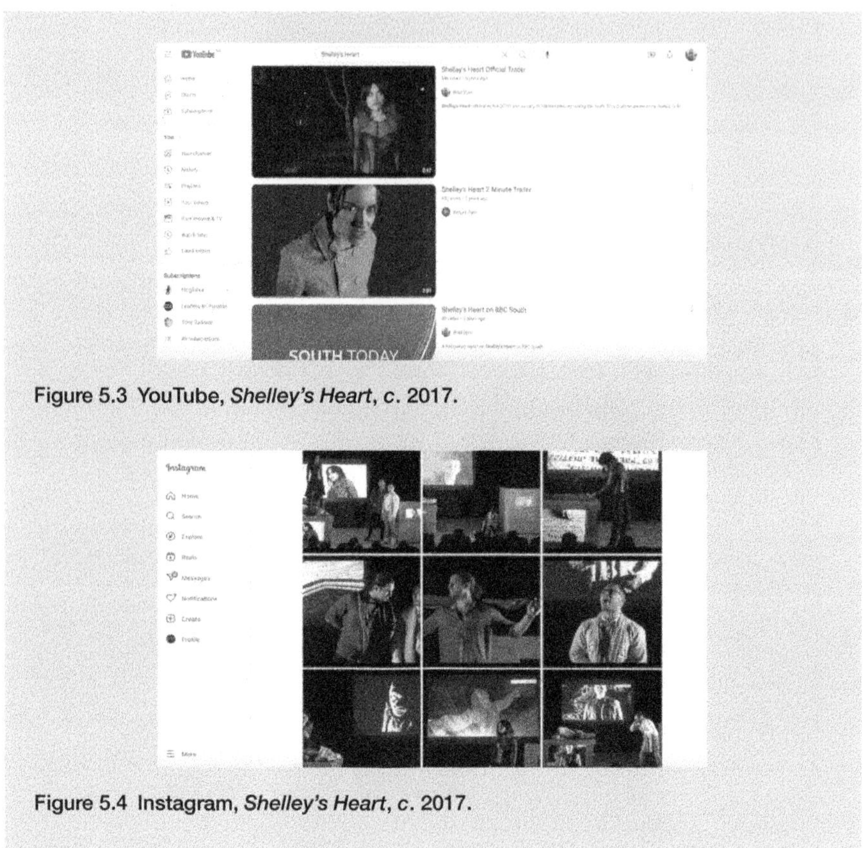

Figure 5.3 YouTube, *Shelley's Heart, c*. 2017.

Figure 5.4 Instagram, *Shelley's Heart, c*. 2017.

External Forum

One effective way to attract players interested in your IDN is by finding forums where people are already discussing similar topics. This strategy allows you to cross-pollinate your ideas with theirs. For example, you could share a link to your IDN in relevant *Discord* (2024) groups focused on interactive narratives or transmedia storytelling. You might also connect with forums that align with the specific topics and themes central to your story.

Alternatively, you could create your own external forum related to the IDN. For instance, consider partnering with an existing subreddit to organize an *Ask Me Anything (AMA)* (2025) where you can discuss the design and development of your IDN.

Link and Backlink

Another way to expand your audience is by linking to websites related to your IDN and asking if they'll link back to yours. This reciprocal approach can attract new players and boost visibility.

Leverage Hashtags

A clever way to attract players is by linking your project to appropriate hashtags. Hashtags act as social media magnets, drawing interest, consolidating discussions, and even generating fresh content. Encourage your existing players to join your marketing efforts by using your hashtag when posting about their experiences, achievements, opinions, and pet theories. They can also include screenshots and fan art. To research trending or niche hashtags related to your genre (e.g., #InteractiveFiction, #StoryGames), use platforms like *Hashtagify* (2025).

Serialized Teasers

Before unveiling your completed IDN, consider tantalizing potential players with sample content. These teasers can attract users by hinting at or showcasing your most engaging elements. Use tools such as *StoryArt* (2025) to create Instagram Story posts or *Loom* (2025) to record short video promos. Here are a few ways to entice your audience:

- **Tasters:** Post story segments, puzzles, or mystery clues on social platforms that tie into the main narrative. Each teaser could hint at a secret feature or storyline in your IDN.
- **Drip drops:** Release content on a scheduled basis, such as a weekly Twitter thread revealing pieces of a backstory that tie into the game, or debuting new story assets.
- **Serialized mystery:** Share cryptic clues tied to story puzzles. Fans who solve them can gain access to an exclusive bonus scene.

Live Promotional Events

Live events are great promotional opportunities as they allow for players to connect with creators, performers, and like-minded fans in real time. Here are some ways to include live events in your marketing strategy:

- **Live voting opportunities:** Host livestreams on platforms like *Twitch* (2025), *YouTube Live* (2025), or *Instagram Live* (2025), allowing players to influence the narrative by voting on key story decisions.

- **Q&A sessions with creators and/or cast:** Give players a chance to engage directly with you and your team.
- **Story previews:** Host live events where you unveil new or exclusive content to build anticipation.

Collaborate with Influencers and Content Creators

You don't have to market your IDN alone. Partner with influencers and content creators in gaming, literature, and interactive media. These creators are often eager to showcase new projects to their dedicated followers. Use platforms such as *Heepsy* (2025) to locate influencers whose interests align with your project or connect with creators in your niche via *Raptive* (2025).

Ways influencers can promote your IDN:

- **Playthroughs:** Invite influencers to explore your IDN on platforms like YouTube or Twitch, helping you reach their audiences.
- **Sneak peeks:** Provide early access to the full IDN or exclusive preview content.

Gamify Social Sharing

Encourage players to share your project on social media by rewarding their participation. Tools like *Woobox* (2025) and *Trello* (2025) can help you design and manage these experiences.

Examples of social sharing incentives:

- **Trade-offs:** Offer players something in return for sharing your project. For instance, players who post a screenshot of their favorite scene could receive downloadable bonus content.
- **External spotlight:** Highlight top contributors on your social media channels. For example, feature UGC in "Fan Friday" posts.
- **Contests and challenges:** Organize fan art or story extension contests, with rewards tied to deeper engagement. Example: "Decode this cipher to unlock an exclusive scene!"

Giveaways

Rewarding players for engaging with your IDN can build loyalty and encourage participation. Make sure giveaways are relevant to your project and provide meaningful value. To coordinate giveaways tied to contests or social sharing, use tools such as *Rafflecopter* (2025) and *Gleam* (2025).

Examples of digital giveaways include:

- **eBooks** (2024)**:** Share related stories or behind-the-scenes content created with platforms like *Canva Create eBooks templates* (2025).

- **Tutorials:** Offer guidance with tools like Easy Tutorial Video Maker (2024).
- **Discount codes:** Use a free random code generator (2024) to provide players with exclusive offers.
- **Loyalty cards and gift certificates:** Create these using free online editable loyalty card templates (2024) and *Canva Gift Certificates templates* (2025).
- **Media downloads:** Share items such as a downloadable scene, soundtrack, or wallpaper (2025) via file-sharing platforms (Indeed Editorial Team 2024).

Monetize

With a bit of planning, your IDN can become a money-making venture. Prospective audiences may adopt a "try it before you buy it" attitude, so consider hooking them with free content upfront. **Free-to-play** models offer substantial content at no cost but require players to pay to see how the story ends. A variation of this is the **freemium** approach, which provides basic or limited features for free while charging a premium for supplemental or advanced features. This strategy is commonly used by creators of mobile stories, often including **in-app purchases** within free episodes. For example, players can purchase extra outfits, new friends, supplementary scenes, and more.

Merch

If you're looking for an easy way to monetize your IDN, consider selling merchandise. There's no need to manufacture products or store them in a spooky warehouse out by the docks. Instead, create a few logos and partner with a service that can print them on T-shirts, mugs, keychains, salad tongs, and all sorts of other items, then ship them directly to consumers (Figure 5.5). Online merch malls (Spreadshop 2024) take a sizable cut (up to 70 percent) of the profits, but they save you hassles and can help you capitalize on untapped opportunities with zero overhead.

Figure 5.5 Merch store—*Shelley's Heart Website, c.* 2018.

Here are some instructive anecdotes related to both social media mechanics and social media marketing.

Cautionary Tales: Social Media Misfires

When adding social media mechanics to your IDN, it's essential to ensure these features feel thematically relevant. One student team I taught liked the idea of including polls, quizzes, and surveys to increase interaction between players. However, they implemented these features haphazardly. As a result, many elements had little connection to their chosen topic and seemed arbitrary or confusing. Unsurprisingly, player engagement was minimal.

In terms of social media marketing, another team created an iDoc about the hazards faced by women returning from a night of drinking. The project was well-produced, with immersive POV footage that placed the player in the shoes of a young woman negotiating various risks, including verbal harassment, spiking, and physical assault. It also incorporated compelling statistics and interviews with a psychologist discussing these issues. However, the outreach and promotion were underwhelming. The team didn't create a social media campaign or connect with forums, websites, and organizations focused on related topics, such as feminist activists and public safety advocates. Despite its potential to reach a wide audience, the IDN went largely unnoticed due to a lack of targeted promotion.

Takeaways

- Tailor your social media mechanics to the topic of your IDN.
- Promote your work to target audiences.

Success Stories: Social Media Triumphs

One of the best examples of embedding a social media interface inside an IDN came from an iDoc about eating healthy. It featured an embedded survey where players picked the junk food that most resembled their personality. After completing the survey, players could see how others had responded to the same questionnaire. They were also able to click on different junk food items to discover their per-ounce calorie count. This playful yet informative approach engaged users while delivering a serious message.

A success story in social media marketing involved a team who created an iDoc about Staffordshire Bull Terriers (Staffies). These stocky dogs share an ancestor with modern pit bulls and are often confused with that more aggressive breed. The project offered tips for raising and protecting Staffies. To promote their work, the students launched an extensive social media campaign, reaching out to Staffy enthusiasts across multiple platforms and sharing links to their iDoc on breed-specific forums.

Within days, the team was thrilled to see their IDN receive thousands of views and their social media pages garner nearly as many likes.

Takeaways

- A quirky interface can motivate engagement with a serious topic.
- Be sure to target groups emotionally invested in your IDN's subject matter.

Key Tasks: Socials

Task 1. Create Marketing Plan

Using the Marketing Plan form available from our website to brainstorm ideas related to promoting your IDN, and list the following items you hope to incorporate:

- **Social media platforms:** A website or app that allows users to create, share, and interact with content.
- **Guerilla marketing strategies:** Unconventional methods to promote a product or service.
- **Live events:** Gatherings that take place in real time, either in person or virtually.
- **Online groups and forums:** Communities that meet in person or virtually where ideas and views on a particular issue can be exchanged.
- **Influencers:** People with the ability to influence potential users by promoting or recommending your IDN on social media.
- **Testimonials:** Statements testifying to the qualities of your IDN.
- **Links:** Clickable items that direct users to another page, document, or other online content.
- **SWOT Analysis:** A strategic planning tool that helps identify and assess the **Strengths**, **Weaknesses**, **Opportunities**, and **Threats** related to your project.
- **Value proposition:** A statement that explains the benefits the IDN offers users and how these differ from the features of competitors (Figure 5.6).

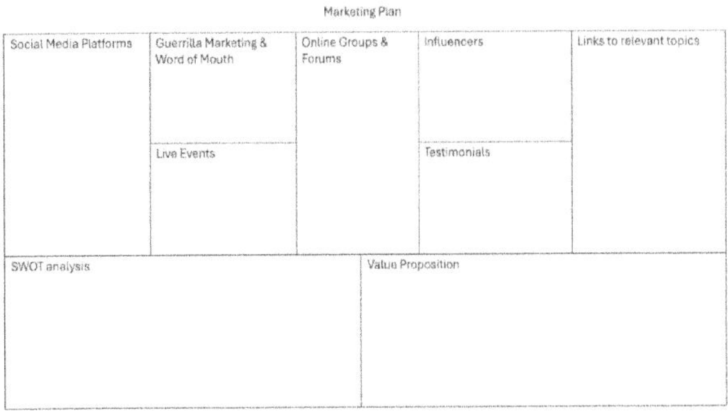

Figure 5.6 Marketing plan.

6   Curation

At the age of twenty-five, the Romantic poet John Keats succumbed to tuberculosis. Convinced his work would be forgotten, he insisted the inscription on his tombstone should read: "Here lies one whose name was writ in water." Anyone who has created a work of digital art can relate. While some papyrus scrolls from classical Greece have survived to this day, media technologies change so quickly that some digital projects produced only a few years ago are no longer functional or accessible. Because of this, creating IDNs can sometimes feel like writing on water. Bit rot, link rot, hacking, software upgrades, and technological obsolescence are constant threats. Just because you've completed a functioning project doesn't mean it will continue to exist. That's why effective curation practices are so important.

The Flashpocalypse

Back in 2009, Adobe's Flash Player was installed on 99 percent of all computers. But then the new generation of iPhones appeared—and they weren't compatible with Flash. Soon, the more efficient and flexible HTML5 was invented, driving another nail into Flash's coffin. By 2017, Adobe announced it would stop supporting Flash Player, and at the start of 2021, Flash was officially discontinued. Adobe began prompting users to uninstall Flash and removed all download links for Flash installers. Around the same time, every major browser removed Flash Player. The internet, as we had known it, was over.

During the early days of Flash, an indie ethos reigned supreme. Creators could produce IDN content free from quality control guidelines or content restrictions. But when Flash disappeared, hosting platforms grew more cautious. This led to additional gatekeeping for creators and more handholding for players. The death of Flash also marked the loss of countless Flash-based projects, including many innovative and intriguing IDNs.

Happily, some Flash-based interactive narratives have been salvaged. Some are hosted on *the Internet Archive* (2024). And a few websites featuring Flash content have managed to pivot. Some, like *Armor Games* (2024) and *Kongregate* (2024), feature interfaces that allow downloadable IDN player to play on their platforms. Others, such as *Newgrounds* (2024), feature a downloadable player that makes it possible to explore Flash content offline.

Future-proofing Your IDN

Sadly, there are no iron-clad strategies that will keep your project safe from all conceivable threats to its longevity. Just as there is no universal approach to creating your IDN, there is no universal approach to preserving it. Any work with digital content is susceptible to corruption and obsolescence. The same can be said for this book. It features references to tons of digital sources, and some will certainly become defunct in the years—possibly weeks—ahead. Rather than lament this fate, here are a few crucial best practices that can help future-proof your IDN:

PRO TIPS

- **Curate with care.** To keep your IDN safe and functioning, do the following:
    - Create on platforms with technical support staff or an open-source structure with a committed and active community of users.
    - Duplicate your files and frequently back them up.
    - Use a journaling file system like ext4 (2024) to ensure metadata is correctly written and ordered on your disks even when the write cache loses power.
    - Store files in two high-quality external hard drives, on a computer, and in the cloud.
    - Perform Data Checks to make sure your files and links are still functioning, and their quality hasn't been compromised.

LANDMINES

- **Beware of curation pitfalls.** To ensure the longevity of your IDN, avoid the following:

    - Don't create on outdated, soon-to-be obsolete, or poorly supported platforms.
    - Don't forget to update your software. If you don't do this, the original version may be discontinued, and your IDN will cease to function.
    - Don't store your hard drives in a leaky shed in the middle of a swamp. Keep them in a safe, dust-free, temperature-controlled environment: perfectly dry and cool (but not freezing), with no direct sunlight, and no electronic or magnetic interference.

Reputation Curation

In addition to keeping your IDN alive and well, it pays to curate your reputation as an IDN creator. One of the best ways to do this is to connect with other IDN makers by attending interactive storytelling conferences like *i-Docs* (2025) or *International*

Conference on Interactive Digital Storytelling (2024). You can also analyze your work in scholarly publications such as *The Journal of Interactive Narrative* (2024), *The Rosebush: Interactive Fiction Theory and Criticism* (2024), *The International Journal of Interactive Storytelling* (2024), *New Media and Society* (2024), and *Media Practice in Education* (2024). To showcase your work, explore interactive fiction journals and zines like *Voidspace* (2024) and *Plotpolis* (2024). Additionally, you can enter interactive writing contests such as *The New Media Writing Prize* (2024), *The Interactive Fiction Competition* (2024), *Parser Comp* (2024), *Peabody Awards Immersive and Interactive* (2024), and *Tribeca: Immersive* (2024).

From the Trenches

Cautionary Tale—Genarrator

One of the most heartbreaking tales related to curation is the saga of the Genarrator platform. Back in 2012, my BU colleague Jim Pope and tech wizard Andy Campbell (*Dreaming Methods* 2024) teamed up to create a user-friendly drag-and-drop IDN creator they titled Genarrator (Gen + narrator—get it?). It functioned as both a story editor and a curation platform. The interface was user-friendly and accessible to anyone on the web.

Jim and Andy received a small amount of funding to support the project, but because they wanted to keep Genarrator free and available to the public, the platform never gained much support from academia or the private sector. Despite this, it worked perfectly for years and proved highly popular with users.

Building on the foundation of Genarrator, Jim created *The New Media Writing Prize* (2024), an international contest celebrating works that combine writing with digital media. Many of the annual entries were hosted on Genarrator. Jim also created two higher education classes titled "Interactive Fiction," one for undergraduates and one for master's students, both of which used Genarrator to construct IDN projects.

Finally, Jim and I collaborated on an outreach project titled: *Digital Interactive Storytelling in the Community* or DISC (Gyori & Pope 2023, 2021). Working with at-risk teens, secondary school students, and young offenders, we used Genarrator to co-create a variety of IDN narratives.

Despite a lack of funding and technical support, Jim and Andy kept Genarrator up and running for eleven years. However, the platform eventually suffered a fatal blow. Chinese characters began appearing across the site, revealing that hackers had accessed and corrupted the source code. Although Andy was able to temporarily fix the issue, he estimated that permanent safeguards and ongoing maintenance would require regular funding. Unable to secure support, he and Jim reluctantly said goodbye to their labor of love as it faded into internet oblivion.

If you want to see a few of the content pages, some are still accessible via the *The Wayback Machine* (2024), but the IDN projects hosted on the platform are no

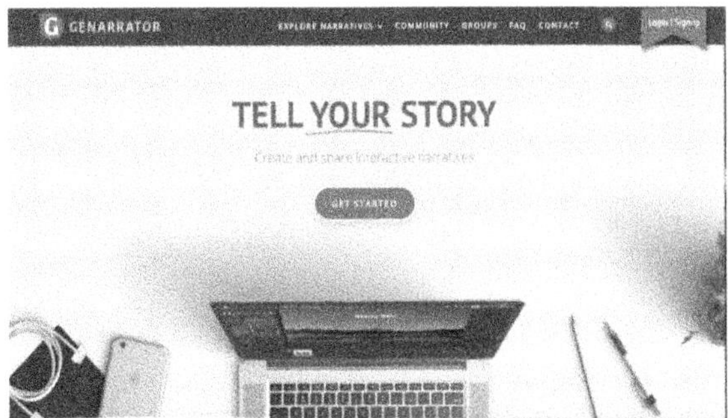

Figure 6.1 Genarrator RIP.

longer functional. As of this writing, Jim and Andy are exploring ways to salvage the hundreds of stories curated on Genarrator. Perhaps they can partner with *The British Library* or another large institution interested in preserving new media texts. For now, however, Genarrator is no more (Figure 6.1).

Takeaways

- Establish a reliable funding model.
- Consider going open source and fostering an active community of creators and programmers to support the evolution of your platform.
- Take as many steps as possible to safeguard against hackers.

Success Story—DISC Project Debut

The glow coming off the projection screen can't compete with the luminous faces of the participants as they take a bow before their friends, family, teachers, and project facilitators. There's nothing quite like an IDN screening in front of an enthusiastic crowd. As the story arrives at each decision point, people shout out their preferred choice. The loudest voices win, which encourages rowdy audience participation. Through the years, I've seen IDN creators from all sorts of backgrounds radiate pride at having accomplished a feat of digital wizardry in a short period of time. This is because producing an IDN is more than a creative act—it's an invitation to connect with others while showcasing the immersive world you've created.

Takeaways

- Let participants revel in the afterglow.
- Share co-creation projects with friends, family, and peers in an informal setting.
- There are few things more gratifying than helping others create. Savor the experience.

Task 1. Create a Curation Plan for Your IDN

Make sure it is on a stable platform and has been tested to confirm there are no bugs. Then back everything up—at least three times.

Conclusion

It's impossible to predict exactly how IDN creation will evolve in the future. That's what makes this such an exciting field to explore. However, we can consider some important technological trends likely to influence this rapidly changing field. The following section speculates about the future of IDNs by chasing the dragon's tail of emerging innovations. Here are five areas that will likely exert a strong influence on IDNs in the years ahead:

Artificial Intelligence (AI)

The most promising, frightening, and paradigm-shattering technology of the current era is AI. While still in its infancy, AI is learning by leaps and bounds and is likely to radically change all aspects of life as we know it, including the process of IDN creation.

By using machine learning algorithms and data analytics, AI-driven content creation will soon be able to reshape interactive storytelling by tailoring narrative experiences to the passions and preferences of individual players. For example, an AI system like *Google Duplex* (Callaham & Fingas 2024) can already engage in small talk and carry out tasks like scheduling appointments over the phone, but this is just the beginning.

In the future, AI will likely blur the line between personalization and pandering. It could generate stories featuring protagonists modeled after users, complete with their names and physical traits—but with thinner physiques, better abs, and perfect hair. These enhanced avatars might engage in extraordinary feats like flying through space or breathing underwater, all while attracting droves of adoring virtual admirers. Imagine your AI-generated alter ego wooing a love interest to a soundtrack of your favorite songs in a world constructed from cherished vacation videos. Or you could ditch the love interest and dive into an orgy of avatars rendered from your favorite selfies, taking digital narcissism to a whole new level.

On a more positive note, in the future, AI could be programmed to broaden your horizons, as well. By exposing you to unfamiliar forms of stimuli, it could challenge you to explore other minds and bodies, seeing the world in new ways and hopefully achieving comfort zone escape velocity.

Spatial Computing

New wearable technologies are making storytelling increasingly immersive and interactive. Welcome to the era of spatial computing. The *Apple Vision Pro* (Apple 2023) responds to hand gestures, voice commands, and eye movements, eliminating the need for a controller in most interactions. The *Meta Quest 3* (2024) enables users to congregate in VR hangouts for both business and social interactions. This means you could create a future IDN by collaborating with people inside a virtual space and then have participants explore the project in another simulated environment.

Spatial computing is likely to continue merging with other cutting-edge technologies, producing new forms of interaction. When combined with AI and location-tracking systems, it could transform the world around us into a narrative-rich environment filled with story nodes that users can unlock with a literal blink of an eye.

Ultimately, virtual and real-world environments will begin to merge so seamlessly that it will be hard to distinguish where one ends and the other begins. For example, spatial journalism (R&D 2021) is already allowing readers to experience stories in three dimensions on phones, web browsers, and VR headsets. This type of reporting is particularly emotive, helping players develop empathy by experiencing what it's like to be a migrant in a leaky boat or a member of an endangered species. Spatial computing can also allow users to embody fictional personae—soaring through space as an alien or swimming through an artery as an anthropomorphic red blood cell. It can also enable users to experience the world through the lens of someone with mental health challenges, or to imagine old photographs coming to life and speaking to them. In addition to all this, spatial computing can extend human abilities—simulating processes such as seeing through walls, reading minds, or photosynthesizing nutrients.

Another innovation is spatial audio (SA), which functions as virtual reality for the ears. In environments designed with SA, sounds emanate from specific locations in 3D space. Paired with VR headsets or AR displays, SA enhances immersive visuals, making them more lifelike and intuitive. For example, as you approach a dragon, its roars grow louder, and stepping into virtual water produces splashing sounds around your ankles. Dynamic head tracking keeps the sound aligned with the visual source, enhancing the sense of immersion. SA also offers educational possibilities, like simulating the experience of being a blind person navigating a subway without risk. Though SA isn't yet widely available, it's a technology to watch—or rather, listen for.

The Internet of Things (IoT)

When was the last time your refrigerator recited a racy limerick, or your toilet sang a song that made you cry? With the IoT, the objects around us can connect to the web and enhance our lives in countless ways. Common applications include self-driving cars, thermostats that begin cooling your house when you're five miles away, or patches that release medicine at specific times.

But smart objects can also be tagged with bits of narrative, like museum audio guides that provide details about a particular painting. This technology could enhance personal mementos in your home by linking them to media assets containing personal anecdotes, enriched with images and sounds.

It's easy to imagine how an array of technological gadgets could tell a story. Every morning, your coffee machine might greet you with the opening scene of a new IDN and offer you a choice of narrative options. You pick one, and it directs you to your exercise bike, which expands on the story and presents another choice, and so on. This approach would transform your smart devices into interactive nodes working together to form a complete story through a game of narrative connect-the-dots.

Holography

While we won't be able to replicate the *Star Trek* holodeck anytime soon, holography still holds great promise for the future of IDN creation. It would be thrilling to have holographic figures walk among us, but the laws of physics preclude this. Such images can only be seen from particular angles after being projected onto a screen.

The simpler version of this is a nineteenth-century technology known as **Pepper's Ghost.** It consists of an offstage figure reflected onto a pane of glass placed between an onstage performer and the audience. This makes it appear as if the performer is interacting with a wraithlike specter.

Contemporary holography is far more advanced but still requires images to be projected onto screens, often cubes in the center of a stage made of holographic gauze or "holo-gauze." This translucent fabric, with a metallic coating, reflects projections without obstructing the view of performers behind it.

Due to these technological limitations, holographic images are best experienced in theatrical settings where audiences remain seated in fixed locations. For more immersive engagement with 3D figures, AR images on phone screens are your best bet.

But while holography is constrained by the laws of physics, the images it conjures are not. It can bring beloved performers back from the dead, as with *The Whitney Houston Hologram Concert* (The Ritz Herald 2021) or Tupac Hologram Snoop Dogg and Dr. Dre Perform Coachella Live 2012 (SnoopDoggTV). It can make old pop stars young again, as with *Abba Voyage* (2022). And it can allow contemporary pop stars to bend reality and minds, such as *Drake performing with sperm cells hologram* (2023), or Madonna performing with the cartoon band *Gorillaz* (2006). The latter is a virtual band created by *Blur* singer Damon Albarn and visual artist Jamie Lewis. Holographs can also construct completely virtual pop stars, like the Japanese sensation Hatsune Miku (Bloomberg 2017). She was created in the early two-thousands from a bit of voice synthesis software and has since released over 100,000 songs in multiple languages and opened shows for Lady Gaga.

As holographic performances grow increasingly common, they are likely to become more interactive. Platforms such as *Holoconnects* (2025) are busy envisioning what the next generation of interactive holography will look like, and this tech hybrid is likely to yield all sorts of interesting offshoots and mutations. We may not want to vote on whether Willy Loman springs back to life at the end of *Death of a Salesman*, but it could be fun to select from an array of dearly departed or fictional avatars to perform with our favorite actors and performers. Spider-Man cast to play Macbeth? Maybe not. But King Kong breakdancing with Celine Dion? Bring it!

Biometric Interfaces

Current uses of biometrics include fingerprint scanners, facial recognition cameras, DNA matching, voice recognition, and retinal scanning. These technologies are used to unlock phones, start cars, research heritage, and perform crime scene analysis. But they can also be harnessed to enhance IDN creation.

Much of this potential involves pairing biometrics with AI to monitor physical reactions to unfolding narratives. This takes the old showbiz adage, "Give the audience what they want," to a new extreme, as biometrics can react to a person's physical responses in real time. Is your pulse quickening? Are your pupils dilating? Is your face showing interest or disgust? Any of these biometric cues can become triggers, shaping elements such as plot, characterization, backstory, or production values.

A recent example is the interactive film *Before We Disappear* (2025), which uses facial recognition cameras to track audience moods and adjust the narrative based on shifting expressions.

As this form of storytelling grows more sophisticated, individual players may want to customize their experiences by guiding the system to interpret their biometric feedback in specific ways. For example, a horror story fan might adjust settings so the narrative intensifies as their heart rate increases, while a timid player might prefer a biometric safe word, allowing a single utterance or gasp to pause the story. A traffic light system could also be implemented, with different biometric responses triggering varying levels of narrative intensity.

Most likely, creators will continue crafting core elements like characters, settings, and major plot points. However, more granular details—such as atmosphere, tone, and suspense—could organically shift based on player reactions. This type of interactivity would make the narrative deeply personalized, akin to a tailored suit for the psyche.

Success Story and/or Cautionary Tale—Your IDN

Creating an IDN involves becoming the protagonist of your own real-life narrative. If acts of God or internal clashes cause the project to crash and burn, the story of your story will become a tragedy. If everything clicks and the result is something you're proud of, the creative process will turn out to be the feel-good hit of the season. In either case, the production of your IDN is certain to be a memorable saga. Like a player navigating an interactive tale, you'll make consequential choices each step of the way. At times, you may feel as if you're wandering in the woods blindfolded. Gradually, however, a clear storyline will emerge, one that, in many respects, resembles the classic monomyth identified by Joseph Campbell, also known as "The Hero's Journey", a term from his book *The Hero with a Thousand Faces* (1949).

It starts with the "call to action," when the creator feels an itch to tell a story. The first act break occurs when you leave the "ordinary world" and enter the "special world" of creative brainstorming. Along the way, there will be breakthroughs and stumbling blocks—"rising and falling action." Grappling with the complexities of the production process during the second act, you may begin to lose heart. This involves confronting setbacks and experiencing self-doubt, culminating in the "midpoint crisis," where you rethink the entire project and arrive at new insights that clarify its meaning. This clarity will give you the energy needed for the final push to the big creative "climax." At that point, everything will come together as the assembly process ties up the remaining loose threads. Afterward, you'll return to the ordinary world ready to showcase your completed project and reflect on everything you've discovered along the way, savoring a gratifying sense of "resolution."

PRO TIP

- **Don't forget the victory lap.** Your project should culminate in a screening for everyone involved and anyone even marginally interested, including friends, family, and curious strangers. You might not have the budget for a lavish wrap party, but this isn't just good karma—it's an important bonding experience. It offers participants and facilitators a chance to showcase their work and reflect on the creative process.
- **Include a postpartum discussion.** After the wrap party, reconvene as many facilitators and participants as possible to reflect on the twists and turns of your creative process. Some creators call this a "postmortem," but "postpartum" is a more fitting term. After all, it's unlikely anyone died during the production, and you've just given birth to a bouncing baby IDN. Looking back on the birthing process involves evaluating what you've achieved, where you stumbled, how you recovered, and what you learned along the way. These insights will never be more vivid. If you forget to jot them down, many will slip away, only to come flooding back when you encounter similar challenges during future projects. However, if you pause to reflect while the production is still fresh in your mind and note best practices, pain points, pitfalls,

and strategic workarounds, you'll stand a much better chance of drawing on these hard-won insights when creating your next IDN. This is also a good time to capture final thoughts via surveys, which can serve as a basis for future research, analysis, or funding bids.

Takeaways

- Accept that every creative process is a mix of pros and cons.
- Learn from setbacks and move forward.
- Celebrate successes and build on them.
- Take time to reflect on what you've learned along the way.
- Keep creating magic.

Worksheets

Contact Sheet

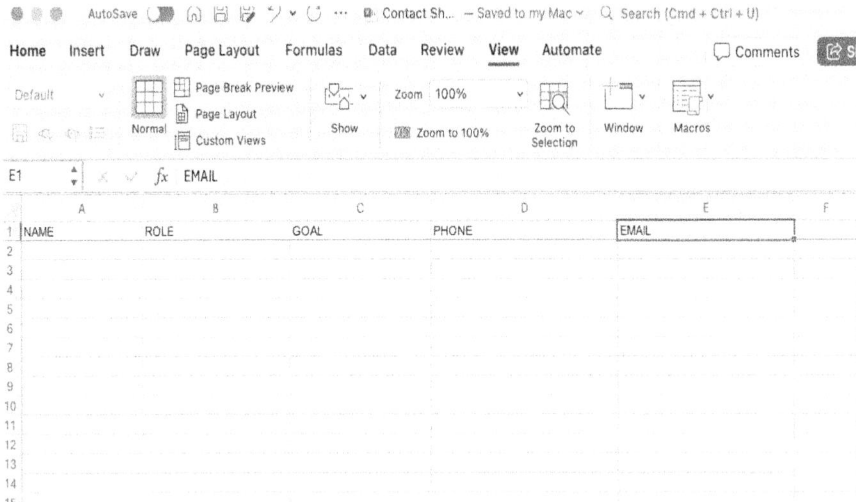

Marketing Plan

Marketing Plan

Social Media Platforms	Guerrilla Marketing & Word of Mouth	Online Groups & Forums	Influencers	Links to relevant topics
	Live Events		Testimonials	

SWOT analysis	Value Proposition

Production Schedule

	A	B	C	D	E	F
1	DATE	DAY	TIME	TASK	OWNERS	LOCATION
2	07/07/2025	Monday	10AM-3PM	DIS planning	Full team	Campus, room WG05
3	07/08/2025	Tuesday	10AM-3PM	Scene Improvs, Location Scout	Full team	Campus, room WG05
4	07/09/2025	Wednesday	10AM-3PM	Filming, Audio Recording, Prototype Assembly	Small Teams	Campus, room WG05, Recording Studio, Locations TBD
5	07/10/2025	Thursday	10AM-3PM	Filming, Audio Recording, Prototype Assembly	Small Teams	Campus, room WG05, Recording Studio, Locations TBD
6	07/11/2025	Friday	10AM-3PM	Edit Media Assets. Assemble DIS	Small Teams	Campus, room WG05
7	OFF	Saturday				
8	OFF	Sunday				
9	07/14/2025	Monday	10AM-3PM	Edit Media Assets. Assemble DIS	Small Teams	Campus, room WG05
10	07/15/2025	Tuesday	10AM-3PM	Edit Media Assets. Assemble DIS	Small Teams, Public	Campus, room WG05, Screening Room
11						
12						
13						
14						

Resource Inventory

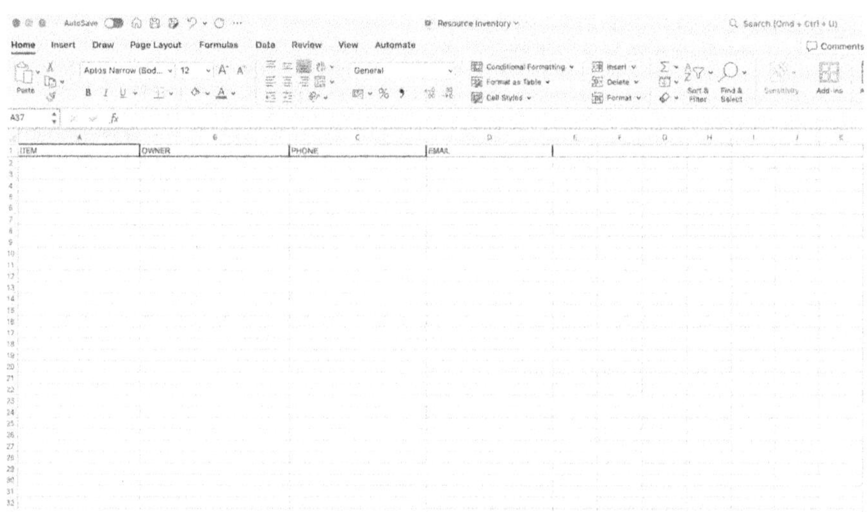

	A	B	C	D
1	ITEM	OWNER	PHONE	EMAIL

Skill Inventory

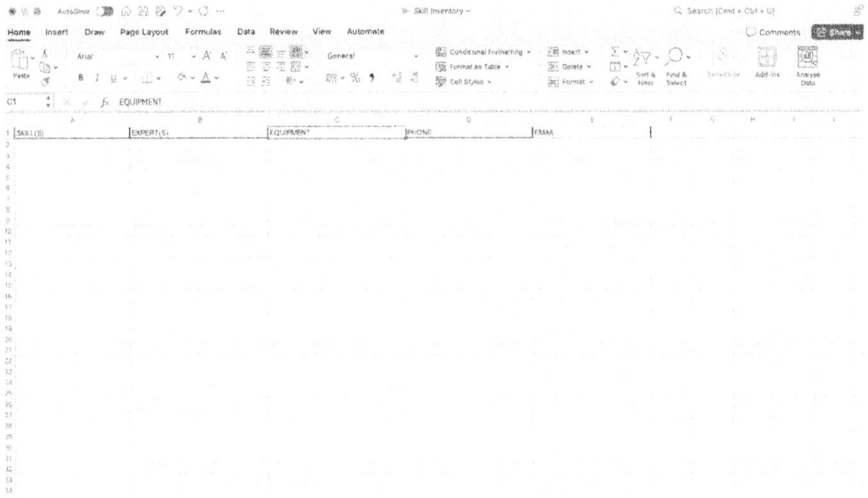

Glossary

First person POV: The player sees what the character sees as they move through the story world.

Third person POV: The player sees an avatar or icon representing them navigating through the story world.

360-image: A picture that captures a complete 360-degree view of the player's surroundings.

4D film: A movie presentation system that combines 3D visuals with synchronized physical effects to create an immersive, multisensory experience.

Abilities: Character skills.

Ad hoc: Not planned before it happens, occurring spontaneously.

Accessibility: Design strategies ensuring that disabled people can play and create IDNs.

Action point: A narrative option triggering an instance of dramatic action.

Aesthetics: The overall look and sound of the IDN.

Affordance: An option the IDN offers to the user/player.

Aggregation: When users or creators enhance the IDN by bookmarking or embedding related assets discovered online, clustering similar items together.

Ambient Copresence: The feeling of being with others, even without direct interaction.

Amusement (theme, water) park: A place with attractions made up of rides, such as roller coasters and Ferris wheels.

Analog: A story or game that does not require digital technology to function.

Animated GIFs: A short looping sequence of still images.

Arborescent: A hypertext structure that branches into multiple pathways often with several endings.

Arrow: A symbol directing the player how to proceed.

Artificial Intelligence (AI): Computer systems that are able to perform tasks that normally require human intelligence.

Asset: Files that create, store, or distribute digital content.

Asynchronous: Not existing or occurring at the same time.

Audio file: A digital container storing audio data.

Audio-only IDN: An Interactive Digital Narrative with no visuals, only audio files.

Augmented reality (AR): A technology that superimposes a computer-generated image onto a user's view of the real world.

Avatar or player icon: An image representing the player.

Axial: A hypertext structure where one node leads to the next in a linear fashion.

Backlinking: Attracting new players by contacting sites you have linked to and asking if they will link back to your site.

Bilinear path: A path where the player can move in two directions: forward or backward.

Binaural audio (360 audio): A mix that surrounds the listener with sounds coming from many different directions.

Biometrics: Body measurements and calculations related to human characteristics and features.

Bit rot: The corruption of digital data that occurs when bits flip from their intended state to the opposite.

Blog: A regularly updated website or web page, typically one run by an individual or small group, that is written in an informal or conversational style.

Branching pattern: A design that starts with a single node containing two or more decision points and continues branching and growing exponentially.

Branching bottleneck pattern: A branching pattern with bottlenecks that fold back into the main narrative.

Buffing: Giving a temporary advantage to a character.

Character: A person in a fictional story.

Character types: Common archetypes, including traders, hunters, monsters, quest givers, bosses, and so on.

Choice-based IF: A style of storytelling where players make choices that impact the narrative's outcome.

Choke Point: A decision that leads to a bottleneck where paths are forced to pass through a single node. This help limit the branching of paths.

Cinemagraph: A photographic image where most of the scene is stationary while the viewer's eye is drawn to a bit of seamlessly looping movement.

Cloud, The: A network of remote servers that provide access to computing resources and services over the internet.

Color palette: The signature hues that define the IDN's visuals.

Community Wall: A digital grid of users in a community displaying content and interactions.

Concentric pattern: An array of choices offered at the same time.

Concept art: A visual representation conveying the look of a project before it's created.

Conditions: Environment or gameplay variables.

Consistency: A design strategy in which recurring elements in the IDN follow predictable patterns.

Constraint: A restriction the IDN design imposes on the user.

Contact sheet: A list of project participants, including phone numbers and emails.

Content warning: A statement alerting players that an IDN contains potentially distressing material.

Copresence: When two or more things occur at the same place, either simultaneously or asynchronously.

Coverage: Shooting the same sequence of dramatic action from various angles.

Creative Nonfiction: A genre of writing that uses literary techniques to tell factual stories.

Creator: An individual working alone or as part of a team to design and produce an IDN.

Crowdfunding: Raising money from many people in small amounts to finance the creation of a project.

Cue Cards: Cards with written prompts to help speakers or actors remember what to say.

Cumulative feedback: A type of feedback that summarizes a series of responses to help a student understand how well they did.

Curation: Safeguarding an IDN to ensure its longevity.

Customization: The ability of the user to tailor an interface to the player's needs or preferences.

Cutscene: A linear scene in a video game that plays when the player reaches a particular point.

Data analytics: The process of inspecting, cleansing, transforming, and modeling data with the goal of discovering useful information, informing conclusions, and supporting decision-making.

Data-glove: A glove-like device with sensors that detects hand and finger movements and sends that information to a computer.

Data-suit: An electronic body covering that transmits a wearer's movements to a computer in virtual reality.

Dead Cat: A furry microphone cover designed to reduce wind noise.

Decision point: A juncture where a player chooses between narrative options.

Deconstructed interview: A question-and-answer sequence broken into an array of responses triggered by options the player can choose from.

Demonstration: A practical exhibition and explanation of how something works or is performed.

Design bible: A comprehensive guide describing all aspects of a project's aesthetic identity.

Dialogue tree (conversation tree): A design mechanic that offers the Player Character dialogue options to choose from, triggering different responses from Non-Player Characters (NPCs).

Diamond pattern: A narrative structure that branches and quickly closes back in on itself.

Digital: Characterized by electronic and especially computerized technology.

Digital Collaboration: The use of technology to enable teamwork, information sharing, and communication.

Divergent thinking: A thought process that involves generating multiple creative solutions to a problem.

Drag and drop: Moving items by placing the cursor over them, pressing the mouse key, and pulling them in a particular direction.

Dramatic conflict: The central struggle between opposing forces in a story that drives the plot forward.

Dramatization (dramatic recreation, dramatic reconstruction): A film sequence depicting a particular incident.

Editorial: Non-technical guidance regarding how production elements should be created, refined, and implemented.

Editorial guidelines: A set of rules that dictate the style, structure, and strategy for an organization's content.

Effects (FX): Visual or audio illusions created to enhance storytelling in films, television, or games.

Embed code: A block of HTML code that allows a user to add content from another website to their own web page.

Embedding: Incorporating external content into a web page, including multimedia elements, documents, or interactive features, without hosting the content yourself.

Emergent storytelling (emergent narrative, procedural narrative): A narrative that develops from the player's interactions with a game.

Engine: The driving force behind the interaction.

Entry point: The location where a narrative strand begins.

Environment: The setting or location of specific scenes or levels.

Escape room: A room where players solve a series of puzzles within a set time to unlock a door and exit.

Experience inventory: A list of lived experiences from team members that can be drawn on for story ideas.

Experience points: Credits acquired by playing a game; the more you play, the more powerful you become.

Exposition Title: A graphic revealing key information about a story's plot.

Extended reality (XR): Immersive technologies that combine physical and digital worlds to create new ways of interacting and perceiving.

Facilitation plan: A scheme to organize an overall production process.

Facilitator: A logistical planner and supervisor of an entire IDN project or group of projects (e.g., a teacher or community organizer).

Feedback: Information conveyed about the user's progress through the IDN.

Field Audio (Wild Audio): The act of recording sound outside of a studio setting.

File-sharing platform: A digital tool that allows users to exchange files over the internet.

Filter: A mechanism that alters a media asset.

Final assembly: The completed version of the IDN.

Fishbone (zipper) pattern: A design that allows the player to veer off and explore occasional tangents before returning to the main narrative path.

Foldback: A narrative path that returns to a previous node.

Font: A typeface with distinct and consistent features.

Formative feedback: A process that provides students with information while they are learning, so they can adjust their learning in real time.

Forum: A digital space where users share information, solve problems, and brainstorm ideas.

Free Loop Video: A short, repeating video clip available for free.

Freemium: A monetization model offering basic features for free while charging for advanced or supplemental options.

Free roam: When a player can move around in a virtual world without limits or restrictions.

Free-to-Play: A monetization strategy that offers substantial content for free but requires payment to unlock certain features or endings.

Full Motion Video Game: A video game that uses pre-recorded video footage to display game action, rather than 3D models, vectors, or sprites.

Game hackathon: A collaborative event where participants work together to create a game within a set time frame.

Game jam: An event where participants try to make a video game from scratch. Depending on the format, participants might work independently, or in teams.

Game studio: A software developer that creates video games and/or IDNs.

Gamification: The application of typical elements of game playing (e.g., point scoring, competition with others, rules of play) to activities such as learning and marketing.

Gauntlet pattern: A fishbone structure modified with complex tangents and foldbacks.

Geo-tag: An electronic tag that assigns a geographical location to a photograph or video, a posting on social media, and so on.

GIF Compressor: A tool that reduces the file size of a GIF without sacrificing quality, allowing for faster loading times.

Giveaway: Free content or benefits provided to loyal users.

Graphic: A chart, diagram, infographic, or icon that conveys information while adhering to a uniform aesthetic.

Grid node: A specific type of landing node with a patchwork structure that displays multiple images.

Guerilla marketing strategies: Unconventional methods to promote a product or service

Guided practice: A teaching method where an educator helps students learn new skills or concepts, then allows them to practice independently.

Hieratic Scale: A visual design technique in which important elements are made larger to indicate their significance.

Holographic gauze (holo-gauze): A translucent, silvered projection screen that creates holographic illusions.

Holography: The study or production of holograms.

Homebrew: The creation of an unofficial IDN or game by exploiting vulnerabilities in proprietary software and game consoles.

Home node: The central hub the story paths extend from. It displays important information about the IDN, including entry points and possibly instructions.

Home return: An icon that directs the player back to the home page.

Hub: The center of an activity, region, or network.

Hypertext fiction (hyperfiction, digi fiction): A genre of digital literature that uses hypertext links to create a nonlinear narrative experience where readers can choose their own path through the story.

Icon: A symbol that indicates an opportunity for interaction.

iDoc (interactive documentary): A nonlinear work of digital nonfiction that gives users multiple ways to navigate through multimedia content.

iFrame: A tool that allows a creator to display multimedia content within an HTML document.

Immersive: Characterized by deep absorption in an artificial environment.

In-App Purchases: Extra content or services that can be bought within an app.

Influence POV: A perspective not tied to any character that influences the story in general.

Influencer: Person with the ability to influence potential users by promoting or recommending the IDN on social media.

Instances: Moments in narrative time when events occur.

Instruction node: A web page displaying information about how to navigate the IDN.

Interactive AI: A type of artificial intelligence that can communicate with users in real time, enabling two-way conversations.

Interactive book (choose your path, choose your own adventure): A physical volume that includes interactive features.

Interactive cinema: A type of storytelling that allows the audience to actively participate in the film and influence the plot.

Interactive digital narrative (IDN): A digital story that lets you make choices.

Interactive fiction (IF): A type of storytelling where the reader's choices impact the story's outcome, often resulting in multiple possible endings.

Interactive map: A diagram tagged with information about a particular physical space.

Interactive theater (immersive theater): A performance where the audience is directly involved with the action of the play, making them active participants instead of passive observers.

Interactive video: A digital video that allows viewers to interact with the content.

Interactivity: An exchange of information between a computer program and a human user.

Internet of Things (IoT): Technology that facilitates communication between devices and the cloud, and between the devices themselves.

Intrinsic motivation: The drive to do something because it is personally satisfying rather than due to external incentives or rewards.

Intro node: A web page with a button that triggers a media asset (video and/or audio file) with introductory information about the IDN.

Interview: A structured conversation where one participant asks questions, and the other provides answers.

Jigsaw/puzzle: An object or concept that needs to be built piece by piece (e.g., assembling a spaceship).

Kicking in the door: When a story master breaks a story lull by leaping forward or inventing a new plot twist.

Landing node: Any node—except the intro node and home node—the player lands on after selecting a decision point.

Landscape Aspect Ratio: The ratio of an image's width to its height, where the width is greater than the height (e.g., 16:9).

Launch asset: A short video or audio file that introduces key concepts related to the Interactive Digital Narrative.

Launch node: An Interactive Digital Narrative page that launches an introductory asset or node.

Launch point: A trigger that starts the introduction to an interactive story.

Law: A rule defining limits of interactivity within the story world (e.g., the player can switch paths without having to start over).

Layered: A hypertext structure where page of text features multiple links to various multimedia enhancements.

Level: A space where a player completes an objective.

Leveling: When experienced players gain more power, and new players struggle to reach that level.

Linear pattern: A unidirectional, chronological trajectory

Link: Clickable item that directs users to another page, document or other online content.

Link rot: The deterioration of hyperlinks over time, leading to broken links, data loss, and other issues.

Live-action footage: Cinematography or videography that captures images of actual physical locations and characters.

Live events: Gatherings that take place in real time, either in person or virtually.

Location scout: The search for a suitable location to film a dramatic sequence.

Location Title: A graphic revealing key information about a story's setting.

Locative (location-aware ambient, in situ) storytelling: A narrative designed to be experienced in a particular location using a combination of images, audio files, texts, and geo-tagged maps.

Lock-and-key (gating) pattern: A story element requiring the player to solve a puzzle, master a skill, or answer a question correctly before proceeding.

Logo: An emblem representing the IDN or specific character(s).

Loop-and-grow pattern: A structure that rotates through the same path multiple times, unlocking and shutting down features with each cycle.

Loop pattern: A foldback structure that involves repeatedly returning to a starting point.

Low-fi: A low-quality aesthetic with grainy images and distorted audio.

Ludic: Involving interactive choices, related to or characterized by play.

Machinima: A short film created by manipulating the real-time computer graphics of a video game.

Makeup test: The process of applying special-effects makeup before filming to ensure it looks good on camera.

Mapping: The use of symbols and colors to signpost navigational options.

Mashup: A mixture or fusion of disparate elements.

Maximalism: A high-impact aesthetic that uses the largest range of materials and colors possible, along with complicated shapes or forms.

Media maker: A digital platform that helps creators produce multimedia assets.

Menu: A feature that displays an array of navigation options.

Merch: Items related to an IDN that users can purchase.

Message window: A design feature that allows a Non-Player Character (NPC) or narrator to send a text responding to a choice made by the player.

Mind map: A visual diagram that organizes ideas and concepts using words, colors, and images.

Minimalism: An austere aesthetic that emphasizes simplicity and repetition.

Mixed reality (MR): A medium in which elements of physical and virtual environments are combined.

Mobile story: A narrative experienced on a mobile device, often a smartphone or tablet.

Modding: The act of modifying hardware, software, or anything else to perform a function not originally intended by the designer.

Modification point: An interactive option that alters some aspect of a node or asset.

Monetize: To make money from a project using strategies such as free-to-play or freemium.

Motif: A recurring visual or sound element.

Motion control sensor: A device that detects movement and converts it into electrical signals.

Multimedia (multimodal, digital) story: A narrative that employs multiple forms of media to enhance or portray the story.

Multiplayer: An IDN or game designed for multiple users.

Multiple endings: A story that concludes in different ways depending on the player's choices.

Multisensory Cinema: A movie-watching experience that engages multiple senses, such as sight, sound, touch, smell, and more.

Narrative: A spoken or written account of connected events.

Nerfing: Temporarily disadvantaging a character.

Networked: A hypertext structure that is radically nonlinear with no clear beginning, middle, or end.

News Game: A video game that incorporates journalistic principles to inform players about real-world news events.

Node: A location where paths converge and branch away.

Nonlinear: Not sequential or straightforward.

Non-Player Character (NPC): A character in the story world who is not controlled by the player.

Online communication hub: A site for sharing editable production schedules, location addresses, prop lists, shot plans, story designs, and more.

Online groups and forums: Communities in person or virtually where ideas and views on a particular issue can be exchanged.

Open world (open map): A structure that allows players to move in any direction for as long as they wish.

Overlay: A visual element placed on top of existing media, such as an image, video, or webpage.

Pantomime: A theatrical entertainment, mainly for children, which involves music, topical jokes, and slapstick comedy and is based on a fairy tale or nursery story, usually produced around Christmas.

Parallel pattern: Two linear stories placed side by side with links between them.

Parser-based IF: A type of narrative where players type natural-language commands, which are analyzed by software to determine the next action or scene.

Participant: A team member collaborating to create an IDN.

Path: A route between two nodes.

Pattern: A collection of nodes and paths representing or constituting the design of an IDN.

Permission marketing (pull marketing): Giving people an opportunity to opt in or out of receiving promotional materials and other content.

Permissions: The rights given to users to access and perform actions within an IDN.

Penalty: A punishment or handicap given to a player or team for breaking a rule or playing illegally.

Pepper's Ghost: a nineteenth-century technology that consists of an offstage figure reflected onto a pane of glass placed between an onstage performer and the audience. This makes it appear as if the performer is interacting with a wraithlike specter.

Personalization (customization): Designing or producing something to meet an individual's requirements.

Physical items: Valuables and curiosities acquired via gameplay and narrative interaction.

Platform: A software-based product or service that provides a foundation for other products or services to be developed.

Player: The person navigating through an IDN.

Player Character (PC): The perspective adopted by the player.

Player vs. environment: Conflict between the player and the level location.

Player vs. player: Conflict between characters.

Playthrough: The act of playing a game or activity from start to finish.

Plot: The main events of a story presented by the writer as an interrelated sequence.

Point and click: Unlocking information, events, tools, or actions with the cursor arrow.

Poll: A survey in which participants communicate responses via the internet, typically by completing a questionnaire on a webpage.

Pop-up window: An overlay that appears on top of a node, revealing a media element such as a still image, slideshow, video, audio file, or block of text.

Portrait Aspect Ratio: The ratio of an image's height to its width, where the height is greater than the width (e.g., 2:3).

Post hoc: Occurring or done after the event.

Post-it (sticky note) plan: A group of Post-it notes covered with story beats, tacked to a wall in different configurations to help organize a narrative.

POV interview: When the subject addresses the camera directly, as if speaking to the character represented by the player's first-person perspective.

Production plan: A scheme for designing and creating an IDN.

Production schedule: A detailed plan outlining the timeline and all stages of an IDN project, from preproduction to postproduction.

Progress bar: A design feature that indicates how much of the IDN the player has explored.

Projection mapping (video mapping, spatial augmented reality): A technique used to project dynamic two- and three-dimensional images onto previously static surfaces.

Project pitch: A brief written or verbal overview of the IDN.

Prop Master: A team member responsible for procuring and coordinating the use of props.

Prototype: A preliminary model, paper or digital, from which other forms are developed.

Pseudo-plat: A spoof of an existing media platform.

Pseudo-tool: A whimsical variation of an existing media tool.

Puppeteering: When a character in a game acts without input from the player.

Puzzle: A mechanism requiring the player to align images and texts to unlock information or progress the narrative.

QR code: A machine-readable code consisting of an array of black and white squares, typically used for storing URLs or other information for reading by the camera on a smartphone.

Quest: A task the Player Character is attempting to complete.

Quest pattern: A collection of concentric patterns loosely linked by branching paths.

Quiz: An interactive questionnaire embedded in the IDN.

Railroading: Forcing a player to follow a rigid, predetermined storyline.

Ramping: Acquiring tools, strength, skills, reputation points, and so on.

Randomization (Aleatory Mechanics): When each item has an equal chance of being assigned to any group.

Real Life (RL): Life as it is lived in reality, as distinct from a fictional or idealized world.

Real-Time Digital Collaboration: A team of creators working simultaneously to produce an IDN.

Recce (location scout): The process of visiting an area where the team plans to film to evaluate its suitability.

Rehearsed Reading: A script-in-hand performance of a theatrical piece with some preparation.

Reskinning: When a story master directs players to enter an unexplored part of the narrative.

Resource inventory: A list of all elements that might benefit the creation of an IDN.

Rewards: Bonuses given to a player for achieving things, for example, a spare player or ghost powers.

Riddle: A short obstacle that helps the player learn more about the world.

Role-playing: Adopting a fictional persona.

Roles and Goals: The specialized responsibilities team members take on and what they plan to accomplish.

Rough Assembly: A loosely configured version of the IDN.

Royalty-Free Media: Third-party media IDN creators can use without paying royalties.

Sandbox: An area for experimentation and testing.

Scoreboard/Scorecard: A tally of points received for performing a task or winning an honor.

Scrolling Story: A storytelling format in which visual and textual elements appear or change as the reader scrolls vertically or horizontally.

Seed book: A document for gathering ideas that can inspire the creation of an IDN.

Shooter: A type of action video game where players use weapons to defeat enemies.

Shot plan: A list of camera angles that the director and/or cinematographer plans to shoot.

Sim-plat: A simulation that imitates the functions of an online platform.

Sim-tool: A simulation that mimics a familiar media interface.

Single Player: A game or narrative played by one person.

Single-Player Choice-Based Interactive Digital Narrative (SCIDN): A digital story for a single user with interactive options.

Site-Specific Theater (Collaborative Mixed Reality, Performance Art): A dramatic production performed at an adapted location other than a theater, such as a factory or church.

Skill inventory: A list of the talents and expertise team members possess that may benefit the production process.

Skip point: An interactive element that allows the player to move ahead, avoiding tedious or redundant content.

Slideshow: A series of pictures that may advance automatically or by player input.

Socials: Online applications that enable users to create and share content or participate in social networking.

Social media mechanics: The way an online application functions.

Social media platform: A website or app that allows users to create, share, and interact with content.

Social media marketing: Using an online application as a promotional tool.

Sound design: Recurring musical themes and sound effects for the IDN.

Sound editing: Combining and mixing audio files.

Sound Effects (SFX): Artificially created or enhanced audio.

Spatial audio: A technology that creates the illusion of sound coming from multiple directions and distances.

Spatial computing: Forms of human-computer interaction taking place in the real world, in and around natural bodies and physical environments.

Splash Page: A page displayed before users can access other pages, often used as an introduction.

Spoke: Each of a set of radial tangents projecting from a central hub.

Spoke and hub pattern: A structure with major branches flowing to and from a central node or set of nodes.

State: A player's status, indicated by a menu, title, or play options, such as score, number of lives, or time remaining.

State tracking (delayed branching): When key choices are remembered and reflected later without requiring entirely new narrative paths. Variables that can be tracked include score, character reputation, skill level, items acquired or lost, time elapsed, and objectives achieved.

Stats Scorecard: A tool summarizing key details to track and improve performance.

Status meter: A design feature that indicates levels of various things gained or lost via state tracking, such as food, money, or love.

Still: A two-dimensional photographic image.

Stop-Motion Animation: The manipulation of objects (dolls, clay figures, LEGO) shot one frame at a time with a stationary camera so they appear to be moving.

Story app: A digital application that tells a story using a combination of images, sound, and print.

Storyboard: A sequence of drawings, often with directions and dialogue, representing the planned shots for a film or video production.

Story concept: The central premise of the IDN.

Storylet: Content unlocked by a set of prerequisites that have specific effects on the story world.

Story map: A graphic organizer that helps creators plot story sequences.

Story world: The fictional universe of a story, including its characters, settings, and events.

String of pearls (rivers and lakes) pattern: A plot that flows in a single direction, occasionally interrupted by free-roam moments when the player can explore nonlinear choices.

Style guide: A collection of elements that inform the audio and visual aesthetic of the IDN.

Summative feedback: Information aimed at helping students understand how well they have done in meeting the overall learning goals of the course.

Survey: A questionnaire that IDN users fill out, providing creators with helpful feedback as they seek to refine their work.

SWOT Analysis: A strategic planning tool that helps identify and assess the strengths, weaknesses, opportunities, and threats involved in a project or organization.

Tag: A special class of decision point that unlocks embellishments that don't directly influence the plot, such as a pop-up window appearing with expositional text.

Teledildonics: The practice of using networked electronic sex toys to remotely control a sexual experience.

Teleprompter (Autocue): A device that projects a speaker's script onto a transparent panel in front of a television camera lens so the speaker can read it while looking into the camera.

Testimonial: Statement testifying to the qualities of the IDN.

Theme: The main idea around which a story revolves.

Threaded pattern: A collection of intertwined threads representing different perspectives, locations, eras, and so on.

Ticking Clock: A plot device requiring the player to accomplish a task within a tight time frame.

Tile: A square on a playing field.

Time cave pattern: A branching sequence with little or no bottlenecking.

Timer: A ticking clock indicating time elapsed and time remaining.

Title: A textual element conveying key bits of information.

Tokens: Discs, medallions, badges, chips, coins, or money.

Transmedia story: A narrative distributed across multiple platforms, such as a blog, a comic, and a video game.

Treasure hunt: A game in which players search for hidden objects by following a trail of clues.

Triple-A video game: Video game produced or distributed by a major publisher with a large development and marketing budget.

Unilinear path: A narrative trajectory that moves in a single direction.

Upskilling: Mastering new abilities.

URL: A Uniform Resource Locator, colloquially known as an "address" on the Web, is a reference to a resource that specifies its location on a computer network.

User: A person navigating through an IDN.

User Experience (UX): The overall experience of a player when they are interacting with digital media.

User-Generated Content (UGC): Material created by users and uploaded to an IDN.

User testing: The process of having different users navigate your IDN and provide feedback.

Value Proposition: A feature or service that makes a product appealing to customers.

Variables: Customizable components related to the player.

Ventriloquism: When a character in a game speaks without input from the player.

VHS board game: An interactive game that combines a board game with a videotape to create gameplay.

Video: Moving images recorded digitally.

Video game (digital game): A game played by electronically manipulating images produced by a computer program on a display screen.

Video editing: Cutting and combining moving images with the help of digital tools.

Virtual Reality (VR): A computer-generated simulation of a three-dimensional image or environment that a person can interact with.

Virtual world: A computer-simulated environment, which may be populated by many simultaneous users.

Visibility: A design strategy that makes the structure of the IDN clear and straightforward.

Visual Effects (VFX): The process by which imagery is created or manipulated outside the context of a live-action shot in filmmaking.

Visual novel: A type of interactive fiction that combines text with static or animated illustrations, and sometimes video footage.

Visual Novel Maker: A software program for designing illustrated interactive stories.

Voting system: A digital interface that allows players to vote to influence outcomes.

VR headset: A device that you wear over your eyes to create a 3D virtual environment that you can explore.

Wallpaper: A digital image used as a decorative background for a device's graphical user interface.

Wearable VR: Headset, suit, or gloves that allow users to immerse themselves in a simulated virtual world.

Web Content Accessibility Guidelines (WCAG): A group of recommendations about improving digital accessibility by refining the design process.

Widget: An interactive element that can be inserted into an IDN.

Wiki: A shared document multiple users can edit simultaneously.

Wiki novel: A novel created collaboratively by multiple authors on a site allowing any user to add and edit content.

Bonus Sources

Readers of the print edition of this book can find clickable links available on the Bloomsbury online resource: https://www.bloomsburyonlineresources.com/creating-the-interactive-digital-narrative

360 Images

TeliportMe Blog (2024), "How to Make a 360° Image: A Comprehensive Guide," *TeliportMe Blog*, January 29. Available online: https://teliportme.com/blog/how-to-make-a-360-image-a-comprehensive-guide/ (accessed August 17, 2024).

Thinglink (2023), "The Best Methods to Create Your Own 360° Content," *Thinglink Blog*, August 9. Available online: https://www.thinglink.com/blog/create-your-own-360-content/ (accessed August 14, 2024).

Analog Games

Analog Games (2024), *Analog Games: World of Non-digital Games.* Available online: http://www.analoggames.com/about/ (accessed August 14, 2024).

Pulsipher, L. (2011), Boardgamegeek, ""Analog" versus "Digital" in Games." Available online: https://boardgamegeek.com/blogpost/5697/analog-versus-digital-in-games (accessed August 16, 2024).

Trammel, A. (2019), "Analog Games and the Digital Economy," *Analog Game Studies*. Available online: https://analoggamestudies.org/2019/03/analog-games-and-the-digital-economy/ (accessed August 17, 2024).

Animation

Animaker (2024), Available online: https://www.animaker.com/ (accessed August 19, 2024).

Artificial Intelligence (AI)

Gibson, C. (2024), "The Future of Interactive Content: AI-Driven Innovations," Medium. April 3. Available online: https://medium.com/@chasegison/the-future-of-interactive-content

-ai-driven-innovations-02061e44baf9#:~:text=The%20future%20of%20interactive
%20content%20is%20closely%20linked%20with%20AI,immersive%20and
%20personalized%20content%20experiences. (accessed August 19, 2024).

Audio

Malinverno, M. (2022), "What is Binaural Audio? How Binaural Recording Works," *Splice Blog*, June 28. Available online: https://splice.com/blog/what-is-binaural-audio/ (accessed August 19, 2024).

Gyori, B. (2022b), "Mr Illusion Taster Trailer," *YouTube*, August 15. Available online: https://www.youtube.com/watch?v=9amccMTSMB8 (accessed August 19, 2024).

Gyori, B. (2023), "Mr Illusion," *Soundcloud,* August 7. Available online: https://www.youtube.com/watch?v=9amccMTSMB8 (accessed August 19, 2024).

Augmented Reality (AR)

Ediiie (2024), "Storytelling with AR: How Augmented Reality is Revolutionizing Storytelling," *Ediiie.com*. Available online: https://www.ediiie.com/blog/storytelling-with-augmented-reality-ar/ (accessed August 14, 2024).

FasterCapital (2024b), "Immersive Storytelling Through Augmented Reality," *FasterCapital*. Available online: https://fastercapital.com/topics/immersive-storytelling-through-augmented-reality.html (accessed August 14, 2024).

Tomi, A.B. and Rambli, D.R.A. (2013), "An Interactive Mobile Augmented Reality Magical Playbook: Learning Number with the Thirsty Crow," *Procedia Computer Science*, 25: 123–130. Available online: https://www.sciencedirect.com/science/article/pii/S1877050913012209 (accessed August 17, 2024).

Biometric

Harpy (2023), "The Ever-Unfolding Plot: How AI and Biometrics Could Allow Stories to Adapt to Each Reader's Experience," *Kadaxis*, December 27. Available online: https://kadaxis.com/blog/2023/12/27/the-ever-unfolding-plot-how-ai-and-biometrics-could-allow-stories-to-adapt-to-each-readers-experience (accessed August 19, 2024).

Budget

11+ Production Budget Templates (2014), *Template.net.* Available online: https://www.template.net/business/budget-templates/production-budget-template/ (accessed August 14, 2024).

A Guide to Media Production Costs and Budgets (2024), *Flywheel Film.* Available online: https://www.flywheelfilm.com/learn/a-guide-to-media-production-costs-and-budgets (accessed August 17, 2024).

Budgeting for Digital Media (2024), *Vervaunt*. Available online: https://vervaunt.com/contact (accessed August 16, 2024).

What are the most effective ways to manage media project budgets? (2024), *Linkedin*. Available online: https://www.linkedin.com/advice/0/what-most-effective-ways-manage -media-project-fkzmc (accessed August 14, 2024).

Choice-based IF

Berkley, K. (2024), "Creating Interactive Fiction: Best Tools for Beginners," *Kim Berkley*. Available online: https://storytellerkim.com/index.php/creating-interactive-fiction-best -tools-for-beginners/ (accessed August 14, 2024).

Dutton, L. (2017), "Creating a Choose Your Own Adventure Story in Google Forms," *YouTube*. Available online: https://www.youtube.com/watch?v=vQt4EhX0Bbo (accessed August 14, 2024).

Five College Digital Humanities (2016), "How to Use Twine to Make Your Own Text Adventure Games!" *YouTube*, June 30. Available online: https://www.youtube.com/ watch?v=M41FFILqu_M (accessed August 14, 2024).

Hartnell, T. (1983), *Creating Adventure Games on Your Computer,* New York: Ballantine Books. Available online: https://colorcomputerarchive.com/repo/Documents/Books /Creating%20Adventure%20Games%20on%20Your%20Computer%20(Tim%20 Hartnell).pdf (accessed August 14, 2024).

Parodi, T. (2015), "Choose Your Own Adventure Powerpoint," *YouTube*. Available online: https://www.youtube.com/watch?v=REj3pmOVACM (accessed August 14, 2024).

Rossi, G.C. (2023), "Writing Tools for Interactive Fiction – an Updated List," *British Library: Digital Scholarship Blog*, August 2. Available online: https://blogs.bl.uk/digital -scholarship/2023/08/writing-tools-for-interactive-fiction-an-updated-list.html (accessed August 17, 2024).

Tech with Tim (2023), "Tython AI Choose Your Own Adventure Game," *YouTube*. Available online: https://www.youtube.com/watch?v=nhYcTh6vw9A (accessed August 17, 2024).

Zinnea (2022), "How to Make a Choose Your Own Adventure Game in Scratch," *YouTube*. Available online: https://www.youtube.com/watch?v=vQt4EhX0Bbo (accessed August 17, 2024).

Cinemagraph

Kerekes, C. (2021), "How to Animate a Cinemagraph in Photoshop," *YouTube*. Available online: https://www.youtube.com/watch?v=Jvpgfob2X-0 (accessed August 19, 2024).

Cinematography

Katz, S.D. (1991), *Film Directing Shot by Shot: Visualizing from Concept to Screen,* Waltham, MA: Focal Press. Available online: https://www.craftfilmschool.com/userfiles/files/Film%20Directing%20Shot%20by%20Shot_%20Visualizing%20from%20Concept%20to%20Screen.pdf (accessed August 19, 2024).

Night, B. (2020), "Film Coverage – A Step-by-Step Guide to Shot Listing Efficiently," *Studiobinder*, May 24. Available online: https://www.studiobinder.com/blog/film-coverage/ (accessed August 19, 2024).

Studiobinder (2020), "The Ultimate Guide to Camera Shots (50+ Types of Shots and Angles in Films)," *Studiobinder*, September 13. Available online: https://www.studiobinder.com/blog/ultimate-guide-to-camera-shots/ (accessed August 19, 2024).

Wu, R. (2020), "A Beginners Guide to Shooting Coverage for a Film Project," *The Beat*, March 27. Available online: https://www.premiumbeat.com/blog/shooting-coverage-film-project/ (accessed August 19, 2024).

Clearance

How to Find and Use Media Assets (Legally) (2020), *Berkeley: Advanced Media Institute.* Available online: https://multimedia.journalism.berkeley.edu/tutorials/media-assets/ (accessed August 19, 2024).

What is Rights Clearance? (2024), *IndieClear.* Available online: https://indieclear.com/what-is-rights-clearance/ (accessed August 19, 2024).

Coding

Capella, W. (2024), "Best Online Coding Bootcamps," *Computer Science.* Available online: https://www.computerscience.org/bootcamps/rankings/best-online-bootcamps/ (accessed August 17, 2024).

Juviler, J. (2024), "How to Start Coding: The Ultimate Guide for Beginner Programmers," *Hubspot,* July 9. Available online: https://blog.hubspot.com/website/how-to-start-coding (accessed August 14, 2024).

Crowdfunding

Crowdfunder (2024), Available online: https://www.crowdfunder.co.uk/ (accessed August 19, 2024).

Gofundme (2024), Available online: https://www.gofundme.com/en-gb (accessed August 19, 2024).

Indiegogo (2024), Available online: https://www.indiegogo.com/ (accessed August 19, 2024).

Kickstarter (2024), Available online: https://www.kickstarter.com/?ref=nav (accessed August 19, 2024).

Smith, T. (2024), "Crowdfunding: What It Is, How It Works, and Popular Websites," *Investopedia*, May 30. Available online: https://www.investopedia.com/terms/c/crowdfunding.asp (accessed August 19, 2024).

Crowdsourcing

Riserbato, R. (2020), "The Ultimate Guide to Crowdsourcing," *HubSpot*, April 22. Available online: https://blog.hubspot.com/marketing/crowdsourcing (accessed August 19, 2024).

Curation

Das, T. (2024), "What is Bit Rot and How to Prevent it?" *Geekflare*, January 2. Available online: https://geekflare.com/bit-rot-prevention/ (accessed August 14, 2024).
Christison, C. (2024), "Content Curation in 2024: Everything You Need to Know," *Hootsuite*, July 9. Available online: https://blog.hootsuite.com/beginners-guide-to-content-curation/ (accessed August 22, 2024).
Clark, L. (2019), "Collecting Interactive Fiction," *British Library: UK Web Archive Blog*, March 29. Available online: https://blogs.bl.uk/webarchive/2019/03/archiving-interactive-fiction.html (accessed August 22, 2024).

Desktop

Gyori, B. (2019b), *Shelley's Heart Desktop Version*. Available online: http://maps.shelleysheart.com/#Mary_Map_1 (accessed August 17, 2024).

Directing

Weston, J. (1996), *Directing Actors: Creating Memorable Performances for Film and Television*, Los Angeles: Michael Wiese Productions. Available online: https://www.scribd.com/document/497418414/Directing-Actors-25th-Anniversary-Edition (accessed August 19, 2024).

Editorial

Lambert, C. (2022), "Embeds, Links and Interactive Content Editorial Guidelines," *Google for Creators*. Available online: https://creators.google/en-us/content-creation-guides/modern-storytelling-with-web-stories/embeds-links-and-interactive-content-editorial-guidelines/ (accessed August 19, 2024).
Porter, J. (2024), "How to Create Editorial Guidlines that are Actually Useful," *Optimizely*, March 13. Available online: https://www.optimizely.com/insights/blog/how-to-create-editorial-guidelines-that-are-actually-useful-template/ (accessed August 19, 2024).

Editing Film/Video

Abreu, R. (2022), "What is Film Editing—Editing Principles & Techniques Explained," *Studiobinder*, February 13. Available online: https://www.studiobinder.com/blog/what-is -film-editing-definition/ (accessed August 19, 2024).

Murch, W. (2001), *In the Blink of an Eye: A Perspective on Film Editing*, Los Angeles: Silman-James Press. Available online: https://www.craftfilmschool.com/userfiles/files/Walter %20Murch%20-%20In%20the%20Blink%20of%20an%20Eye%20Revised%202nd %20Edition%20(2001%2C%20Silman-James%20Pr).pdf (accessed August 19, 2024).

Emergent Narrative

Emergent Narrative (2024), TV Tropes. Available online: https://tvtropes.org/pmwiki/pmwiki .php/Main/EmergentNarrative#:~:text=An%20%22emergent%20narrative%22%20or %20%22,interactions%20with%20various%20gameplay%20subsystems (accessed August 19, 2024).

Warner, N. (2022), "The Art of Make Believe: Emergent Narrative in Games," *Destructoid.co m.* Available online: https://www.destructoid.com/emergent-narrative-video-games-art -of-make-believe/ (accessed August 19, 2024).

Escape Room

Billock, J. (2024), "World-Competitive Escape Rooms Are Darker, Scarier, and More Scientific," *Atlas Obscura*, April 25. Available online: https://questfactor.us/blog/escape -room-theory/#:~:text=Here"s%20what%20escape%20room%20theory,another%20 riddle%20in%20the%20room (accessed August 17, 2024).

Escape Room Theory (2024), *Quest Factor*. Available online: https://questfactor.us/blog/ escape-room-theory/#:~:text=Here"s%20what%20escape%20room%20theory,anoth er%20riddle%20in%20the%20room (accessed August 17, 2024).

Extended Reality (XR)

Skult, N. and Smed, J. (2020), "Interactive Storytelling in Extended Reality: Concepts for the Design," *Game User Experience and Player-Cantered Design*, April 7. Available online: https://link.springer.com/chapter/10.1007/978-3-030-37643-7_21 (accessed August 14, 2024).

Malik, F. (2024), "Difference Between Mixed Reality and Extended Reality," *Educative.io* . Available online: https://www.educative.io/answers/difference-between-mixed-reality -and-extended-reality (accessed August 14, 2024).

Feed

Easiest way to add a Social Feed to Your Site for Free, The (2024), *Curator*. Available online: https://curator.io/ (accessed August 21, 2024).

Flash

Rowley, R. (2023), "Two Years On: What Did We Really Lose When Flash Player Died?" *Overclockers UK*, February 24. Available online: https://www.overclockers.co.uk/blog/two-years-on-what-did-we-really-lose-when-flash-player-died/#:~:text=The%20Death%20of%20Flash%20Player,download%20links%20for%20Flash%20installers (accessed August 22, 2024).

Newton, C. (2021), "Winding Down: The Death of Flash and a Critical Review of 'Coil'," *Idols and Realities: Monsters, Media and Metaphysics*, April 18. Available online: https://idolsandrealities.wordpress.com/2021/04/18/winding-down-the-death-of-flash-and-a-critical-review-of-coil-2008/ (accessed August 22, 2024).

Form

Blasbalg, C.L. (2024), "10 Best Forums for Online Communities (Free and Paid)," *WIXBlog*, March 3. Available online: https://www.wix.com/blog/best-forum-software (accessed August 21, 2024).

Giveaway

Lore, J. (n.d.), "How to Do a Facebook Giveaway: A Step-By-Step Guide," *Wishpond*, Available online: https://blog.wishpond.com/post/115675437312/how-to-run-a-giveaway-on-facebook (accessed August 21, 2024).

Palka, K. (2023), "Instagram Story Giveaway: How to Pick a Winner from Stories," *Easypromos*, May 11. Available online: https://www.easypromosapp.com/blog/en/instagram-story-giveaway/ (accessed August 21, 2024).

Sumon, S. (2024), "How to Do a Giveaway: 7 Tips to Go Viral in 2024," *Wedevs,* April 9. Available online: https://wedevs.com/blog/451511/how-to-do-a-giveaway/ (accessed August 21, 2024).

Holograph

Network, The (2024), "Holographic Entertainment: Step into the Future of Immersive Experiences," *The Nework*, January 18. Available online: https://tothenetwork.com/holographic-entertainment-step-into-the-future-of-immersive-experiences/ (accessed August 17, 2024).

Perry. J. (2016), "Holographic Storytelling: The Stories of Holocaust Survivors are Brought to Life with the Help of Interactive 3D Technologies," *VML*, June 16. Available online: https://www.vml.com/insight/holographic-storytelling (accessed August 19, 2024).

Hypertext Fiction (Hyperfiction, Digi Fiction)

Clifton, M. (2021), "Hypertext Fiction: The Literary Genre that was Theorized Before it was Written," *Berkeley Fiction Review*, August 2. Available online: https://berkeleyfiction

review.org/2021/08/02/hypertext-fiction-the-literary-genre-that-was-theorized-before-it
-was-written/ (accessed August 14, 2024).

Rizer, A. (2021), "A Guide to Hypertext Literature," *Book Riot*, November 15. Available
online: https://bookriot.com/a-guide-to-hypertext-literature/ (accessed August 16, 2024).

Icebreakers

Cserti, R. (2024), "61 Ice Breaker Games [That Your Team Won't Find Cheesy],"
SessionLab. Available online: https://www.sessionlab.com/blog/icebreaker-games/
(accessed August 14, 2024).

iDoc (Interactive Documentary)

Gyori, B. and Charles, M. (2017), "Designing Journalists: Teaching Journalism Students
to Think Like Web Designers," *Journalism and Mass Communication Educator*, 73 (2).
Available online: https://journals.sagepub.com/doi/abs/10.1177/1077695817713424
(accessed August 14, 2024).

I-docs (2024), *I-docs.org.* Available online: https://www.facebook.com/groups/iDocs/
(accessed August 17, 2024).

Wagner, V. (n.d.), "Crafting Digression: Interactivity and Gamification in Creative Nonfiction,"
Assay: A Journal of Nonfiction Studies. Available online: https://www.assayjournal.com/
vivian-wagner-crafting-digression-interactivity-and-gamification-in-creative-nonfiction-51
.html (accessed August 19, 2024).

iFrame

Best iFrame Widgets, The (2024), *Elfsight*. Available online: https://elfsight.com/iframe
-widgets/ (accessed August 19, 2024).

iFrame Generator (2024), Available online: https://www.iframe-generator.com/ (accessed
August 19, 2024).

Juviler, J. (2022), "What is an IFrame? [+ How to Embed Content With Iframes]," *HubSpot*,
June 17. Available online: https://blog.hubspot.com/website/what-is-an-iframe#:~:text
=The%20iframe%20element%20is%20specified,within%20a%20different%20web
%20page (accessed August 19, 2024).

Interactive AI

AI Writing (2023), "AI and Interactive Storytelling: Exploring the Possibilities of AI-Powered
Narratives," *On-Page by Traffic Research*, June 9. https://blog.on-page.ai/ai-and
-interactive-storytelling/ (accessed August 17, 2024).

Storynest (2024), *Storynest.ai.* Available online: https://storynest.ai/ (accessed August 16,
2024).

Interactive Book

Choose Your Own Adventure Book List (2024), *Goodreads*. Available online: https://www
.goodreads.com/list/tag/choose-your-own-adventure (accessed August 16, 2024).
Chooseyourownstory.com (2024), *Halogen Studios Entertainment*. Available online: https://
chooseyourstory.com/ (accessed August 16, 2024).

Interactive Cinema

Matt, L. (2021), "Video Games and Film: Understanding Interactive Cinema," *University Of
Washington*. Available online: https://uw.pressbooks.pub/cat2/chapter/video-games
-and-film-understanding-interactive-cinema/ (accessed August 17, 2024).
Walker, A. (2023), "Interactive Cinema: How Films Could Alter Plotlines in Real Time by
Responding to Viewers" Emotions," *The Conversation*, March 20. Available online:
https://theconversation.com/interactive-cinema-how-films-could-alter-plotlines-in-real
-time-by-responding-to-viewers-emotions-200145 (accessed August 14, 2024).

Interactive Digital Narrative (IDN)

Accessible Interactive Fiction (2024), *intfiction.org*. Available online: https://intfiction.org/t/
accessible-interactive-fiction/61668 (accessed January 19, 2025).
Crawford, C. (2006), "Dragon Speech 'I Had a Dream'," *YouTube*. Available online: https://
www.youtube.com/watch?v=CBrj4S24074 (accessed August 17, 2024).
Failbetter Games (2024), Available online: https://www.failbettergames.com/ (accessed
August 19, 2024).
Making-Of Articles (n.d.), *The Interactive Fiction Wiki*. Available online: https://www.ifwiki
.org/Craft#Making-Of_Articles (accessed August 14, 2024).
Short, E. (2014), "Writing in Collaboration with the System," *Emily Short's Interactive
Storytelling*. Available online: https://emshort.blog/2014/10/29/writing-in-collaboration
-with-the-system/ (accessed August 17, 2024).
Twine Cookbook (2021), "Welcome to the Twine Cookbook," *Twinery*. Available online:
https://twinery.org/cookbook/ (accessed August 14, 2024).

Interactive Fiction (IF)

Emshort (2024), "IF Interfaces," *Pinterest*. Available online: https://www.pinterest.com/
emshortif/if-interfaces/ (accessed August 16, 2024).
Hardjono, H. (2022), "Simulating a Parser in Twine?" *Intfiction.org: the Interactive Fiction
Community Forum*. Available online: https://intfiction.org/t/simulating-a-parser-in-twine
-split-from-the-art-of-language-agnostic-design/54883 (accessed August 16, 2024).
Locke (2018), "Parser Vs. Hyperlinks?" *Intfiction.org: the Interactive Fiction Community
Forum*. Available online: https://intfiction.org/t/parser-vs-hyperlinks/13004 (accessed
August 17, 2024).

Mattchelen (2024), "Another Interactive Fiction Engine List," *Google Sheets*. Available
online: https://docs.google.com/spreadsheets/d/1-B1yKlateTpwTdRNT9W
_ZjDzC6XnFpHXrcZ4nr_x7LQ/edit?gid=0#gid=0 (accessed August 17, 2024).

Porpentine (2012a), "Creation Under Capitalism and the Twine Revolution," *Nightmare
Mode*, November 25. Available online: https://nightmaremode.thegamerstrust.com
/2012/11/25/creation-under-capitalism/ (accessed August 17, 2024).

Reed, A. (2023), "50 Years of Text Games," *Substack*, October 21. Available online: https://
if50.substack.com/p/print-on-demand-edition-of-50-years (accessed August 17, 2024).

Interactive Theater (Immersive Theater)

Immersology: Structures and Theories of Immersive Theatre (2017), *Strange Bird
Immersive*, July 27. Available online: https://strangebirdimmersive.com/immersology/
category/immersive-101/ (accessed August 17, 2024).

Wellham, K. (2024), "Immersive and Interactive Theatre," *Immersive Experience Network*.
Available online: https://immersiveexperience.network/articles/immersive-and-
interactive-theatre/ (accessed August 16, 2024).

The Internet of Things (IoT)

Kardoyianni, S. (2024), "The Importance of Interactivity in Modern Digital Experiences,"
Yodeck, August 14. Available online: https://www.yodeck.com/news/future-of
-interactivity/ (accessed August 30, 2024).

Kumar, A. (2024), "The Future of Interaction Design," *Medium*, April 24. Available online:
https://medium.com/@adhundhara/the-future-of-interaction-design-596f4a64962d
(accessed August 17, 2024).

Link

Dean, B. (2024), "What are Backlinks?" *Backlinko,* August 16. Available online: https://
backlinko.com/hub/seo/backlinks (accessed August 19, 2024).

Location

MasterClass (2021), "Location Scouting Guide: How to Scout Locations for a Film,"
MasterClass, September 8. Available online: https://www.masterclass.com/articles/how
-to-scout-locations-for-a-film (accessed August 19, 2024).

Locative (Location-Aware Ambient, In-Stu) Storytelling

Abba, T. (2017), "A Manifesto for Ambient Literature," *Ambient Literature*, May. Available
online: https://research.ambientlit.com/index.php/a-manifesto-for-ambient-literature/
(accessed August 17, 2024).

Craven, E. (2022), "Locative Storytelling and Writing for Apps," *Story City*, February 3. Available online: https://research.ambientlit.com/index.php/a-manifesto-for-ambient -literature/ (accessed August 17, 2024).

Gottstein, J., Johnson, L., Macpherson, J., Morgan, R., and Peters, S. (2017), "The World as Your Canvas: Telling Location Based Stories," *Game Developers Conference*, December 15. Available online: https://www.youtube.com/watch?v=9sGDQRc-NA8 (accessed August 17, 2024).

How to Put Your Location on Snapchat Story (2023), *How to Wisdom*, December 2. Available online: https://www.youtube.com/watch?v=HDtRqYBbQbM (accessed August 14, 2024).

Jarvis, J. (2008), "Ambient Intimacy," *BuzzMachine,* May 6. Available online: https:// buzzmachine.com/2008/05/06/ambient-intimacy/ (accessed August 19, 2024).

Nance, T. (2023), "How To Add Custom Location to Instagram Story," *YouTube*, February 13. Available online: https://www.youtube.com/watch?v=T-Wcr_wyYqM (accessed August 17, 2024).

Packer, H.S., Hargood, C., Howard, Y., and Papadopoulos, P. (2017), "Developing a Writer's Toolkit for Interactive Locative Storytelling," *10th International Conference on Interactive Digital Storytelling*, November. Available online: https://www.researchgate.net /publication/320766852_Developing_a_Writer"s_Toolkit_for_Interactive_Locative_Stor ytelling (accessed August 14, 2024).

Ludic and Narrative Pleasures

Brislin, S. (2013), "Balancing Narrative and Gameplay," *Game Developer*. Available online: https://www.gamedeveloper.com/design/balancing-narrative-and-gameplay (accessed August 14, 2024).

Failbetter Games (2024), Available online: https://www.failbettergames.com/ (accessed August 19, 2024).

Homebrew (2025), *Wikipedia*. Available online: https://en.wikipedia.org/wiki/Homebrew_ (video_games) (accessed January 1, 2025).

Ikonomi, J. (2022), *Issuu*. Available online: https://issuu.com/polisuniversity/docs/ikonomi _thesis_final_19_june_2022_pdf_a/101 (accessed August 19, 2024).

Kehoe, J. 2017 (2017), "Ludology vs. Narratology: The Story and the Sandbox," *The Writer's Block*. Available online: https://thewritersblockonline.wordpress.com/2017/02 /11/ludology-vs-narratology-the-story-and-the-sandbox/ (accessed August 17, 2024).

Open World (2024), *Wikipedia*. Available online: https://en.wikipedia.org/wiki/Open_world (accessed August 19, 2024).

Sandbox Game (2024), *Wikipedia*. Available online: https://en.wikipedia.org/wiki/Sandbox _game (accessed August 14, 2024).

Short, E. (2020), "IF Meetup Jan 2020 Storylets," *YouTube*, February 23. Available online: https://www.youtube.com/watch?v=0zDXcVc5zv0 (accessed August 19, 2024).

Video Game Modding (2024), *Wikipedia*. Available online: https://en.wikipedia.org/ wiki/Video_game_modding#:~:text=Video%20game%20modding%20(short%20 for,sub%2Ddiscipline%20of%20general%20modding (accessed August 19, 2024).

Machinima

Machinima (2024), *Wikipedia.* Available online: https://en.wikipedia.org/wiki/Machinima (accessed August 17, 2024).

Media Asset

Spacey, J. (2023), "41 Examples of Media Assets," *Simplicable*, July 10. Available online: https://simplicable.com/en/media-assets (accessed August 19, 2024).

Merch

Sayana (2022), "How to Create and Sell Merch as an Artist," *Splice Blog*, January 31. Available online: https://splice.com/blog/how-to-make-sell-merch-as-an-artist/ (accessed August 22, 2024).

Mind Map

Free Online Mind Maps (2024), *Canva.* Available online: https://www.canva.com/graphs/mind-maps/ (accessed August 19, 2024).
How to Make a Mind Map (2024), *Lucidchart.* Available online: https://www.lucidchart.com/pages/how-to-make-a-mind-map (accessed August 19, 2024).

Mixed Reality (MR)

Gera, E. (2019), "Not Quite Film, or Games … Is Interactive Mixed Reality the Future of Storytelling?," *The Guardian*. Available online: https://www.theguardian.com/games/2019/may/02/vr-mixed-reality-storytelling-sundance-festival-new-frontier-narratives (accessed August 16, 2024).
Mixed Reality Applications for Interactive Storytelling (2024), Available online: https://newdiscovery.agency/mixed-reality-applications-for-interactive-storytelling/ (accessed August 16, 2024).

Mobile Story

Creating Interactive Stories with Mobile Apps (2024), July 16. Available online: https://developersappindia.com/blog/creating-interactive-stories-with-mobile-apps (accessed August 17, 2024).
Karlin, M. (2017), "Lightwell: Create and Publish Your Own Interactive Story App," *The Ed Tech Round Up.* Available online: http://www.edtechroundup.org/reviews/lightwell-create-and-publish-your-own-interactive-story-app (accessed August 16, 2024).

Multimedia Story (AKA Multimodal, Digital)

Koon-Stack, C. (2020), "How to Incorporate Multimedia into Your Storytelling," *Storytelling.* Available online: https://www.storytelling.comnetwork.org/explore/172/how-to -incorporate-multimedia-into-your-storytelling (accessed August 14, 2024).

Sapega, M. (n.d.), "How to get Started with Multimedia Storytelling," *Shorthand.* Available online: https://shorthand.com/the-craft/tips-tools-guides-for-multimedia-storytellers/ (accessed August 19, 2024).

Multiplayer Game

8 Factors of Multiplayer Game Development, The (2024), *Go Create.* Available online: https://unity.com/how-to/multiplayer-game-development-factors (accessed August 17, 2024).

Ixie (2024), "A Beginner's Guide to Multiplayer Game Development," *Ixie.* Available online: https://www.ixiegaming.com/blog/guide-to-multiplayer-game-development/ (accessed August 16, 2024).

Moy, T.W. (2023), "Multiplayer Narrative Games: Do They Exist?" *Intfiction.org.* Available online: https://intfiction.org/t/multiplayer-narrative-games-do-they-exist/55117 (accessed August 19, 2024).

Node Assembly

Phillipps, C. (2019), "All Choice No Consequence: Efficiently Branching Narrative," *YouTube.* Available online: https://www.youtube.com/watch?v=TEa9aSDHawA&t=1s (accessed August 19, 2024).

Otome

Otome Game (2024), *Wikipedia.* Available online: https://en.wikipedia.org/wiki/Otome _game#:~:text=In%20the%20visual%20novel%20examples,minigames%20or%20by %20raising%20stats (accessed August 19, 2024).

Paths

Cid, D. (2024), "Linear or Nonlinear, That is the Question," *Scruffy Dog Creative Group,* January 9. Available online: https://www.scruffydogltd.com/linear-or-not-linear-that-is -the-question/ (accessed August 19, 2024).

Freed, A. (2014), "Branching Conversation Systems and the Working Writer, Part 2: Design Considerations," *Game Developer,* September 9. Available online: https://www .gamedeveloper.com/design/branching-conversation-systems-and-the-working-writer -part-2-design-considerations (accessed August 19, 2024).

Holcomb, A. (2015), "String of Pearls: An Alternative Way to Create a Story," *Creative Screenwriting*, August 19. Available online: https://www.creativescreenwriting.com/string-of-pearls-an-alternative-way-to-create-a-story/ (accessed August 19, 2024).

Kolte, A. (n.d.), "Hub and Spoke Progress System for Character Individuality," *Into the Echo*. Available online: https://intotheecho.online/blog/hub-and-spoke-progression-for-character-individuality (accessed August 19, 2024).

Short, E. (2024), "Multilinear IF," *Emily Short's Interactive Storytelling*. Available online: https://emshort.blog/how-to-play/writing-if/my-articles/multilinear-if-older (accessed August 19, 2024).

Quest Video Games (2024), *Wikipedia*. Available online: https://en.wikipedia.org/wiki/Quest_(video_games) (accessed August 19, 2024).

Taylor, S. (2016), "Sara Taylor on Multi-threaded Narratives," *Penguin*, February 26. Available online: https://www.penguin.co.uk/articles/2016/02/sara-taylor-on-multi-threaded-narratives (accessed August 19, 2024).

Parser-based IF

Code with Huw (2022), "How To Parse User Input (Complete Course in Adventure Game Programming)," *YouTube*. Available online: https://www.youtube.com/watch?v=mgjwjd3Led4 (accessed August 14, 2024).

Crowther, W. (1976), "Colossal Cave Adventure," *Colossal Cave Adventure Page*. Available online: https://rickadams.org/adventure/ (accessed August 14, 2024).

Wright, E. (2017), "Making a Text Adventure Parser," *YouTube*. Available online: https://www.youtube.com/watch?v=ll3O1CJA-x8&t=1259s (accessed August 16, 2024).

Infocom-type Parser (2006), *IFWiki*. Available online: https://www.ifwiki.org/Infocom-type_parser (accessed August 17, 2024).

Permissions

Rusbridge, A. (2024), "Permissions Management: A Developers" Perspective on Authorization," *PingIdentity*, April 15. Available online: https://www.pingidentity.com/en/resources/blog/post/permissions-management-authorization-perspective.html (accessed August 19, 2024).

Permission Marketing

Godin, S. (2008), "Permission Marketing," *Seth's Blog*, January 31. Available online: https://seths.blog/2008/01/permission-mark/ (accessed August 21, 2024).

Personalization

Newman, D. (2023), "The Future of Personalization: What You Need to Know," *Forbes*. Available online: https://www.forbes.com/sites/danielnewman/2023/05/07/the-future-of-personalization-what-you-need-to-know/ (accessed August 21, 2024).

Poll (Survey)

Rebelo, M. (2023), "The 12 Best Free Survey Tools and Form Builders," *Zapier*. Available online: https://zapier.com/blog/best-free-survey-tool-form-app/ (accessed August 19, 2024).

Post-it (Sticky note) Plan

Barrera, J. (2022), "How to use Post-it Notes to Visually Organize your Story," *Story Embers*. Available online: https://storyembers.org/how-to-use-post-it-notes-to-visually -organize-your-story/ (accessed August 19, 2024).
Easy Planning Using Post-it Notes (2024), *Canva*. Available online: https://www.canva.com /graphs/mind-maps/ (accessed August 19, 2024).
Freehand - the All-in-one Collaborative Workplace (2024), *Invision*. Available online: https:// www.invisionapp.com/ (accessed August 19, 2024).

Production Planning

Brewer, D. (2024), "Basics of Project Development for a Media Organization," *Media Helping Media*. Available online: https://mediahelpingmedia.org/strategy/basics-of -project-development-for-a-media-organisation/ (accessed August 19, 2024).
Jovan (2017), "What is a Production Schedule and Why is it Important," *Squaredaisy*, August 15. Available online: https://www.squaredaisy.com/video-production-schedule/ (accessed August 19, 2024).
Price, L. (2017), "Robert Rodriguez's "Make a Film With What You've Got" Method," *Raindance*. Available online: https://raindance.org/robert-rodriguezs-make-film-youve -got-method/ (accessed August 19, 2024).
Shorr, A. (2019), "15 Pro Tips to Create a More Encouraging Production Schedule," *Studiobinder*, July 18. Available online: https://www.studiobinder.com/blog/15-PRO TIPs-to-create-a-better-production-schedule (accessed August 19, 2024).
Srinivasan, P. (2024), "10 Production Schedule Templates for Production Planning," *ClickUp*. Available online: https://clickup.com/blog/production-schedule-templates/ (accessed August 19, 2024).

Projection Mapping

Build an Interactive Projection Mapping Installation (2021), *Bare Conductive*, February 9. Available online: https://www.bareconductive.com/blogs/resources/create-an -interactive-projection-mapping-installation (accessed August 16, 2024).
What is Interactive Projection Mapping (2024), *Dominion*. Available online: https://www .dominionprint.com/what-is-interactive-projection-mapping-and-how-does-it-work/#:~ :text=The%20difference%20between%20interactive%20and,include%20interactive %20floors%20and%20walls (accessed August 17, 2024).

Prototyping

Figma Prototyping (2024), *Figma*. Available online: https://www.figma.com/prototyping/ (accessed August 19, 2024).

Lucidchart (2024), *Lucid*. Available online: https://www.lucidchart.com/pages/? (accessed August 19, 2024).

Prototyping for All (2024), *Proto.io*. Available online: https://proto.io (accessed August 19, 2024).

Ranking

How to Create an Online Ranking System (2024), *KeepTheScore*. Available online: https://keepthescore.com/blog/posts/ranking-leaderboards/ (accessed August 19, 2024).

Real Time Digital Collaboration

Mahas, G. (2019), "Folktale Let's You Create and Add to Other People's Stories," *Trendhunter*, November 11. Available online: https://www.trendhunter.com/trends/collaborative-storytelling-platform (accessed August 16, 2024).

Nichols, E., Gao, L., and Gomez, R. (2020), "Collaborative Storytelling with Large-scale Neural Language Modes," *Association for Computing Machinery*, October 1. Available online: https://dl.acm.org/doi/fullHtml/10.1145/3424636.3426903 (accessed August 17, 2024).

Remix Culture. (2024), *Wikipedia*. Available online: https://en.wikipedia.org/wiki/Remix_culture (accessed August 14, 2024).

Role Playing

DM Lair, The (2022), "10 Tricks to Improve Your Roleplaying in Dungeons & Dragons." Available online: https://www.youtube.com/watch?v=-Szzvnz2fDg&ab_channel=theDMLair (accessed January 1, 2025).

Townshend, K. (2023), "Live and Let Larp: Playing a Medieval Ruler in a Magical Kingdom Could Change Your Life," *Independent*. Available online: https://www.independent.co.uk/life-style/larping-uk-live-action-role-playing-b2369244.html (accessed August 16, 2024).

Williams, C. (1990), "D&D Beyond," *Wizards of the Coast*. Available online: https://www.dndbeyond.com/how-to-play-dnd (accessed August 14, 2024).

Scrolling Story

Publish Scrollytelling Stories with Shorthand (2024), *Shorthand.* Available online: https://shorthand.com/lp/scrolltelling/index.html?utm_source=google&utm_medium=cpc&utm_campaign=18146304662&utm_content=142171011924&utm_term=scrollytelling&gad

_source=1&gclid=CjwKCAjwzIK1BhAuEiwAHQmU3jcRQVE0R9Mp14QTd4hUtZIXM3L
aZgWTf1LtKyxHII8n1Sw9lEDzVBoCkMQQAvD_BwE (accessed August 14, 2024).

What is Scrollytelling Anyway? (2024), *Shorthand*. Available online: https://shorthand.com/
the-craft/an-introduction-to-scrollytelling/index.html (accessed August 14, 2024).

Site-Specific Theater (Collaborative Mixed Reality, Performance Art)

Bowditch, R., Tobin, D.B., Pace, C., and Devine, M. (2018), "Four Principles about Site-
Specific Theatre: A Conversation on Architecture, Bodies, and Presence," *Theatre
Journal*, March 1. Available online: https://www.jhuptheatre.org/theatre-topics/online
-content/issue/theatre-topics-volume-28-number-1-march-2018/four-principles
(accessed August 14, 2024).

Hamburger, A. (2019), "The Why and How of Site-Specific: From Then to Now," *Howlround
Theatre Commons,* May 2. Available online: https://howlround.com/why-and-how-site
-specific (accessed August 16, 2024).

Social

Bartimus, A. (n.d.), "10 Resources to Help Run Social Media," *Healthy Dash of Social*.
Available online: https://www.healthydashofsocial.com/blog/10-resources-to-help-you
-run-social-media (accessed August 19, 2024).

Social Media Marketing

Baker, K. (2024), "Social Media Marketing: The Ultimate Guide," *Hubspot*. Available online:
https://blog.hubspot.com/marketing/social-media-marketing (accessed August 21,
2024).

Spatial Storytelling

Taledeck (2024), "The Sensations of Spatial Storytelling," *Inlusio Interactive*. Available online:
https://www.taledeck.com/en/spatial-storytelling-field-guide (accessed August 14, 2024).

Zaunschirm, M. (2024), "The Power of 3D Audio in Immersive Experiences," *Linkedin,*
February 22. Available online: https://www.linkedin.com/pulse/power-3d-audio
-immersive-experiences-markus-zaunschirm-j7cmf/ (accessed August 19, 2024).

Story Map

Jones, S.K. (2022), "Getting Started with Interactive Fiction," *Write More with Simon*,
June 27. Available online: https://simonkjones.substack.com/p/getting-started-with
-interactive (accessed August 19, 2024).

Pereira, G. (2012), "How to Create a Story Map," *diyMFA*, May 15. Available online: https://diymfa.com/writing/mapping-out-your-story/ (accessed August 19, 2024).

Story Structures

MasterClass (2022), "Unique Story Structures: 5 Unconventional Story Structures," *MasterClass*, July 22. Available online: https://www.masterclass.com/articles/unique-story-structures (accessed August 19, 2024).

Style Guide

Patel, N. (2024), "How to Create an Editorial Style Guide," *NeilPatel*. Available online: https://neilpatel.com/blog/editorial-style-guide/ (accessed August 19, 2024).

Theme Entertainment

Cabolis, Y. (2024), "Spatial Computing and its role in Themed Entertainment," *Electrosonic*. Available online: https://www.electrosonic.com/blog/spatial-computing-and-its-role-in-themed-entertainment (accessed August 29, 2024).

Transmedia Story

Mcerlean, K. (2018), *Interactive Narratives and Transmedia Storytelling: Creating Immersive Stories Across New Media Platforms*, New York: Routledge.

Video Game

Learn to Design Video Games with GameDesigning.org (2024), *Game Designing*. Available online: https://gamedesignskills.com/game-design/ (accessed August 14, 2024).

Stefyn, N. (2020), "Game Design Basics," *CG Spectrum*, May 1. Available online: https://www.cgspectrum.com/application (accessed August 17, 2024).

What is Video Game Design? (2024), *Game Designs Skills*. Available online: https://gamedesignskills.com/game-design/ (accessed August 17, 2024).

Virtual Reality (VR)

FasterCapital (2024a), "Interactive Storytelling with VR," *FasterCapital*. Available online: https://fastercapital.com/topics/interactive-storytelling-with-vr.html (accessed August 17, 2024).

Vallance, M., and Towndrow, P.A. (2022), "Perspective: Narrative Storyliving in Virtual Reality Design," *Perspective*, March 31. Available online: https://www.frontiersin.org /journals/virtual-reality/articles/10.3389/frvir.2022.779148/full (accessed August 17, 2024).

Wardrobe

Landis, D.N. (2014), "Costume Design Instructional Guide," *Academy of Motion Picture Arts and Sciences*. Available online: https://www.oscars.org/sites/oscars/files/ teachersguide-costumedesign-2015.pdf (accessed August 19, 2024).

Widget

Distribute Web Stories on Your Own Site Using Widgets (2024), *MakeStories*. Available online: https://makestories.io/embed-google-web-stories/ (accessed August 19, 2024).

Wiki

Wikinovel.net (2024), Available online: http://www.wikinovel.net/ (accessed August 17, 2024).

References

Readers of the print edition of this book can find clickable links available on the Bloomsbury online resource: https://www.bloomsburyonlineresources.com/creating-the-interactive-digital-narrative.

4K Resolution (2024), *Wikipedia*. Available online: https://en.wikipedia.org/wiki/4K _resolution (accessed August 30, 2024).

4X (2024), *Wikipedia*. Available online: https://en.wikipedia.org/wiki/4X (accessed August 17, 2024).

8K Resolution (2024), *Wikipedia*. Available online: https://en.wikipedia.org/wiki/8K _resolution (accessed August 30, 2024).

A Guide to Media Production Costs and Budgets (2024), *Flywheel Film.* Available online: https://www.flywheelfilm.com/learn/a-guide-to-media-production-costs-and-budgets (accessed August 17, 2024).

Abba Voyage (2022), Available online: https://www.youtube.com/watch?v=JxWNxGymi4U &ab_channel=ABBAVoyage (accessed January 15, 2025).

Abstract Strategy Game (2024), *Wikipedia.* Available online: https://en.wikipedia.org/wiki/ Abstract_strategy_game (accessed August 17, 2024).

Action-Adventure Game (2024), *Wikipedia.* Available online: https://en.wikipedia.org/wiki/ Action-adventure_game (accessed August 14, 2024).

Action Game (2024), *Wikipedia.* Available online: https://en.wikipedia.org/wiki/Action_game (accessed August 14, 2024).

Action Role-Playing Game (2024), *Wikipedia.* Available online: https://en.wikipedia.org/wiki/ Action_role-playing_game (accessed August 17, 2024).

Adobe Audition (2024), Available online: https://www.adobe.com/uk/products/audition.html (accessed August 19, 2024).

Adobe Creative Cloud (2024), Available online: https://www.adobe.com/uk/creativecloud .html (accessed August 19, 2024).

Adobe Express (2025), Available online: https://www.adobe.com/express/business (accessed January 8, 2025).

Adobe Illustrator (2024), Available online: https://www.adobe.com/uk/products/illustrator .html (accessed August 19, 2024).

Adobe InDesign (2024), Available online: https://www.adobe.com/uk/products/indesign/ free-trial-download.html (accessed August 19, 2024).

Adobe Photoshop (2024), Available online: https://www.adobe.com/uk/products/ photoshopfamily.html (accessed August 19, 2024).

Adobe Premiere Pro (2024), Available online: https://www.adobe.com/products/premiere .html (accessed August 19, 2024).

Adobe Premiere Rush (2024), Available online: https://www.adobe.com/uk/products/premiere-rush.html (accessed August 19, 2024).

ADRIFT (2024), Available online: https://www.adrift.co/ (accessed August 17, 2024).

Adventure Game (2024), *Wikipedia.* Available online: https://en.wikipedia.org/wiki/Adventure_game (accessed August 14, 2024).

AJAX Introduction (2024), *W3 Schools.* Available online: https://www.w3schools.com/js/js_ajax_intro.asp (accessed August 19, 2024).

Alexa (2025), Available online: https://en.wikipedia.org/wiki/Amazon_Alexa (accessed January 15, 2025).

Alston, J. and Campbell, A. (2010), *Dreaming Methods.* Available online: https://dreamingmethods.com/about/ (accessed August 14, 2024).

Alternate Reality Game (2024), *Wikipedia.* Available online: https://en.wikipedia.org/wiki/Alternate_reality_game (accessed August 17, 2024).

Amusement Park (2024), *Wikipedia.* Available online: https://en.wikipedia.org/wiki/Amusement_park (accessed August 31, 2024).

Animatrik (2022), "Animatrik Powers Bieber's Interactive Virtual Experience Concert," *Animatrik*, March 24. Available online: https://www.animatrik.com/blog/animatrik-powers-biebers-interactive-virtual-experience-concert (accessed August 14, 2024).

Anthropy, A. (2013), "Queers in Love at the End of the World," *The Interactive Fiction Database.* Available online: https://ifdb.org/viewgame?id=622aq9w92sxoym4p (accessed August 16, 2024).

ANTLR (2024), Available online: https://www.antlr.org/ (accessed August 14, 2024).

Apple (2023), "Apple Vision Pro," *YouTube.* Available online: https://www.youtube.com/watch?v=TX9qSaGXFyg (accessed August 19, 2024).

Appleton, M. (2024), "Ambient Copresence," *Maggie.* Available online: https://maggieappleton.com/ambient-copresence (accessed August 19, 2024).

Applications for Interactive Storytelling (2024), *New Discovery*, July 3. Available online: https://newdiscovery.agency/mixed-reality-applications-for-interactive-storytelling/ (accessed August 14, 2024).

Armor Games (2024), Available online: https://armorgames.com/category/flash-games (accessed August 22, 2024).

Articulate 360 (2014), "PowerPoint tips: How to Create an Interactive Story with Links, Part 1," *YouTube.* Available online: https://www.youtube.com/watch?v=J0ikAP3is6M&t=1s (accessed August 19, 2024).

Articy Draft (2024), *Articy.* Available online: https://www.articy.com/en/ (accessed August 19, 2024).

Artlist (2024), Available online: https://artlist.io/ (accessed August 19, 2024).

Ashell, S.K. (2015), "Standard Patterns in Choice-Based Games," *These Heterogenous Tasks*, January 26. Available online: https://heterogenoustasks.wordpress.com/2015/01/26/standard-patterns-in-choice-based-games/ (accessed August 19, 2024).

Ask Me Anything (AMA) (2025), Available online: https://www.reddit.com/r/AMA/ (accessed January 9, 2025).

Aston, J. (2016), "Interactive Documentary – What Does it Mean and Why Does it Matter?" *IDocs*, March. Available online: http://i-docs.org/interactive-documentary-what-does-it-mean-and-why-does-it-matter/ (accessed August 19, 2024).

Astron Belt (2024), *Wikipedia.* Available online: https://en.wikipedia.org/wiki/Astron_Belt (accessed August 14, 2024).

Atkin, M. & Milen, T. (2008), *Curation.* Available online: https://xolabs.co.uk/ (accessed August 16, 2024).

Audacity (2024), Available online: https://www.audacityteam.org/ (accessed August 19, 2024).

Auto Battler (2024), *Wikipedia.* Available online: https://en.wikipedia.org/wiki/Auto_battler (accessed August 16, 2024).

Avid (2024), Available online: https://www.avid.com/ (accessed August 19, 2024).

Baamboozle (2025). Available online: https://www.baamboozle.com/ (accessed 25 May 2025).

Badge Maker (2024), *Google Play.* Available online: https://play.google.com/store/apps/details?id=com.gombosdev.badgemaker&hl=en&gl=US&pli=1 (accessed August 21, 2024).

Bandersnatch (2024), Black Mirror, *Wikipedia.* Available online: https://en.wikipedia.org/wiki/Black_Mirror:_Bandersnatch (accessed August 19, 2024).

Barác, Z. (2018), "Collaborative Storytelling – A Presentation with Many (maybe too many Triangles)," *Secret Story Network: YouTube,* November 28. Available online: https://www.youtube.com/watch?v=qvzAr1l7ZUk (accessed August 17, 2024).

Barnhart, B. (2024), "What's an Animatic? Benefits, Uses, and Real-World Examples," April 8. Available online: https://www.linearity.io/blog/animatic/#:~:text=At%20its%20core%2C%20an%20animatic,timing%2C%20pacing%2C%20and%20composition (accessed August 19, 2024).

Bartimus, A. (n.d.), "10 Resources to Help Run Social Media," *Healthy Dash of Social.* Available online: https://www.healthydashofsocial.com/blog/10-resources-to-help-you-run-social-media (accessed August 19, 2024).

Basecamp. (2024), Available online: https://basecamp.com/ (accessed August 19, 2024).

Battle Royal Game (2024), *Wikipedia.* Available online: https://en.wikipedia.org/wiki/Battle_royale_game (accessed August 17, 2024).

BBC Storyformer (2024), Available online: https://www.bbc.co.uk/makerbox/tools/storyformer (accessed August 19, 2024).

Before we Disappear (2025), *Albino Mosquito Productions.* Available online: https://www.albinomosquito.com/before-we-disappear/ (accessed 25 May 2025)

Bishōjo Game (2024), *Wikipedia.* Available online: https://en.wikipedia.org/wiki/Bish%C5%8Djo_game (accessed August 19, 2024).

Bitsy (2024), Available online: https://bitsy.org/ (accessed August 19, 2024).

Blanc, W. (2013), "Perrier Secret Place," *Quad Productions.* Available online: https://perrier-secret-place.soft112.com/ (accessed August 16, 2024).

Blast Theory (2024), Available online: https://www.blasttheory.co.uk/ (accessed August 14, 2024).

Bloom, A. (2016), "Creating an Interactive Digital Story using PowerPoint 1," *YouTube,* October 11. Available online: https://www.youtube.com/watch?v=KzENmFK0fag&t=1s (accessed August 19, 2024).

Bloomberg (2017), "One of Japan's Biggest Pop Stars Isn't Human." Available online: https://www.youtube.com/watch?v=vPBRj0bE55w&ab_channel=BloombergTelevision (accessed January 15, 2025).

Blue Man Group (2024), Available online: https://www.blueman.com/ (accessed August 16, 2024).

Blue Vertigo (2024), Available online: https://www.bluevertigo.com.ar/ (accessed August 19, 2024).

Bogost, I. (2003), *Persuasive Games*. Available online: https://persuasivegames.com/about/ (accessed August 14, 2024).

Bomo Audio (2024), Available online: https://www.productionbase.co.uk/profile/862872/employer/BOMO-Audio (accessed August 30, 2024).

Bortnick, J. (2016), "IFTF Grants Guidelines," *Interactive Fiction Technological Foundation*. Available online: https://iftechfoundation.org/committees/grants/grants-guidelines/ (accessed August 14, 2024).

Brain-controlled cinema: Introducing the interactive film that watches you watch it (2023), *Connectivity*, March 2. Available online: https://www.connectivity4ir.co.uk/article/196207/Brain-controlled-cinema--Introducing-the-interactive-film-that-watches-you-watch-it.aspx (accessed August 14, 2024).

Branch, J. (2012), "Snow Fall: the Avalanche at Tunnel Creek," *New York Times*, February 19. https://www.nytimes.com/projects/2012/snow-fall/index.html#/?part=tunnel-creek (accessed August 14, 2024).

British Library, The (2024), Available online: https://www.bl.uk/ (accessed August 16, 2024).

Buffer (2025), Available online: https://buffer.com/ (accessed January 8, 2025).

Burg, K. and Beck, J. (n.d.), "Cinemagraphs," *Cinemagraphs.com*. Available online: https://cinemagraphs.com/ (accessed August 19, 2024).

Buta, A. (2010), *Fan Studio*. Available online: https://www.fanstudio.co.uk/ (accessed August 16, 2024).

BUZZ (2024), Available online: https://buzz.bournemouth.ac.uk/ (accessed August 19, 2024).

Byrne, R. (2019), "How to Use Keynote to Build Choose Your Own Adventure Stories," *YouTube*. Available online: https://www.youtube.com/watch?v=EUFllttcFWc&t=1s (accessed August 19, 2024).

Cage, D. (1997), *Quantic Dream*. Available online: https://www.quanticdream.com/en (accessed August 14, 2024).

Callaham, J. and Fingas. R. (2024), "What is Google Duplex and How do You Use it?" *Android Authority*, April 4. Available online: https://www.androidauthority.com/what-is-google-duplex-869476/ (accessed August 14, 2024).

Campbell, A. and Bedford, M. (2000), "The Virtual Disappearance of Miriam," *Dreaming Methods*. Available online: https://dreamingmethods.com/portfolio/the-virtual-disappearance-of-miriam/ (accessed August 14, 2024).

Campbell, J. (1949), "The Hero with a Thousand Faces," *Pantheon Books*. Available online: https://archive.org/details/herowiththousand0000camp_x3m0/mode/2up (accessed September 2, 2024).

Canva Create eBooks templates (2025), Available online: https://www.canva.com/create/ebooks/ (accessed January 9, 2025).

Canva Create Gift Certificate templates (2025), Available online: https://www.canva.com/create/gift-certificates/ (accessed January 9, 2025).

Canva Infographics (2024), Available online: https://www.canva.com/create/infographics/ (accessed August 19, 2024).

Card Game (2024), *Wikipedia*. Available online: https://en.wikipedia.org/wiki/Card_game (accessed August 17, 2024).

Casey, R. (2020), *Baamboozle*. Available online: https://www.baamboozle.com/ (accessed August 16, 2024).

Casual Game (2024), *Wikipedia*. Available online: https://en.wikipedia.org/wiki/Casual_game (accessed August 14, 2024).

Charades (2024), *Wikipedia*. Available online: https://en.wikipedia.org/wiki/Charades (accessed August 14, 2024).

Charles, M., Gyori, B., Wolters, S., and Peñuela, J.A.U. (2015), "Target BACRIM: Blurring Fact and Fiction to Create an Interactive Documentary Game," *Interactive Storytelling - 8th International Conference on Interactive Digital Storytelling*, November 30. 349–352

Chatbot (2024), *Wikipedia*. Available online: https://en.wikipedia.org/wiki/Chatbot (accessed August 14, 2024).

ChatGPT (2024), Available online: https://openai.com/chatgpt/ (accessed August 14, 2024).

Choice of Games (2024), Available online: https://www.choiceofgames.com/ (accessed August 21, 2024).

Choice Script, Introduction to (2024), *Choice of Games*. Available online: https://www.choiceofgames.com/make-your-own-games/choicescript-intro/ (accessed August 19, 2024).

Choose Your Own Adventure (2024), *Wikipedia*. Available online: https://en.wikipedia.org/wiki/Choose_Your_Own_Adventure (accessed August 19, 2024).

Christiansen, S. (2013), "Trapped in Time," *Interactive Fiction Database*. Available online: https://ifdb.org/viewgame?id=juj5b61griyoswn2 (accessed August 19, 2024).

Chroma Key (2024), *Wikipedia*. Available online: https://en.wikipedia.org/wiki/Chroma_key (accessed August 19, 2024).

CinemaFlow (2024), Available online: https://www.cinemaflow.ai/home-lp?gad_source=1&gclid=Cj0KCQjw0Oq2BhCCARIsAA5hubXltv-S46P28hP4Obd7DwWer5gD0gkNljiB7CKchL8h_28y4EjvgmoaApj9EALw_wcB (accessed August 19, 2024).

Cinnamon (2024), Available online: https://projects.linuxmint.com/cinnamon/ (accessed December 23, 2024).

Claude (2024), Available online: https://claude.ai/login?returnTo=%2F%3F (accessed August 22, 2024).

Clip Champ (2025), Available online: https://clipchamp.com/en/ (accessed January 13, 2025).

Collaborative Fiction (2024), *Wikipedia*. Available online: https://en.wikipedia.org/wiki/Collaborative_fiction (accessed August 19, 2024).

Collapsus: Interactive Experience (2010), Available online: https://submarine.nl/project/collapsus/ (accessed August 14, 2024).

Colligan, P. (2009), *The Raspberry Pi Foundation*. Available online: https://www.raspberrypi.org/about/ (accessed August 16, 2024).

Color Gel (2024), *Wikipedia*. Available online: https://en.wikipedia.org/wiki/Color_gel (accessed August 19, 2024).

CommonNinja (2024), Available online: https://www.commoninja.com/widgets/comments (accessed August 21, 2024).

Computer Wargame (2024), *Wikipedia*. Available online: https://en.wikipedia.org/wiki/ Computer_wargame (accessed August 14, 2024).

Concept Art (2024), *Wikipedia*. Available online: https://en.wikipedia.org/wiki/Concept_art (accessed August 19, 2024).

Connected Learning Alliance (2011), "Games and Education Scholar James Paul Gee on Video Games, Learning, and Literacy," *YouTube*. Available online: https://www.youtube .com/watch?v=LNfPdaKYOPI (accessed August 19, 2024).

Console Mods (2025), "Magnavox Odyssey Homebrew Games." Available online: https:// consolemods.org/wiki/Odyssey:Magnavox_Odyssey_Homebrew_Games

Countingdownto (2024), Available online: https://countingdownto.com/ (accessed August 19, 2024).

Cox, M.A. (2015), *Wikinovel.net*. Available online: http://www.wikinovel.net/ (accessed August 19, 2024).

Create ebooks (2024), *Canva*. Available online: https://www.canva.com/create/ebooks/ (accessed August 21, 2024).

Dark Souls (2024), *Wikipedia*. Available online: https://en.wikipedia.org/wiki/Dark_Souls (accessed August 14, 2024).

DaVinci Resolve 19 (2024), Available online: https://www.blackmagicdesign.com/products/ davinciresolve/edit (accessed August 19, 2024).

DcheJ (2022), "Wild Thing (1967), Monterey Pop Festival," *YouTube*. Available online: https://www.youtube.com/watch?v=xVN8_7wVSG0 (accessed August 14, 2024).

Dead Cat (2024), *Wiktionary*. Available online: https://en.wiktionary.org/wiki/dead_cat (accessed August 19, 2024).

Deafverse (2025), Available online: https://deafverse.com/ (accessed 25 May 2025).

Deck-Building Game (2024), *Wikipedia*. Available online: https://en.wikipedia.org/wiki/Deck -building_game (accessed August 14, 2024).

Dues Ex (2024), *Wikipedia*. Available online: https://en.wikipedia.org/wiki/Deus_Ex (accessed December 24, 2024).

Dialog (2024), Available online: https://www.linusakesson.net/dialog/ (accessed December 23, 2024).

Diegesis (2024), *Wikipedia*. Available online: https://en.wikipedia.org/wiki/Diegesis (accessed August 19, 2024).

Digital Productions Arte (2025), "Notes on Blindness," Available online: https://www.arte.tv/ digitalproductions/en/notes-on-blindness/ (accessed 25 May 2025).

Discord (2024), Available online: https://discord.com/ (accessed August 19, 2024).

Discord Bots (2025), Available online: https://discordbotlist.com/ (accessed January 8, 2025).

Disney (2021), "Disney Develops New Spider-Man Attraction Using Technology that Empowers Guests to Discover Web-Slinging Super Powers," *Walt Disney Company*, June 3. Available online: https://thewaltdisneycompany.com/disney-develops-new -spider-man-attraction-using-technology-that-empowers-guests-to-discover-web -slinging-super-powers/ (accessed August 19, 2024).

Docubase (2024), *MIT Open Documentary Lab*. Available online: https://store .steampowered.com/ (accessed August 21, 2024).

Downpour (2024), Available online: https://downpour.games/ (accessed August 19, 2024).

Drake performing with sperm cells hologram (2023), Available online: https://www.youtube
.com/shorts/v_1PaGTJrzw (accessed January 15, 2025).

Dramatization (2024), *Wikipedia*. Available online: https://en.wikipedia.org/wiki/
Dramatization (accessed August 19, 2024).

Dreaming Methods (2025), Available online: https://dreamingmethods.com/ (accessed
May 25, 2025).

Easy Planning Using Post-it Notes (2024), *Canva*. Available online: https://www.canva.com
/graphs/mind-maps/ (accessed August 19, 2024).

Easy Tutorial Video Maker, The (2024), *Animoto*. Available online: https://animoto.com
/make/tutorial-videos#:~:text=Partner%20of-,The%20easy%20tutorial%20video
%20maker,template%20to%20publishing%20in%20minutes (accessed August 21,
2024).

Echo (2025), Available online: https://en.wikipedia.org/wiki/Amazon_Echo (accessed
January 15, 2025).

Echoes (2024), Available online: https://echoes.xyz/ (accessed August 14, 2024).

Edström, M. (2015), "Exploring the World's Largest Cave," *National Geographical*. Available
online: https://www.nationalgeographic.com/news-features/son-doong-cave/2/#s
=pano37 (accessed August 14, 2024).

Eduk8me (2021), "Create Interactive Fiction in Google Docs," *YouTube*. Available online:
https://www.youtube.com/watch?v=RNdyjHq5zFY (accessed August 19, 2024).

Edward Packard (2024), *Wikipedia*. Available online: https://en.wikipedia.org/wiki/Edward
Packard(writer) (accessed August 16, 2024).

Eko (2024), Available online: https://eko.com/eko-studio-visual-commerce-platform
(accessed August 19, 2024).

Elder Scrolls V: Skyrim, The (2024), *Wikipedia*. Available online: https://en.wikipedia.org/wiki
/The_Elder_Scrolls_V:_Skyrim (accessed December 24, 2024).

Epstein, M. (2005), "History Unwired: Venice," *Walking Cinema*. Available online: https://
www.walkingcinema.org/project-history-unwired (accessed August 16, 2024).

Ext4 (2024), *Wikipedia*. Available online: https://en.wikipedia.org/wiki/Ext4#:~:text=ext4
%20enables%20write%20barriers%20by,and%20delete%20many%20small%20files
(accessed August 31, 2024).

External Storage (2024), *Wikipedia*. Available online: https://en.wikipedia.org/wiki/External
_storage (accessed August 16, 2024).

Ezgif (2024), Available online: https://ezgif.com/maker (accessed August 19, 2024).

Fabulich, D. and Strong-Morse, A. (2009), "Choice of the Dragon," *Choice of Games*.
Available online: https://www.choiceofgames.com/dragon/ (accessed August 17,
2024).

Facebook (2024), Available online: https://www.facebook.com/ (accessed August 21,
2024).

Fighting Fantasy (2024), *Wikipedia*. Available online: https://en.wikipedia.org/wiki/Fighting
_Fantasy (accessed August 14, 2024).

Fighting Game (2024), *Wikipedia*. Available online: https://en.wikipedia.org/wiki/Fighting
_game (accessed August 14, 2024).

Figma (2025), Available online: https://www.figma.com/ (accessed 26 May 2025).

Final Cut Pro X (2024), Available online: https://www.apple.com/uk-business/shop/product
/D61097M/A/final-cut-pro-x (accessed August 19, 2024).

Final Fantasy (2024), *Wikipedia*. Available online: https://en.wikipedia.org/wiki/Final
Fantasy(video_game) (accessed December 24, 2024).

Find a Bristol Tree on the Move (2024), *Bristol Tree Forum*. Available online: https://
bristoltreeforum.org/2017/03/06/finding-a-bristol-tree-on-the-move/ (accessed August
14, 2024).

Firebase (2025), Available online: https://firebase.google.com/ (accessed January 5,
2025).

Firewatch: Campo Santo (2024), *Wikipedia*. Available online: https://en.wikipedia.org/wiki/
Firewatch (accessed August 14, 2024).

First-Person Shooter Games… In 1909? Meet "Motographic Target Shooting (2019),
Movies Silently, February 2. Available online: https://moviessilently.com/2019/02/02/first
-person-shooter-games-in-1909-meet-motographic-target-shooting/ (accessed August
17, 2024).

Flash Mob (2024), *Wikipedia*. Available online: https://en.wikipedia.org/wiki/Flash_mob
(accessed August 16, 2024).

Flesser, S. and Gardebäck, M. (2010), "Projects," *Simogo*. Available online: https://simogo
.com/ (accessed August 17, 2024).

Flicking (2024), *Boardgamegeek*. Available online: https://boardgamegeek.com/
boardgamemechanic/2860/flicking (accessed August 14, 2024).

Flickr (2025), Available online: https://www.flickr.com/ (accessed January 8, 2025)

Flourish (2024), Available online: https://flourish.studio/ (accessed August 19, 2024).

Flowxo (2024), Available online: https://flowxo.com/ (accessed August 19, 2024).

Forumotion.com (2024), Available online: https://www.forumotion.com/ (accessed August
21, 2024).

Free AI Plot Generator for Interactive Fiction Games (2024), *Writecream*. Available online:
https://www.writecream.com/free-ai-plot-generator-for-interactive-fiction-games/
(accessed August 19, 2024).

Freed, A. (2014), "Branching Conversation Systems and the Working Writer, Part 2:
Design Considerations," *Game Developer*, September 9. Available online: https://www
.gamedeveloper.com/design/branching-conversation-systems-and-the-working-writer
-part-2-design-considerations (accessed August 19, 2024).

Free HTML Email Templates (2024), *Beefree*. Available online: https://beefree.io/templates
(accessed August 21, 2024).

Free Loop Videos (2024), *Pexels*. Available online: https://www.pexels.com/search/videos/
loop/ (accessed August 19, 2024).

Free Music Archive (2024), Available online: https://freemusicarchive.org/ (accessed August
19, 2024).

Free Online Editable Loyalty Card Templates (2024), *WEPIK*. Available online: https://wepik
.com/templates/loyalty-cards (accessed August 21, 2024).

Free Online Polls (2024), *SmartSurvey*. Available online: https://www.smartsurvey.co.uk/
free-online-polls (accessed August 19, 2024).

Free Random Codes Generator (2024), *Voucherify*. Available online: https://www.canva
.com/create/ebooks/ (accessed August 21, 2024).

Freesound (2024), Available online: https://freesound.org/ (accessed August 19, 2024).

Full Motion Video Game (2024), *Wikipedia*. Available online: https://en.wikipedia.org/wiki/
Full-motion_video (accessed August 19, 2024).

Fulltime Filmmaker (2022), 8 Steps to Shooting Interviews // Job Shadow. Available online: https://www.youtube.com/watch?v=Xmn5JhIL3PI (accessed August 19, 2024).

Game Developer (2024), Available online: https://www.gamedeveloper.com/latest-news #close-modal (accessed August 21, 2024).

Game Hackathon Guide: Everything You Need to Know (2022), *Hackathon.com*, May 4. Available online: https://corporate.hackathon.com/articles/game-hackathon-guide -everything-you-need-to-know (accessed August 16, 2024).

Game Jams on itch (2024), *itch.io* Available online: https://itch.io/jams (accessed August 14, 2024).

GameMaker (2025), Available online: https://gamemaker.io/en (accessed January 5, 2025).

Gaudenzi, S. (2015), "The 3 Levels on the Spectrum of Interactive Storytelling," *Journalism .co.uk*. Available online: https://www.journalism.co.uk/news/the-3-levels-on-the -spectrum-of-interactive-storytelling-/s2/a565674/ (accessed August 19, 2024).

Gaylor, B. (2015), "Do Not Track." Available online: https://donottrack-doc.com/en/intro/ (accessed August 14, 2024).

Geocaching (2024), Available online: https://www.geocaching.com/play (accessed August 16, 2024).

Giannchi, G., Rowland, G., Brenford, S., Foster, J., Adams, M., and Chamberlain, A. (2010), "Blast Theory's *Rider Spoke*, its Documentation and the Making of its Replay Archive," *Contemporary Theatre Review,* 20: 353–367. Available online: https://www .tandfonline.com/doi/abs/10.1080/10486801.2010.489047 (accessed August 16, 2024).

Gibson, C. (2024) "The Future of Interactive Content: AI-Driven Innovations," *Medium,* April 3. Available online: https://medium.com/@chasegison/the-future-of-interactive-content -ai-driven-innovations-02061e44baf9#:~:text=The%20future%20of%20interactive %20content%20is%20closely%20linked%20with%20AI,immersive%20and %20personalized%20content%20experiences. (accessed August 19, 2024).

GIF Compressor (2024), *Free Convert*. Available online: https://www.freeconvert.com/gif -compressor (accessed August 19, 2024).

Gift Certificates (2024), *Canva*. Available online: https://www.canva.com/create/gift -certificates/ (accessed August 21, 2024).

Gimbal (2024), *Wikipedia*. Available online: https://en.wikipedia.org/wiki/Gimbal (accessed August 19, 2024).

Gingold, C. (2015), "Earth: A Primer." Available online: https://www.earthprimer.com/ (accessed August 16, 2024).

GitHub (2024), Available online: https://github.com/ (accessed August 14, 2024).

Gleam (2025), Available online: https://gleam.io/ (accessed January 9, 2025).

GNOME Shell. Available online: Available online: https://extensions.gnome.org/ (accessed December 23, 2024).

Gobo (lighting) (2024), *Wikipedia*. Available online: https://en.wikipedia.org/wiki/Gobo_ (lighting)#:~:text=A%20gobo%20is%20an%20object,emitted%20light%20and%20 its%20shadow (accessed August 19, 2024).

Godin, S. (2008), "Permission Marketing," *Seth's Blog*, January 31. Available online: https://seths.blog/2008/01/permission-mark/ (accessed August 21, 2024).

Godot (2024), Available online: https://godotengine.org/ (accessed August 19, 2024).

Google Drive (2024), Available online: https://accounts.google.com/AccountChooser /signinchooser?service=writely&theme=mn&ddm=0&flowName=GlifWebSignIn &flowEntry=AccountChooser (accessed August 19, 2024).

GoPro (2024), Available online: https://gopro.com/en/gb/ (accessed August 19, 2024).

Gorillaz ft. Madonna (2006), Available online: https://vimeo.com/340169963 (accessed January 15, 2025).

Grabowska, K. (2019), "Warsaw Rising," *Warsaw Rising Museum.* Available online: http:// www.warsawrising.eu/ (accessed August 17, 2024).

Guncho (2024), Available online: https://www.guncho.com/ (accessed August 14, 2024).

Gyori, B. (2013), IMDB "Brad Gyori Writer, Producer, Director." Available online: https:// www.imdb.com/name/nm0350507/ (accessed August 14, 2024).

Gyori, B. (2018a), *Shelley's Heart.* Available online: https://www.shelleysheart.com/ (accessed August 14, 2024).

Gyori, B. (2018b), *Shelley's Heart Locative Version.* Available online: https://storyplaces .bournemouth.ac.uk/#/story/5c94ccff5d1c3f1944672a8a (accessed August 17, 2024).

Gyori, B. (2019a), "Reanimating Shelley's Heart: Breathing New Life into Locative Learning with Dual Process Design," *Media Practice and Education*, August 2019, 21 (1): 1–22. Available online: https://www.researchgate.net/publication/335170999_Reanimating _Shelley"s_Heart_breathing_new_life_into_locative_learning_with_dual_process_design (accessed August 31, 2024).

Gyori, B. (2019b), *Shelley's Heart Desktop Version.* Available online: http://maps .shelleysheart.com/#Mary_Map_1 (accessed August 17, 2024).

Gyori, B. (2022), "Target BACRIM Teaser Trailer," *YouTube.* Available online: https://www .youtube.com/watch?v=1LhCdGZ8o6s&t=4s (accessed August 17, 2024).

Gyori, B. (2023), "Mr Illusion," *Soundcloud,* August 7. Available online: https://www .youtube.com/watch?v=9amccMTSMB8 (accessed August 19, 2024).

Gyori, B. and Charles, M. (2017), "Designing Journalists: Teaching Journalism Students to Think Like Web Designers," *Journalism and Mass Communication Educator*, 73 (2). Available online: https://journals.sagepub.com/doi/abs/10.1177/1077695817713424 (accessed August 14, 2024).

Gyori, B. and Pope, J. (2021), "Decision Points: Designing Student-centered Learning for Digital Interactive Storytelling," *Writing in Education*, 84 (Summer): 19–25. Available online: https://eprints.bournemouth.ac.uk/36022/ (accessed August 17, 2024).

Gyori, B. and Pope, J. (2023), "Branching Paths: Using Digital Interactive Storytelling To Encourage Marginalised Young People To Engage With Creative Writing," *Writing in Education*, 89 (Spring): 41–48. Available online: https://eprints.bournemouth.ac.uk /39109/ (accessed August 16, 2024).

Gyori, B. and Zaluczkowska, A. (2022), "How we Role: The Collaborative Role-playing Poetics of the Secret Storytelling Network," *Journal of Screenwriting*, 23 (2): 207–230. Available online: https://eprints.leedsbeckett.ac.uk/id/eprint/8934/1/HowWeRoleAM -ZALUCZKOWSKA.pdf (accessed August 16, 2024).

Hanako Games (2013), "Long Live the Queen," *Steam*, November 8. Available online: https://store.steampowered.com/app/251990/Long_Live_The_Queen (accessed August 19, 2024).

Hashtagify (2025), Available online: https://hashtagify.app/ (accessed January 8, 2025).

Hauser, E. (2013), "Raspberry Pi Start up Page," *Trinket*. Available online: https://trinket.io/python/cee37619b0 (accessed August 17, 2024).

Heepsy (2025), Available online: https://www.heepsy.com/ (accessed January 9, 2025).

Henkel, G. and Lee, K. (2017), "Planescape: Torment: Enhanced Edition," *Steam,* April 11. Available online: https://store.steampowered.com/app/466300/Planescape_Torment_Enhanced_Edition/ (accessed August 19, 2024).

Hennessy, B.P. (2015), "Birdland," *The Interactive Fiction Database*. Available online: https://ifdb.org/viewgame?id=ap1651hvjldbuugj (accessed August 14, 2024).

Henrysson, R. (2022), *Supermassive Games*. Available online: https://www.supermassivegames.com/ (accessed August 17, 2024).

Hero's Journey (2024), *Wikipedia*. Available online: https://en.wikipedia.org/wiki/Hero%27s_journey (accessed August 19, 2024).

Hidden Object Game (2024), *Wikipedia*. Available online: https://en.wikipedia.org/wiki/Hidden_object_game (accessed August 14, 2024).

Holoconnects (2025), Available online: https://www.holoconnects.com/ (accessed January 15, 2025).

Holodeck (2024), *Wikipedia*. Available online: https://en.wikipedia.org/wiki/Holodeck (accessed August 19, 2024).

Hootsuite (2025), Available online: https://www.hootsuite.com/ (accessed January 8, 2025).

Hopscotch (Cortázar Novel) (2024), *Wikipedia*. Available online: https://en.wikipedia.org/wiki/Hopscotch_(Cort%C3%A1zar_novel) (accessed August 14, 2024).

Humfrey, J. (2014), "80 Days," *Inkle*. Available online: https://www.inklestudios.com/80days/ (accessed August 17, 2024).

Huneualt, M. (2018), "Roxham." Available online: https://roxham.nfb.ca/intro-1-en (accessed August 17, 2024).

Huynth, M. (2015), "The Boat," *SBS Online*. Available online: https://www.sbs.com.au/theboat/ (accessed August 19, 2024).

iFrame (2024), *W3 Schools*. Available online: https://www.w3schools.com/tags/tag_iframe.ASP (accessed August 19, 2024).

I Love Bees (2024), *Wikipedia*. Available online: https://en.wikipedia.org/wiki/I_Love_Bees (accessed August 16, 2024).

Immersive (2024), *Tribeca*. Available online: https://tribecafilm.com/festival/immersive (accessed August 22, 2024).

Incremental Game (2024), *Wikipedia*. Available online: https://en.wikipedia.org/wiki/Incremental_game (accessed August 16, 2024).

Indeed Editorial Team (2024), "Top 10 Secure File Sharing Platforms (with pros and cons)," *Indeed*, June 28. Available online: https://uk.indeed.com/career-advice/career-development/secure-file-sharing-platforms (accessed August 21, 2024).

Inform 6 (2024), Available online: https://github.com/DavidKinder/Inform6 (accessed December 23, 2024).

Inform 7 (2024), Available online: https://ganelson.github.io/inform-website/ (accessed August 16, 2024).

Inklewriter (2024), *Inkle*. Available online: https://www.inklestudios.com/inklewriter/ (accessed August 19, 2024).

Instagram (2024), Available online: https://www.instagram.com/ (accessed August 21, 2024).

Instagram Live (2025), Available online: https://creators.instagram.com/live?locale=en_GB (accessed January 9, 2025).

Instapaper (2024), Available online: https://www.instapaper.com/ (accessed August 21, 2024).

Interactive Fiction Archive, The (2024), Available online: https://www.ifarchive.org/ (accessed August 21, 2024).

Interactive Fiction Competition, The (2024), Available online: https://ifcomp.org/ (accessed August 22, 2024).

Interactive Fiction Database (2024), Available online: https://ifdb.org/ (accessed August 21, 2024).

Interactive Film (2024), *Wikipedia*. Available online: https://en.wikipedia.org/wiki/Interactive_film (accessed August 14, 2024).

Interactive Theatre (2024), *Wikipedia.* Available online: https://en.wikipedia.org/wiki/Interactive_theatre (accessed August 19, 2024).

Intercom (2024), Available online: https://www.intercom.com/ (accessed August 21, 2024).

International Conference on Interactive Digital Storytelling (2024), ARDIN. Available online: https://ardin.online/conferences/icids-interactive-storytelling/ (accessed August 22, 2024).

International Journal of Interactive Storytelling, The (2024), *Global Vision Press*. Available online: https://gvpress.com/journals/IJIS/ (accessed August 22, 2024).

Internet Archive (2024), Available online: https://archive.org/browse.php?field=subject&mediatype=software&collection=softwarelibrary_flash_games (accessed August 22, 2024).

Intrinsic Motivation (2024), *Wikiversity.* Available online: https://en.wikiversity.org/wiki/Intrinsic_motivation (accessed August 19, 2024).

Itch.io (2024), Available online: https://itch.io/ (accessed August 21, 2024).

Jackson, S. (1995), "Patchwork Girl," *Eastgate*. Available online: https://www.eastgate.com/catalog/PatchworkGirl.html (accessed August 14, 2024).

James J. Gibson. (2024), *Wikipedia*. Available online: https://en.wikipedia.org/wiki/James_J._Gibson (accessed August 19, 2024).

James, M. (2019), *Audience of the Future*. Available online: https://audienceofthefuture.live/about/ (accessed August 14, 2024).

Jib (Crane) (2024), *Wikipedia*. Available online: https://en.wikipedia.org/wiki/Jib_(crane) (accessed August 19, 2024).

Jones, A., Gyori, B., Hargood, C., Charles, F., and Green, D. (2018), "Shelley's Heart: Experiences in Designing a Multi-Reader Locative Narrative," *Narrative and Hypertext,* July 9, 2018, Baltimore, USA. Available online: https://eprints.bournemouth.ac.uk/30691/ (accessed August 19, 2024).

Joseph, C. (2024), "Fund Better Games," *Fail Better Games*. Available online: https://chrisjoseph.org/fundbetter-funding-for-narrative-game-projects-and-interactive-fiction/ (accessed August 14, 2024).

Journal of Interactive Narrative (2024), Available online: https://journal.ardin.online/ (accessed August 22, 2024).

Julio Cortázar (2024), *Wikipedia*. Available online: https://en.wikipedia.org/wiki/Julio_Cort%C3%A1zar (accessed August 14, 2024).

The JumiFilm (2024), "Impossible LEGO Animations," *YouTube*. Available online: https://www.youtube.com/watch?v=nv_EsoPzPgk&t=59s (accessed August 19, 2024).

Kahoot (2025), Available online: https://kahoot.com/ (accessed January 8, 2025)

Kennedy, A. and Arendt. P. (2009), *Fail Better Games*. Available online: https://www.failbettergames.com/about (accessed August 16, 2024).

Kick (2025), Available online: https://kick.com/ (accessed January 8, 2025).

Kinoautomat (2024), *Wikipedia*. Available online: https://en.wikipedia.org/wiki/Kinoautomat (accessed August 17, 2024).

Kits.AI (2024), Available online: https://www.kits.ai/ (accessed August 19, 2024).

Klondike (solitaire) (2024), *Wikipedia*. Available online: https://en.wikipedia.org/wiki/Klondike_(solitaire) (accessed August 17, 2024).

Klynt (2024), Available online: https://www.klynt.net/ (accessed August 19, 2024).

Koenitz, H., (2015), "Towards a Specific Theory of Interactive Digital Narrative," *Interactive Digital Narrative: History, Theory and Practice*, Eds. Koenitz, H., Ferri, G., Haahr M., Sezen D., and Ibrahim T. Routledge, 2015.

Koivisto, S. (2016), "Minecraft Education," *Teacher Gaming LLC.* Available online: https://education.minecraft.net/en-us (accessed August 14, 2024).

Kongregate (2024), Available online: https://www.kongregate.com/games (accessed August 22, 2024).

Knight, A. and Harris, R. (1999), "The Lost Temple: An Interactive Puzzle Book," *Brickipedia.* Available online: https://brickipedia.fandom.com/wiki/The_Lost_Temple_-_An_Interactive_Puzzle_Book (accessed January 1, 2025).

Kriebernegg, T. (2015), *App Radar*. Available online: https://appradar.com/blog/mobile-game-engines-development-platforms (accessed August 16, 2024).

Kurosawa, A (1950), "Rashomon," *Daiei Film*, August 26, Japan. Available online: https://watch.plex.tv/movie/rashomon (accessed September 3, 2024).

Last of Us, The (2024), *Wikipedia.* Available online: https://en.wikipedia.org/wiki/The_Last_of_Us (accessed August 19, 2024).

Legend of Zelda: Breath of the Wild, The (2024), *Wikipedia*. Available online: https://en.wikipedia.org/wiki/The_Legend_of_Zelda:_Breath_of_the_Wild (accessed August 19, 2024).

Lialina, O. (1996), "My Boyfriend Came Back From the War," *Net Art Anthology*. Available online: https://sites.rhizome.org/anthology/lialina.html (accessed August 14, 2024).

Li, B. (2020), "Indefinite: Interrogation Game," *Google Play*. Available online: https://play.google.com/store/apps/details?id=air.me.brandlibel.indefinite&hl=en_GB (accessed August 16, 2024).

Life Simulation Game (2024), *Wikipedia*. Available online: https://en.wikipedia.org/wiki/Life_simulation_game (accessed August 19, 2024).

Lighting up Stonehenge (2018), Motion Mapping. Available online: https://motionmapping.co.uk/our-case-studies/lighting-up-stonehenge/ (accessed August 14, 2024).

Light Plot (2024), *Wikipedia*. Available online: https://en.wikipedia.org/wiki/Light_plot (accessed August 19, 2024).

List of Dice Games (2024), *Wikipedia*. Available online: https://en.wikipedia.org/wiki/List_of_dice_games (accessed August 14, 2024).

List Randomizer (2024), *Random.org*. Available online: https://www.random.org/lists/ (accessed August 19, 2024).

Liu, B. (2009), *Pocketgems*. Available online: https://www.pocketgems.com/about/ (accessed August 14, 2024).

Live-Action Role-Playing Game (2024), *Wikipedia*. Available online: https://en.wikipedia.org/wiki/Live_action_role-playing_game (accessed August 14, 2024).

Living Theatre, The (2024), *Wikipedia*. Available online: https://en.wikipedia.org/wiki/The_Living_Theatre (accessed August 16, 2024).

Live Action Role-Playing Game (2024), *Wikipedia*. Available online: https://en.wikipedia.org/wiki/Live_action_role-playing_game (accessed August 14, 2024).

Lizardry (2023), "Refined Self: The Personality Test Game," *Steam*, November 14. Available online: https://store.steampowered.com/app/2514960/Refind_Self_The_Personality_Test_Game/ (accessed August 14, 2024).

Location API (2024), *Unwiredlabs*. Available online: https://unwiredlabs.com/ (accessed August 14, 2024).

Logic Pro (2024), Available online: https://www.apple.com/uk/logic-pro/ (accessed August 19, 2024).

Logo Design (2024), Available online: https://logodesign.ai/?gad_source=1&gclid=CjwKCAjw_ZC2BhAQEiwAXSgCloY5JoGl9j3iWY6mHo3lDZkrkMTCyMDrzbtTO1SE9Fjr7HkaoFgb9xoC5vYQAvD_BwE (accessed August 19, 2024).

Lone Wolf (2024), *Wikipedia*. Available online: https://en.wikipedia.org/wiki/Lone_Wolf_(gamebooks) (accessed August 14, 2024).

Loom (2025), Available online: https://www.loom.com/ (accessed January 9, 2025).

Loominous and Mandarb, D. (2003), *Adventure Game Studio*. Available online: https://www.adventuregamestudio.co.uk/ (accessed August 16, 2024).

Lost (2024), *Wikipedia*. Available online: https://en.wikipedia.org/wiki/Lost_(2004_TV_series) (accessed August 19, 2024).

LostArk: Winter Soloist (2025), Available at: https://www.playlostark.com/en-us (accessed January 1, 2025).

Lost: Via Domus (2024), *Wikipedia*. Available online: https://en.wikipedia.org/wiki/Lost:_Via_Domus (accessed August 19, 2024).

Madagascar (2016), "INVASION! | Animated 360 VR Movie," *Baobab Studios*, December 21. Available online: https://www.youtube.com/watch?v=SZ0fKW5PttM (accessed August 16, 2024).

Mansaray, S. (2022), "Product Demo Videos: Getting Them Right the First Time," *ispring*. Available online: https://www.ispringsolutions.com/blog/product-demo-video (accessed August 19, 2024).

MapHub (2024), Available online: https://maphub.net/ (accessed August 19, 2024).

Mass Effect (2024), *Wikipedia*. Available online: https://en.wikipedia.org/wiki/Mass_Effect (accessed December 24, 2024).

Massively Multiplayer Online Role-Play Game (2024), *Wikipedia*. Available online: https://en.wikipedia.org/wiki/Massively_multiplayer_online_role-playing_game (accessed August 14, 2024).

The Matrix Online (2024), *Wikipedia*. Available online: https://en.wikipedia.org/wiki/The_Matrix_Online (accessed August 19, 2024).

Maureen Murdock's Heroine's Journey Arc (2024), *The Heroine's Journey Project: Exploring and Documenting Life-Affirming Alternatives to the Hero's Journey*. Available online: https://heroinejourneys.com/heroines-journey/ (accessed August 17, 2024).

Maurin, F. (2014), *Prezi*. Available online: https://prezi.com/ilzwxzjz2t5p/narrative-structures
-in-interactive-documentaries/ (accessed August 19, 2024).

McMillion Sheldon, E. (2013), "Hollow: An Interactive Documentary." http://
hollowdocumentary.com/ (accessed August 16, 2024).

Media Practice and Education (2024), *Taylor and Francis Online*. Available online: https://
www.tandfonline.com/journals/rjmp21 (accessed August 22, 2024).

Mendes, J. and Allison, L. (2012), "Bear 71," *National Film Board of Canada*. Available
online: https://bear71vr.nfb.ca/#!/ (accessed August 16, 2024).

Mentimeter (2025), Available online: https://www.mentimeter.com/ (accessed January 8, 2025)

Meta Quest (2024), "Meta Quest 3," *YouTube*. Available online: https://www.youtube.com/
watch?v=Exu7r2vZpcw (accessed August 16, 2024).

Midjourney (2024), Available online: https://www.midjourney.com/home (accessed August
16, 2024).

Miller, I. (2024), "Data Stories," *Hex*. Available online: https://hex.tech/use-cases/
exploratory-analysis/interactive-data-stories/ (accessed August 19, 2024).

Minecraft: Story Mode (2015), *Telltale Games*. Available online: https://steamcommunity
.com/app/376870 (accessed 3 January 2025).

MIT Docubase (2024), Available online: https://docubase.mit.edu/ (accessed August 19,
2024).

Morris, F. (1995), *The Space*. Available online: https://www.thespace.org/ (accessed
August 17, 2024).

Mounts (2024), *GoPro*. Available online: https://gopro.com/en/gb/shop/mounts
-accessories/camera-mounts?term=mounts (accessed August 19, 2024).

Multiplayer Online Battle Arena (2024), *Wikipedia*. Available online: https://en.wikipedia.org/
wiki/Multiplayer_online_battle_arena (accessed August 16, 2024).

Murno, B. (2018), "How Dramatic Reconstruction Transformed the Documentary," *BBC
Arts*, November 30. Available online: https://www.bbc.co.uk/programmes/articles
/hTpnDmGXV219Wd5MWGXw1p/how-dramatic-reconstruction-transformed-the
-documentary (accessed August 19, 2024).

Myers, J. (2017), "Codename Cygnus," *Earplay*. Available online: http://www
.codenamecygnus.com/#about (accessed August 17, 2024).

Myst (2024), *Wikipedia*. Available online: https://en.wikipedia.org/wiki/Myst (accessed
August 19, 2024).

National Deaf Centre (2024), *Deafverse*. Available online: https://deafverse.com/ (accessed
December 21, 2024).

Newgrounds (2024), Available online: https://www.newgrounds.com/flash/player (accessed
August 22, 2024).

New Media and Society (2024), *SAGE Journals*. Available online: https://us.sagepub.com/
en-us/nam/journal/new-media-society (accessed August 22, 2024).

New Media Writing Prize (2024), Available online: https://newmediawritingprize.co.uk/
(accessed August 19, 2024).

Nichols, E. (2020) "Collaborative Storytelling with Large-scale Neural Language Models,"
ACM Digital Library. Available online: https://doi.org/10.1145/3424636.3426903
(accessed August 17, 2024).

Nightmare (2024), *Boardgamegeek*. Available online: https://boardgamegeek.com/
boardgame/5041/nightmare (accessed August 14, 2024).

Nintendo Switch (2024), Available online: https://www.nintendo.com/us/switch/ (accessed December 27, 2024).

Nisi, V. and Haahr, M. (2006), "Weird View: Interactive Multilinear Narratives and Real-Life Community," *Crossings: eJournal of Art and Technology*, 4 (1): 1–13. Available online: https://mf.media.mit.edu/pubs/journal/WeirdView.pdf (accessed January 1, 2025).

Norman, D.A. (2013), *The Design of Everyday Things*, *2nd Revised and Expanded Edition*, Cambridge: MIT Press. Available online: https://ia902800.us.archive.org/3/items/the designofeverydaythingsbydonnorman/The%20Design%20of%20Everyday%20Things %20by%20Don%20Norman.pdf (accessed August 19, 2024).

Notion (2025), Available online: https://www.notion.com/ (accessed January 8, 2025)

Novelab, Atlas V. (2024), *Notes on Blindness on Meta Quest*, ARTE France. Available online: https://www.meta.com/experiences/notes-on-blindness/1946326588770583/ ?srsltid=AfmBOorQMGcDtxYrxbh0kZU-IQSUeQISIQmYVyKII7Z6HF-bVJxYFSyu (accessed December 21, 2024).

Noyes, R. (1996), "Pick Up the Phone Booth and Die," *The Interactive Fiction Database*. Available online: https://ifdb.org/viewgame?id=4gb36vjo20qpvxty (accessed August 14, 2024).

NV Access (2024), Available online: https://www.nvaccess.org/ (accessed December 23, 2024).

Oladipo, T. (2024), "23 Top Social Media Sites to Consider for Your Brand in 2024," *Buffer*, April 24. Available online: https://buffer.com/library/social-media-sites/ (accessed August 21, 2024).

Pantomime (2024), *Wikipedia*. Available online: https://en.wikipedia.org/wiki/Pantomime (accessed August 16, 2024).

Parchment (2024), Available online: https://iplayif.com/ (accessed December 23, 2024).

Parse Platform (2024), Available online: https://opencollective.com/parse-server (accessed August 16, 2024).

ParserComp (2024), Available online: https://parsercomp.itch.io/ (accessed August 22, 2024).

Peabody Awards, The (2024), Available online: https://peabodyawards.com/awards/ immersive-interactive/ (accessed August 22, 2024).

Pepper's Ghost (2024), *Wikipedia*. Available online: https://en.wikipedia.org/wiki/Pepper %27s_ghost (accessed August 22, 2024).

Persson, M. and Bergstein, J. (2011), "Minecraft," *Minecraft.net,* November 18. Available online: https://www.minecraft.net/en-us (accessed August 19, 2024).

Photo Collages (2024), *Canva*. Available online: https://www.canva.com/create/photo -collages/ (accessed August 21, 2024).

Pinterest (2024), Available online: https://www.pinterest.co.uk/ (accessed August 19, 2024).

Platformer (2024), *Wikipedia*. Available online: https://en.wikipedia.org/wiki/Platformer (accessed August 14, 2024).

Playlist Generator (2024), Available online: https://www.playlist-generator.com/ (accessed August 21, 2024).

PlayStation 5 (2024), Available online: https://www.playstation.com/en-us/ps5/ (accessed December 27, 2024).

Plotpolis (2024), Available online: https://plotopolis.com/submissions (accessed August 22, 2024).

Pokémon Go (2025), Available online: https: pokemongolive.com (accessed January 10, 2025).

Porpentine (2012b), "Howling Dogs." Available online: https://xrafstar.monster/games/twine/howlingdogs/ (accessed August 14, 2024).

Porpentine (2013), "Ultra Business Tycoon III." Available online: https://xrafstar.monster/games/twine/tycoon/ (accessed August 17, 2024).

Poulton, L., Panetta, F. Burke, J., and Levene, D. (2014), "The Shirt on Your Back," *The Guardian*, April 16. Available online: https://www.theguardian.com/world/ng-interactive/2014/apr/bangladesh-shirt-on-your-back (accessed August 17, 2024).

Pre Gauntt, J. (2015), "Storytelling for the Internet of Things," *Medium*, April 27. Available online: https://medium.com/iot-storytelling/storytelling-for-the-internet-of-things-7bc3d9e083dc (accessed August 17, 2024).

Proto (2024), Available online: https://proto.io/ (accessed August 19, 2024).

Pro Tools (2024), Available online: https://www.avid.com/pro-tools (accessed August 19, 2024).

Punchdrunk (2024), Available online: https://www.punchdrunk.com/ (accessed August 17, 2024).

PuzzleScript! (2024), Available online: https://www.puzzlescript.net/ (accessed August 19, 2024).

Puzzle Video Game (2024), *Wikipedia*. Available online: https://en.wikipedia.org/wiki/Puzzle_video_game (accessed August 17, 2024).

Quarry, The (2024), *Wikipedia*. Available online: https://en.wikipedia.org/wiki/The_Quarry_(video_game) (accessed August 17, 2024).

Quest (2024), *Textadventures.co.uk.* Available online: https://textadventures.co.uk/quest (accessed August 17, 2024).

Quizmaker (2024), Available online: https://www.quiz-maker.com/ (accessed August 19, 2024).

Quiz Maker: Create a quiz to challenge your audience (2024), *Mentimeter*. Available online: https://www.mentimeter.com/features/quiz-presentations (accessed August 21, 2024).

R&D (2021), "Some Stories are Best Told in Your own Place," *The New York Times*, June 4. Available online: https://rd.nytimes.com/projects/spatial-journalism-vision/ (accessed August 19, 2024).

Racing Game (2024), *Wikipedia*. Available online: https://en.wikipedia.org/wiki/Racing_game (accessed August 14, 2024).

Raconteur (2024), Available online: https://raconteur.readthedocs.io/en/latest/ (accessed August 19, 2024).

Rafflecopter (2025), Available online: https://www.rafflecopter.com/ (accessed January 9, 2025).

Ramis, H. (1993), "Ground Hog Day," *Columbia Pictures*, February 12, United States. Available online: https://w1.nites.is/movies/groundhog-day/ (accessed September 4, 2024).

Random Number Generator (2024), *Calculator.net*. Available online: https://www.calculator.net/random-number-generator.html (accessed August 19, 2024).

Raptive (2025), Available online: https://raptive.com/ (accessed January 9, 2025)

Reiss, A. (2022), "The Sounds of CDMX," *The Pudding*. Available online: https://roxham.nfb.ca/intro 1 on (accessed August 17, 2024).

Rennison, T. (2008), *Tin Man Games*. Available online: https://tinmangames.com.au/ (accessed August 17, 2024).

Resident Evil (2024), *Wikipedia*. Available online: https://en.wikipedia.org/wiki/Resident _Evil_6 (accessed August 19, 2024).

Resnick, M. (2003), *Scratch*. Available online: https://scratch.mit.edu/ (accessed August 16, 2024).

Review Management Software (2024), *Capterra.* Available online: https://www.capterra .com/review-management-software/ (accessed August 19, 2024).

Rhythm Game (2024), *Wikipedia*. Available online: https://en.wikipedia.org/wiki/Rhythm _game (accessed August 16, 2024).

Ritz Herald, The (2021), "The Whitney Houston Hologram Concert." Available online: https://www.youtube.com/watch?v=FVCEXr6Qlkg&t=64s&ab_channel=TheRitzHerald (accessed January 15, 2025).

Rob, Rev. (2009), Project Odball. Available online: https://forums.atariage.com/topic /153337-project-odball-complete/ (accessed December 27, 2024).

Roll and Write Games (2019), *Boardgamegeek*. Available online: https://boardgamegeek .com/geeklist/213815/roll-and-write-games (accessed August 14, 2024).

Role-Playing Game. *Wikipedia*. Available online: https://en.wikipedia.org/wiki/Role-playing _game (accessed December 24, 2024).

The Rosebush: Interactive Fiction Theory and Criticism (2024), Available online: https://the -rosebush.com/ (accessed August 22, 2024).

RPGmaker MZ (2024), Available online: https://plaza-us.komodo.jp/products/rpg-maker -mz (accessed December 24, 2024).

RSS.app (2024), Available online: https://rss.app/ (accessed August 21, 2024).

Runway ML (2025), Available online: https://clipchamp.com/en/ (accessed January 13, 2025).

Sandel, C. and VanEseltine, C. (2013), "Chemistry and Physics," *Interactive Fiction Database.* Available online: https://ifdb.org/viewgame?id=qfvfc6576i90py4w (accessed August 19, 2024).

Schleiner, A.M., Leandre, J., and Condon, B. (2002), "Velvet Strike," *Net Art Anthology.* Available online: https://anthology.rhizome.org/velvet-strike (accessed August 19, 2024).

Search Engine Optimization (2024), *Wikipedia*. Available online: https://en.wikipedia.org/ wiki/Search_engine_optimization (accessed August 21, 2024).

Seaton, J. (2010), "The Zoo Vet," *Twinkl.* Available online: https://www.twinkl.co.uk/ resource/the-zoo-vet-originals-animation-t-1674064740 (accessed August 14, 2024).

Seager, S. (2013), "Beyond the Hero's Journey: Four Innovative Models for Digital Story Design," *Strategy & Story*. Available online: https://www.steveseager.com/heros-journey -four-innovative-narrative-models-digital-story-design/ (accessed August 17, 2024).

Secret Cinema (2024), Available online: https://www.secretcinema.com/ (accessed August 17, 2024).

Secret Story Network (2024), Available online: https://secretstorynetwork.com/ (accessed August 16, 2024).

Seltani (2024), Available online: https://seltani.net/ (accessed August 19, 2024).

Sensorama (2024), *Wikipedia*. Available online: https://en.wikipedia.org/wiki/Sensorama (accessed August 30, 2024).

Shooter Game (2024), *Wikipedia*. Available online: https://en.wikipedia.org/wiki/Shooter
_game (accessed August 14, 2024).

Short, E. (2012), "Counterfeit Monkey," *Emily Short's Interactive Storytelling*. Available
online: https://emshort.blog/2012/12/31/counterfeit-monkey/ (accessed August 16,
2024).

Short, E. (2013), "A Dark and Stormy Entry," *Turn to Page 4*, January 21. Available online:
https://turntopage4.blogspot.com/2013/01/a-dark-and-stormy-entry.html (accessed
August 19, 2024).

SignUp Sheet (2024), *SignUp.* Available online: https://signup.com/Sign-Up-Sheet
(accessed August 21, 2024).

Silent Disco (2024), *Wikipedia*. Available online: https://en.wikipedia.org/wiki/Silent_disco
(accessed August 17, 2024).

Simplified Animation Maker (2024), Available online: https://simplified.com/animation-maker
(accessed August 19, 2024).

Sims, The (2024), *Wikipedia*. Available online: https://en.wikipedia.org/wiki/The_Sims
(accessed August 19, 2024).

Simulation Video Game (2024), *Wikipedia.* Available online: https://en.wikipedia.org/wiki/
Simulation_video_game (accessed August 14, 2024).

Siri (2025), Available online: https://en.wikipedia.org/wiki/Siri (accessed January 15, 2025).

Sirin Orbital Systems (2022), "Extended Reality Lab for Mars Experiments (Mars Xlab)," *The
European Space Agency*. Available online: https://www.esa.int/ESA_Multimedia/Images
/2022/06/Extended_reality_lab_for_Mars_experiments_Mars_Xlab (accessed August
14, 2024).

Slack (2024), Available online: https://slack.com/intl/en-gb (accessed August 19, 2024).

Slideshow Video Templates (2024), *Renderforest*. Available online: https://www
.renderforest.com/Slideshow (accessed August 19, 2024).

Snapchat (2024), Available online: https://www.snapchat.com/ (accessed August 21,
2024).

Snappa (2025), Available online: https://snappa.com/ (accessed January 8, 2025).

SnoopDoggTV (2012), "Tupac Hologram Snoop Dogg and Dr. Dre Perform Coachella Live
2012." Available online: https://www.youtube.com/watch?v=TGbrFmPBV0Y&t=1s&ab
_channel=SnoopDoggTV (accessed January 15, 2025).

Social deduction game (2024), *Wikipedia*. Available online: https://en.wikipedia.org/wiki/
Social_deduction_game (accessed August 17, 2024).

Solano, A. (2023), Dolby Atmos – Understanding Binaural Mixing," *Production Expert*,
October 7. Available online: https://www.production-expert.com/production-expert-1/
dolby-atmos-understanding-binaural-mixing (accessed August 19, 2024).

SonicMaps (2024), "SonicMaps: Locative Auido," *Recursive Arts*. Available online: https://
sonicmaps.xyz/ (accessed August 14, 2024).

Soundraw (2024), Available online: https://soundraw.io/ (accessed August 14, 2024).

Sports Video Game (2024), *Wikipedia*. Available online: https://en.wikipedia.org/wiki/Sports
_video_game (accessed August 17, 2024).

Spreadshop (2024), Available online: https://www.spreadshop.com/?affiliateid=1261186
(accessed August 21, 2024).

Squiffy (2024), *Textadventures.co.uk.* Available online: https://textadventures.co.uk/squiffy
(accessed August 14, 2024).

Stealth Game (2024), *Wikipedia*. Available online: https://en.wikipedia.org/wiki/Stealth _game (accessed August 16, 2024).

Steam (2024), Available online: https://store.steampowered.com/ (accessed August 21, 2024).

Stepworks (2024), Available online: https://step.works/index.php/site (accessed August 19, 2024).

Stevens, M. (2013), "Our Boys in Uniform," *Textadventures.co.uk*, September 29. Available online: https://textadventures.co.uk/games/view/jswkzey41uuskfgcvbumrw/our-boys-in -uniform (accessed August 19, 2024).

Stewart, C. (2020), "How to Shoot TOP DOWN Video! | Make a "Tasty" Style Video," *YouTube*. Available online: https://www.youtube.com/watch?v=ZzygLeDxUC0 (accessed August 19, 2024).

Storch, H. (2023), "Adventures for Siri," *The App Store: Apple*. Available online: https:// apps.apple.com/lt/app/adventures-for-siri/id1564635035 (accessed August 17, 2024).

Story AI (2024), Available online: https://storyai.cc/ (accessed December 30, 2024).

Strategy Video Game (2024), *Wikipedia*. Available online: https://en.wikipedia.org/wiki/ Strategy_video_game (accessed August 17, 2024).

Stream (2025), Available online: https://stream.io/ (accessed January 8, 2025).

StoryArt (2025), Available online: https://storyart.io/ (accessed January 9, 2025).

Story City (2016), Available online: https://about.storycity.app/ (accessed August 16, 2024).

StoryDev (2024), Available online: https://github.com/storydev/sd2 (accessed August 17, 2024).

StoryMaps (2024), Available online: https://storymaps.com/ (accessed August 19, 2024).

StoryNexus (2024), Available online: http://storynexus.com/s (accessed August 19, 2024).

Storyplaces (2025), Available online: https://storyplaces.soton.ac.uk/ (accessed 25 May 2025).

Stott, K. (1995), *BellyFeel*. Available online: https://bellyfeel.co.uk/ (accessed August 16, 2024).

Survey Monkey (2024), Available online: https://uk.surveymonkey.com/?ut_source =homepage&ut_source3=header (accessed August 19, 2024).

Survival Game (2024), *Wikipedia*. Available online: https://en.wikipedia.org/wiki/Survival _game (accessed August 14, 2024).

Svend Åge Madsen (2024), *Wikipedia*. Available online: https://en.wikipedia.org/wiki/ Svend_%C3%85ge_Madsen (accessed August 16, 2024).

Szalat A., Ronez J., and Lotz S. (2008), *Gaza/Sderot, MIT Docubase*. Available online: https://docubase.mit.edu/project/gazasderot-life-in-spite-of-everything/ (accessed January 1, 2025).

Tableau Building (2024), *Boardgamegeek*. Available online: https://boardgamegeek.com/ boardgamefamily/27646/mechanism-tableau-building (accessed August 17, 2024).

Tabletop role-playing game (2024), *Wikipedia*. Available online: https://en.wikipedia.org/wiki /Tabletop_role-playing_game (accessed August 14, 2024).

Tactical Role-Playing Game (2024), *Wikipedia*. Available online: https://en.wikipedia.org/wiki /Tactical_role-playing_game (accessed August 17, 2024).

TADS (2024), Available online: https://www.tads.org/tads3.htm (accessed August 14, 2024).

Talefy (2024), Available online: https://talefy.ai/ (accessed December 30, 2024).

Tascam, Portacapture (2024), *Tascam*. Available online: https://tascam.jp/int/product/ portacapture_x8/top (accessed August 19, 2024).

TAVR Operation (2023), *SmartTek Solutions*. Available online: https://www.youtube.com/ watch?v=7Df6dLmdkh4&t=1s (accessed August 16, 2024).

Taylor-Laird, J. (2018), "The Shapes in Your Story: Narrating Mapping Frameworks," *Game Developers Conference*, March 16. Available online: https://ubm-twvideo01.s3 .amazonaws.com/o1/vault/gdc2016/Presentations/TaylorLaird_Jay_The_Shapes_In.pdf (accessed August 19, 2024).

Teams (2024), Available online: https://www.microsoft.com/en-gb/microsoft-teams/group -chat-software (accessed August 19, 2024).

Teledildonics (2024), *Wikipedia*. Available online: https://en.wikipedia.org/wiki/Teledildonics (accessed August 23, 2024).

Telltale (2024), Available online: https://telltale.com/ (accessed August 21, 2024).

Tetris (2024), *Wikipedia*. Available online: https://en.wikipedia.org/wiki/Tetris (accessed August 21, 2024).

Texture (2024), Available online: https://texturewriter.com/about (accessed August 19, 2024).

TikTok Live (2025), Available online: https://www.tiktok.com/live?lang=en (accessed January 8, 2025).

Tiermaker (2024), Available online: https://tiermaker.com/ (accessed August 19, 2024).

Tile-Based Game (2024), *Wikipedia*. Available online: https://en.wikipedia.org/wiki/Tile -based_game (accessed August 14, 2024).

Tile-Matching Video Game (2024), *Wikipedia*. Available online: https://en.wikipedia.org/wiki/ Tile-matching_video_game (accessed August 14, 2024).

TinyBop (2024), Available online: https://tinybop.com/ (accessed August 14, 2024).

Tower Defense (2024), *Wikipedia*. Available online: https://en.wikipedia.org/wiki/Tower _defense (accessed August 16, 2024).

Toy (2024), *Wikipedia*. Available online: https://en.wikipedia.org/wiki/Toy (accessed August 16, 2024).

Trello (2025), Available online: https://trello.com/ (accessed January 9, 2025).

Trick-Taking Game (2024), *Wikipedia*. Available online: https://en.wikipedia.org/wiki/Trick -taking_game (accessed August 14, 2024).

Trzaska, A. (2021), *Interactive Fiction Database*. "4x4 Archipelago." Available online: https:// ifdb.org/viewgame?id=nmg570ycyex4mty0 (accessed August 17, 2024).

TTSMAKER (2024), Available online: https://ttsmaker.com/ (accessed August 19, 2024).

Tuesday (2024), Available online: https://kirilllive.github.io/tuesday-js/ (accessed August 19, 2024).

Twine (2024), *Twinery*. Available online: http://twinery.org/ (accessed August 19, 2024).

Twitch (2025), Available online: https://www.twitch.tv/ (accessed January 9, 2025).

Uncharted (2024), *Wikipedia*. Available online: https://en.wikipedia.org/wiki/Uncharted (accessed August 19, 2024).

Unity (2024), Available online: https://unity.com/ (accessed August 19, 2024).

Unmanned Aerial Vehicle (2024), *Wikipedia*. Available online: https://en.wikipedia.org/wiki/ Unmanned_aerial_vehicle (accessed August 19, 2024).

Unreal Engine (2024), Available online: https://www.unrealengine.com/en-US (accessed August 19, 2024).

Vio, P. (2014), "Seven Deadly Sins," *The Film Board of Canada and The Guardian*. Available online: http://digital-deadly-sins.theguardian.com/ (accessed August 14, 2024).

Vistacreate (2024), Available online: https://create.vista.com/ (accessed August 19, 2024).

Visual Novel Maker (2025). Available online: https://www.visualnovelmaker.com/ (accessed January 1, 2025)

Vive Arts (2021), "Curious Alice: the VR experience, Behind the scenes," *Victoria and Albert Museum*, May 18. Available online: https://www.youtube.com/watch?v=j1maAW2F2Ug (accessed August 16, 2024).

Viveport (2025), "Curious Alice." Available online: https://www.viveport.com/apps/d1f89b95-788f-4e59-83a0-5d9ccf071c66?hl=en-US&srsltid=AfmBOorBkPlyPC3hKQ5abG1ZlvKeoJABPyGGOKhqL1FKYNzFX0viinXH (accessed 25 May 2025).

Voiceflow (2024), Available online: https://www.voiceflow.com/ (accessed August 16, 2024).

VoiceMap (2024), "VoiceMap: Location Aware Storytelling," *The Lit Platform*. Available online: https://theliteraryplatform.com/news/2016/05/voicemap-location-aware-storytelling/ (accessed August 16, 2024).

Voidspace (2024), *Voidspacezine*. Available online: https://voidspacezine.com/ (accessed August 22, 2024).

Voki (2024), Available online: https://www.voki.com/ (accessed August 19, 2024).

Wallpaper (2025), Available online: https://en.wikipedia.org/wiki/Wallpaper_(computing) (accessed January 9, 2025).

Walton, N. (2019), "AI Dungeon," *Latitude*. Available online: https://play.aidungeon.com/ (accessed August 17, 2024).

Walking Dead, The (2024), *Wikipedia*. Available online: https://en.wikipedia.org/wiki/The_Walking_Dead_(video_game) (accessed August 17, 2024).

Wanwan L., Changyang L., Minyoung K., Haikun H., and Lap-Fai Yu (2023), "Location-Aware Adaptation of Augmented Reality Narratives," *Special Interest Group on Computer-Human Interaction*. Available online: https://www.youtube.com/watch?v=StkAO1fj5M0 (accessed August 17, 2024).

Wayback Machine (2024), Available online: https://web.archive.org/ (accessed August 22, 2024).

WCAG Guidelines (2024), Available online: https://www.w3.org/WAI/standards-guidelines/wcag/ (accessed December 21, 2024).

What is XR? 5 Extended Reality Examples That Explain the Promise (2023), *InContext*, October 6. Available online: https://incontextsolutions.com/blog/extended-reality-examples/ (accessed August 14, 2024).

WhatsApp (2024), Available online: https://www.whatsapp.com/ (accessed August 14, 2024).

What is Backlinking and Why is it Important for SEO. (2024). *Intuit Mailchimp*. Available online: https://makestories.io/embed-google-web-stories/ (accessed August 19, 2024).

Wheel of Names (2024), *Wheelofnames.com*. Available online: https://wheelofnames.com/ (accessed August 19, 2024)

Wickens, K. (2022), "Someone Crafted a Redstone PC in Minecraft to Play Minecraft Inside Minecraft," *PCGamer*, September 9. Available online: https://www.pcgamer.com/minecraftception-redstone-pc-chungus/ (accessed August 19, 2024)

Wikinovel.net (2025). Available online: http://www.wikinovel.net/ (accessed 25 May 2025).

Wireless Microphone (2024), *Wikipedia*. Available online: https://en.wikipedia.org/wiki/Wireless_microphone (accessed August 14, 2024).

The Witcher 3: Wild Hunt (2024), *Wikipedia*. Available online: https://en.wikipedia.org/wiki/The_Witcher_3:_Wild_Hunt (accessed August 14, 2024).

Woobox (2025), Available online: https://woobox.com/ (accessed January 9, 2025).

World of Warcraft (2024), *Wikipedia*. Available online: https://en.wikipedia.org/wiki/World_of_Warcraft (accessed August 19, 2024).

Worth, J. (2014), "If the Moon were a Pixel," *Josh Worth.com*. Available online: https://joshworth.com/dev/pixelspace/pixelspace_solarsystem.html (accessed August 16, 2024).

X (2024), Available online: https://x.com/home (accessed August 21, 2024).

X API (2025), Available online: https://developer.x.com/en/products/x-api (accessed January 8, 2025).

X Box (2024), Available online: https://www.xbox.com/en-US (accessed December 27, 2024).

YouTube (2024), Available online: https://www.youtube.com/ (accessed August 21, 2024).

YouTube Live (2025), Available online: https://www.youtube.com/channel/UC4R8DWoMol7CAwX8_LjQHig (accessed January 9, 2025).

Zarf (2013), "Seltani," *Seltani.net*. Available online: https://seltani.net/ (accessed August 19, 2024).

Zombies, Run! (2024), Available online: https://zrx.app/zombies (accessed August 14, 2024).

Zoom (2025), Available online: https://www.zoom.com/ (accessed January 8, 2025).

Zoom, Handheld Recorders (2024), *Zoom*. Available online: https://zoomcorp.com/en/ca/handheld-recorders/ (accessed August 19, 2024).

Index